T0209427

"Melissa has successfully navigated her way through some of the greatest health challenges a body can face." — Donna Eden

The Road to Gratitude

A Guide to Healing Body~Mind~Spirit
Through Energy Medicine

MELISSA G RICHARDSON

BALBOA.PRESS
A DIVISION OF HAY HOUSE

Balboa Press books may be ordered through booksellers or by contacting:

Balboa Press
A Division of Hay House
1663 Liberty Drive
Bloomington, IN 47403
www.balboapress.com
1 (877) 407-4847

Interior Image Credit: Brandon Alvarado

Print information available on the last page.

ISBN: 978-1-9822-4303-6 (sc)
ISBN: 978-1-9822-4305-0 (hc)
ISBN: 978-1-9822-4304-3 (e)

Library of Congress Control Number: 2020902906

Balboa Press rev. date: 04/30/2020

I would like to dedicate this book to my family and friends, who never gave up on believing that I would actually get it done! I also want to dedicate it to my wonderful clients, who have taught me how to be the best healing facilitator I can be.

Contents

Addendums

Acknowledgments

I'd like to thank my family and friends, who continually believed in my vision to write a book that could help many people to heal. They held that faith for the entire six years it took me to get this book out of me. They stood by me through my own healing journey along the way. I couldn't love you all more!

I especially want to recognize my kids — Claire, Angel, and Rudy — who would have to find me (outside on the couch writing) when they needed me, or they had to run errands because my body decided to learn from yet another healing crisis so that I could share how I healed from it. They are my heart and my biggest cheerleaders in this life.

I want to thank my clients who trust me to help them with the transformational work that we do together. You are my teachers and I am honored.

I would like to thank Donna Eden, Anthony William, and David Feinstein for their dedication to teaching and guiding all of us on our healing journey. Because of their dedication, sacrifices, and examples, we all have more information, and if we use it, the ability to be healthy and happy. There is no bigger gift than that when you have been mysteriously, desperately, or chronically ill. They have dedicated their lives to helping others heal.

I want to thank my amazing editor, Maria Petrova, who not only is a great editor and graphic artist, but also an Eden Method Energy Medicine Practitioner who follows the Medical Medium. I could not have asked for a better editor for this book! She is a beautiful soul of so many talents and has my deepest gratitude for helping me to birth this book.

My kids think I am weird for this one, but I want to thank Ed Sheeran, whose music and vulnerability in his lyrics is an example of love to us all. His beautiful music got me through some really tough times these past eight years, and I am grateful for it still. I am going to meet you someday, Ed, and give you a big hug of gratitude, and of course a signed copy of this book ☺

A big thank you to my beta book readers Meryl Adam, Maryanne O' Brien Stansfield (wordsmith extraordinaire!), and Amy Bisely. I especially want to thank my dear sister-friend, Jill Furtado, who read several drafts tirelessly and was a huge help with my earlier editing and writing. I can't thank you enough, Jilly!

A special thank you to Allyson Magda Photography for the pictures for this book, patiently finding the best way to introduce me to you all. I have deep gratitude for all of the *many* alternative practitioners, authors, and teachers who have helped me on my healing journey. There are so many of you to be grateful for! Thank you to my colleagues in the Medical Medium Practitioner Support Network for all of the information, guidance, mutual support, love, and knowledge we all share to help ourselves and our clients, family, and friends to heal. I love you all!

I am grateful for this life, which has taught me so much and humbled me tremendously. I wouldn't change it. The synchronicities of how this book and all facets of it came to be are directly attributed to Source and my belief in surrendering to Divine for what is for the greater good. Enjoy!

The author in 2002, 38 years old

The author in January 2020, 55 years old

Introduction

"Something very beautiful happens to people when their world has fallen apart: a humility, a nobility, a higher intelligence emerges at just the point when our knees hit the floor."
— *Marianne Williamson*

We are all on a journey in this life. Sometimes the road is open, with beautiful, breathtaking vistas. Sometimes the path is difficult, and we don't know how to move forward. We long for a simple, beautiful life, the fairytale symbols of happiness: a perfect relationship, happy children, beautiful house, and perfect health. Never any problems, everything we desire manifesting easily, everything flowing perfectly according to our will and plan.

And yet it seems we are here to experience at least some form of hardship. All major spiritual traditions and religions teach that we are in relationship to greater spiritual wisdom, to a consciousness higher than our own, that we are part of a greater whole. Christianity, Judaism, Buddhism, and Native American teachings view human life as an imperfect but incredibly valuable learning experience for the benefit of our eternal soul. We are here to learn, be hurt, hurt others, and to learn lessons about non-duality. What I mean by non-duality is our connectedness with each other and everything. We are not separate from each other. We influence each other in countless seen and unseen ways.

I have learned these things by being brought to my knees, healing myself body-mind-spirit and becoming the best Advanced Eden Method Energy Medicine Practitioner possible. I have come from being separate and very sick to becoming part of not one but three powerfully healing communities — Eden Method Energy Medicine, the Medical Medium Practitioner Support Community, and Reconnective Healing. I am continually learning, growing, and advancing in my knowledge and healing to help teach others to learn, grow, heal, and be happy.

We can learn how to see ourselves as part of a greater whole, not as forlorn beings in a clockwork world ruled by chance and chaos. The ancients describe a wise universe that sees all our problems, our overwhelm, our indecision, our dire need for meaning and love. That greater consciousness sees our lives like a tapestry of all of the moments within them. The many colors of the threads in the tapestry represent the moments of our lives with various emotions of pain, anger, joy, anxiety, pleasure, despair, laughter, grief, all contributing to our soul's learning.

The more beautiful and rich our personal tapestry, the more opportunities we've had for growth toward a life based on love rather than fear. We are all on different journeys with our own set of opportunities and challenges. Some of these opportunities are addiction, cancer, loss of a child, abuse, or divorce — trials that can feel like they're ripping our hearts apart. Moments that leave us feeling unable to go on lead us eventually, after days, months, or years of searching, to surrendering to a more enlightened, connected, loving, and peaceful existence. We lose the need for judgment with the knowing that we all have our own challenges and that we are all in this together and always have been.

If you've had a mystery illness that has plagued you for years and even decades, this book is for you. If you've had a cancer diagnosis, have been dealing with mystery or chronic pain, are struggling with panic, anxiety, or depression, have experienced infidelity, or have had the breakup of a long-term marriage leave you in pieces, this book is for you. I have been there. So many of us have. This book will not only help you to heal from these things but also thrive after them.

This book is about my journey from a tired child experiencing headaches, allergies, and rashes as a common occurrence to an adult with a mystery illness for decades that came and went, and eventually an aggressive and irregular skin cancer diagnosis. It is the story of how I was able to transform these things into being a vibrant, happy, healthy fifty-something woman. I've been asked many times how I regained my health and how I am so happy. I can't tell my story in full to everyone individually, so I set out to write this book and share all of the things I have learned and the tools I've used along the way to heal myself. I want to help others to heal and thrive.

I've been blessed with a great education. I have a degree in Finance from California Polytechnic University, which I put to work helping to build a very successful family construction and development company. I also got a teaching credential and a real estate license. And yet despite being a successful woman in California, a state obsessed with health and wellbeing, I was unprepared for these life lessons, which reduced me to a glimmer of my true self. I needed to learn much more, go much deeper, take my healing into my own hands.

My four years of intensive Eden Method training with the astounding healer Donna Eden, along with my studies of Anthony William (Medical Medium)'s work has been the foundation to my healing. This book includes easy energy protocols you can do with your own hands, with no need for a healer. It also includes nutritional and supplement information that has been my "go to" for healing viruses and for being vibrantly healthy in my daily life. I also outline the more commonly needed information I have learned or channeled from my guides to help myself heal and that has subsequently helped my energy medicine clients. I recommend other great books as resources for your own healing.

I have been blessed to work with hundreds of clients to assist them in releasing old emotions that had been causing them dis-ease in their body and emotional and physical pain. I also teach my clients a daily energy wellness routine that takes 3-5 minutes. It changes lives, and I personally do not get out of bed until I have done it. I share this routine and many other powerfully healing protocols with you in this book.

Clients come to me with a myriad of challenges from depression and anxiety to cancer, pain, mystery illness, and blocks in their life that are holding them back. We are able to clear energy contracts with other people that are no longer serving them or us and are holding us back from our vibrantly healthy and happy life. I teach my clients as I assist them in their healing to empower them in their own self-healing journey. This book is a compilation of the biggest-impact and most used protocols that I use in my energy medicine practice.

My light is shining so much brighter along with the lights of the people I have been blessed to help on their healing journey. I see an image of my candle lighting others so that we all shine brighter as more and more of us are passing on this light. This is how we heal and how we help to heal the world. We are all in this together.

I recognize finding the hope to heal is not so easy when you are in the most painful place, but as things happen against our expectations, we find wisdom in going with the flow. You can hold your hands out to the sky and say "really?!" while smiling and surrendering. Afterward you will know why the event happened and eventually be grateful for the learning and growth that came from the experience. You will find humility and trust in the journey. That is the beauty of true healing.

Besides the two biggest influences in my healing, Donna Eden and Anthony William, along the way I've read many books by Wayne Dyer, Louise Hay, Doreen Virtue, Christiane Northrup, to name a few, that have contributed to my healing. I will share what I have learned from them that I used on my journey to joy and vibrancy. In this book is everything I have learned to reverse my aggressive and irregular skin cancer, heavy metal toxicity, chronic fatigue, depression, and to go off thyroid and sleep medication.

I do not have any medical training, nor am I in the medical field. Always research things for yourself or get the guidance of an N.D. or an M.D. if that is what is speaking to you. **Energy is my medicine.** Working with your own energy field is a surprisingly powerful, always at the ready, way to feel significantly better. Much of our fatigue is your energies needing to be corrected, just like you would straighten a crooked picture frame, or something else obviously a bit off in our physical environment. You can do it for yourself — you don't have to travel and see a practitioner.

I will share what I did to make necessary and healthy changes in my life. I will give specific examples of things to eat and supplements that can be taken that will support healthy changes in your life to transform your long-term and chronic illness into vibrant health. You can choose to discuss them with your medical doctor, naturopathic doctor, or nutritionist, or use part or all of them to create a plan that fits your lifestyle and needs. I will share stories from my life and also from sessions I have done with clients that are examples of how our energy body cannot be left out of the healing process. This is not intended to change your beliefs in any way, just to show you the unfolding of my life that consisted of exhaustion, chronic and extreme stress, depression, illness, and judgment into a life of connectedness, grace, love, health, peace, joy, gratitude, forgiveness, and service to others.

This book includes energy protocols to support and balance your energetic body, which will help you to heal your physical body. It is a resource with protocols for you to clear emotions in your energetic field and body that are triggering you and keeping you from living a vibrant life and living your purpose. For your benefit I have also included a protocol that helps you to get rid of energy cords that are draining you and making you feel exhausted. Donna Eden, who can see energies, says that she can see dis-ease in our energy field first before it goes into our physical body. Being vibrant is being in charge of your own energies and not taking on other people's energies. I will also share my routine for better sleep.

My recipe for a happy life: Live in the moment, laugh often and out loud, love like there is no tomorrow, and breathe deeply. When you are stressed and not sure how you are going to get everything done and feed everyone, take just one minute to breathe deeply, look up from your list, ground yourself. Listen to bird song when possible, and while you are slogging through those endless emails, stop and think about something you are grateful for as you look out the window for a minute. Watch sunsets and sunrises by yourself or with your loved ones. Help other people and animals, even insects, plants, and trees. Care for yourself in your thoughts, in the way you feed yourself, and in the ways you manage your energies and emotions. Spend time in nature and move your body. Do things that make your soul sing and open your heart to everyone. Be passionate about your contribution to life and share it. This is success.

I received my cancer diagnosis while I was navigating the ending of my long-term marriage. I thought, "How in the world can I handle this also? I cannot die, my kids need me!" My intention was to experience my divorce with as much love and grace as possible. But I wasn't extending this same love and grace to myself, and I soon realized how much I was out of balance. I was being reactionary instead of being and doing what I needed to do to be healthy. I had not been trusting and honoring my beliefs. I was living a life of worry, fear, and exhaustion from not putting myself first. We are meant to come from love in all ways for a better world. Love can heal so many things if allowed. *But we need to love ourselves first, and then we will be able to truly love everyone and everything else.* This is how situations shift and how true healing happens.

I recently went on a hike with a close friend. We decided it had been too long since we connected, and it was time to get caught up on each other's lives. We shared our love and gratitude for our friendship and each other. It was a beautiful hike in nature with an extraordinary sky. I mentioned that the old Melissa (before my opportunities for my own tapestry to become so beautiful started and changed me) would not have taken this precious time with a friend in the late afternoon. I would have been in my business mindset and would have chosen my to-do list and the pressures of work productivity over this beautiful time that ultimately contributes to a happier, healthier, and more productive me. We laughed a lot, shared insights, and we gave each other the gift of our time and companionship on a beautiful day.

We followed this hike by sharing a meal. During the meal my friend looked at me and said, "Generally, after we get hurt deeply, we end up being even better." I said, "Amen to that. I am living proof!"

Melissa Richardson
San Luis Obispo, CA

Chapter 1
The Early Years

"Nothing ever happened in the past that can prevent
you from being in the present now."
— *Eckhart Tolle*

I WAS BORN IN THE high desert of Southern California in the heat of the summer. Temperatures were often 110 to 115 degrees, and you could see the heat shimmering off the pavement and smell asphalt in the hot air. In the early morning of summer the smell of the grass lawns with water drops from sprinklers was so pungent and fresh before the heat set-in. My sisters and I would savor the last breaths' of moisture and coolness in the air before the sun took over and the habitual quest for moisture set in for the day to combat the heat.

The desert is beautiful, especially in the fall, when the blistering heat is gone, yet it's warm during the day. Water is still on plants and lawns glisten fresh and new in the morning. The days get to be in the mid 80's, and the evenings are like magic during and after the golden sunset.

I grew up riding my bike around town and also in the desert with my twin sister and a pack of friends, creating forts and riding on dirt trails from one house to another. My least favorite time was in the spring, when the winds would start blowing sand at us, making us feel gritty, dirty, and disgruntled. I remember driving my Volkswagen to work when I was in my teens and watching the tumbleweeds keep pace with my car on back roads. My friends and I would joke about our 1980's hair and needing the 60mph hair spray just to get our bangs through the day. We would say that the winds gave a whole new meaning to the "messy sexy look." The "scary crazy look" was more accurate.

My mom used to lie on the hard tile floor under the swamp cooler (cools air through evaporation of water) in the hall to make it through those scorching last few weeks in July and August of her pregnancy until she delivered my twin sister and me. I can't imagine being pregnant with twins, let alone in the middle of the summer in the high desert, with only a swamp cooler for air. I was fourth in my family of all girls, the youngest child by six minutes. My identical twin sister was a full pound and one ounce larger than me turning in our mother's womb at the last minute to be the first one born into this life. She says she is the oldest twin, and to this day she likes to think that she is the boss of me. I often let her. We were three and a half years younger than our next sister, Karen, and our oldest sister, Sherry, was another thirteen months older than Karen.

Having a built-in friend with my sister was very convenient. We each had our own best friends, and we ran in a pack of four or more. The next street over from our busy block was where my childhood best friend, Susan, lived with her mother, brother, and sister. They were a second family to me, complete with their Grandma, whom we all called "Mimi." They had a gaggle of kids on their street, and we'd all play hide and seek in the neighborhood on those beautiful and warm desert summer nights. Sleepovers were our favorite in the summer, followed by riding bikes to the donut shop the next morning and getting four donuts each! Looking back – yikes!

Our dad was a major sports enthusiast and really wanted a son to share that with. He got my twin sister, Dana, and me, and we were the best tomboys we could be for our dad. We grew up at the ballparks during softball season, which seemed to be mostly all year long because when dad wasn't playing men's fast pitch softball he was umpiring it. We went fishing with Dad, and Dana's best friend Paula (another tomboy) would come along as well. Nacho cheese Doritos and RC Cola were the staples of our diet on those trips. Our family went camping, sometimes taking our friends with us for lifelong memories. We played basketball, softball, and volleyball. We rode our bikes everywhere and were always going and doing things.

Dad was mostly raised in California. He has always been a very active and gregarious fellow, knowing no strangers. My Mom is from England and immigrated here with her family when she was seventeen. Mom can be very quiet in her English way, but she has a quick wit and core strength to her, which she fortunately passed on to us girls.

We had your typical 60's and 70's middle-class, blue-collar upbringing. We lived down the tree-lined street from our grade school and within bicycling distance to our junior high school. Most summer days we were kicked out of the house in the morning, after our Captain Crunch, Fruit Loops, Instant Breakfast shake, Pop-tarts or Coco Puffs breakfast. We were allowed back inside for a lunch of Wonder Bread, fried bologna or tuna and pickle sandwiches. Then we were sent outside again to have more adventures riding our bikes in the desert, hanging out at the library, goofing around at our school, playing ping pong in our garage, stomping aluminum cans to take to the recycling center, or sometimes reading while listening to our phonograph until dark, when we had to be home for family dinner.

Our dinners were a family affair with all six of us around the round table in the small kitchen. Dinner was usually a pot roast, barbeque steak, spaghetti or pork chops with canned vegetables, peas, lima beans (which I've never liked), green beans, or carrots. We'd often have iceberg lettuce salads with tomatoes and lots of Girard's dressing on it. Boxed foods and frozen dinners became popular in the late 70's, and, not to be left out, we joined this new food trend. We would have boxed tuna casserole, taco casserole, macaroni and cheese, Hamburger Helper, or whatever frozen meals we liked.

Throughout my childhood I clearly remember being tired. I now can attribute that partially to being constantly dehydrated, since the benefits of drinking water weren't talked about then. We drank a lot of soda because it was so readily available to us. My dad worked in the beverage industry for Pepsi Cola and RC Cola. We grew up on soda, lots of soda, and not much water. The harmful effects of soda were discovered and widely publicized some 20 years later. This habit led to me having lots of cavities and eventually getting nine mercury fillings.

If you are feeling tired, try this:

First, drink a glass of water if you have some handy. Then place your fingers on both collarbones and trace them toward the center of your body as they turn down. You should feel your fingers slide into a dip below your collarbones and next to the center of your chest. These are the K-27 points, which are the end points on your Kidney Meridian. Now tap these points firmly with your fingers until you feel energized or more alert.

Knowing what I know now, besides being "out" energetically and dehydrated, I also believe I was so tired in my childhood because I was toxic from heavy metals, which can be passed down through generations. Heavy metals can pass through the placenta barrier and can be accumulated through generations and passed on. I learned from listening to the Medical Medium's podcast about heavy metals[1] that workers in the hat factories where the felt fedoras and other hats were cured in vats of mercury had a 3–5 year life span. Remember the saying "Mad Hatter?" Now we know where it came from. If your ancestors wore those felt hats like mine did in England then they would have absorbed the mercury when they would wear the hats on their foreheads, sweating and absorbing those toxins. That mercury can be passed on and was. Lead, aluminum, cadmium, can all be

---

[1] https://soundcloud.com/medicalmedium/heavy-metal-detox

passed down as well. It has finally been proven that metal toxicity is passed from mother to baby in utero.[2]

It actually helps the mom to reduce her metal levels by having a baby. This has caused me deep sadness, since my children are showing some of the same symptoms I remember having when I was their age, such as being quick to get sick, exhaustion, bad menstrual cramps, and poor sleep. We also accumulate metals from eating fish containing mercury, taking fish oil supplements, breathing the air (especially jet fuel when flying or living near airports), and drinking water with metals in it.

Happily, my kids are young adults now and are working on eating healthy and getting the heavy metals out of their body and brain. I am able to help my kids to do this the natural way that I used to get the metals out of my body and brain thanks to the Medical Medium, Anthony William.

Anthony William became famous in 2015 with the publication of his book *Medical Medium*. Strange as the title sounds, Anthony is the real deal. I am living and breathing proof of it as well as my clients, friends, and family, whom I help with their healing by using Anthony's protocols for detoxing and healing. Anthony has been hearing guidance from what he calls Spirit — a generic word for "higher power," "spirit guides," or "Creator" — since he was four years old. He diagnosed his grandmother with lung cancer when he was four. She was tested the following week, and it was confirmed. Anthony has helped tens, maybe even hundreds of thousands of people so far in his life. Testimonials of the efficacy of his protocols abound on social media and personal blogs, including statements by celebrities, who usually hesitate to recommend paranormal authors. His current waiting list is around 25,000 people. He has had to close his waiting list because he doesn't have enough time in the remainder of his life to help all of these people.

Since Anthony is physically not able to have private sessions

---

[2] http://www.cnn.com/2010/HEALTH/06/01/backpack.cord.blood/index.html

with everyone who wants and needs it, he has poured his heart and soul into writing books for all of us to read and use as guides to heal ourselves. I learned the protocols from Anthony's books and my own healing experiences. I was blessed to be invited to join and accepted into the Medical Medium Practitioner Support Network. I work with other healing professionals to learn more about Anthony's protocols to help my clients. I will share what I did to heal myself with Anthony's protocols from heavy metals toxicity, toxins, viruses, and bacteria in the following chapters.

There are other ways to be exposed to mercury also. I loved canned tuna and would eat it regularly. This continued into my adult years as well. Unfortunately, we had no idea how bad it was for us with regard to the mercury levels in the tuna. There was also the BPA that was used in the cans back then. It has only been discovered in recent years that the levels of mercury in canned tuna are quite high.

My generation grew up on a lot of processed foods. It was our way of life back then. Us four girls would go to the store with our mom in the panel station wagon. I remember riding in the far back of the car crawling around, goofing off with my sis, and getting on our big sisters' nerves. At the store we would skip the produce section except for iceberg lettuce and tomatoes for the salad and would pick different sugary cereals, canned fruits and vegetables, Vienna sausages, Spam in a can, bologna, canned tuna, cucumber, cottage cheese, Velveeta cheese slices, ice cream, Ding Dongs, and Doritos. What we saw in ads and commercials were all these happy people eating these packaged goods.

Health was not ever a question regarding these foods. A Snickers candy bar or M&M's and a Diet Pepsi were my go-to's as a teenager for a snack or even a meal when I was at work. When we would get home from the grocery store after all of the groceries were put away by all of us, I remember it being a sneaky race to get to the ice cream before anyone else. Whoever got to the ice cream first would try and eat all of the chocolate out of the marble fudge ice cream.

Usually they did a really good job of excavating that chocolate and then disappeared while subsequent blame shifting would ensue with predictable regularity. I was quite accomplished at this.

Our most health-conscious moments came to us when we watched our mom working out with Jack LaLanne on TV in the living room. He was famous for his workouts, but we didn't pay much attention to the food tips he suggested. Instead, we held in our minds the media images of thin and happy models eating crackers and drinking Diet Coke.

Growing up in the Antelope Valley — the high desert in North Los Angeles County — I have had the thought that maybe it was better that we did not drink much water. There were some reports that toxic nuclear waste was being dumped in old abandoned wells far out in the valley. Back then I believe we were all on well water, which pulled from the huge water table that all or most of the wells tap into. If toxins were being dumped into a well, even in a remote area, I would think they would be mixing into the water table that our wells in that valley were drawing from. I have not researched this, but if you've seen *Erin Brockovich*, you would be wondering as I am.

When I was in eighth grade my sister Karen worked at Alpha Beta, a grocery store in town. Karen was a junior in high school that year, and in the spring she started having extreme pains in her arms. It was 1978. Because Karen was a grocery checker, they thought it was tennis elbow from the repetitive motion of that job. All we knew at home was that she would lie awake moaning and crying because the pain was so bad for her. This was a horrible time for all of us but especially for Karen. She was finally diagnosed with Acute lymphocytic leukemia. It was an aggressive childhood leukemia and rare in a 17-year-old. Karen started chemotherapy and got into remission. This was also during the "smog day" times. There would be health alerts for bad air quality in the Los Angeles basin where we would go for Karen's doctor visits and treatments. There were days that we were all breathing in obvious toxins when we were in the Los

Angeles area. I remember vividly leaving the high desert with clear skies, driving the 70 miles toward Los Angeles, and seeing the smog fog hanging over and enveloping the entire Los Angeles valley basin. We would see it and want to hold our breath knowing that it could not be good for us. The water quality and the air quality we were exposed to back then are some things I think about when I think about my sister Karen and her cancer.

My sister fought hard for her life for a year and three months until cancer won. She wore her afro curly hair wig with grace and humor during her senior year of high school when she felt able to attend school, which was amazingly strong of her. My oldest sister had already graduated, but my twin sister and I were freshmen at the time. I was so proud of Karen for her display of grace and humor throughout her illness.

Toward the end, all of us from our family went to City of Hope to get tested to see if any of us were potential bone marrow transplant matches. This was in 1979 and it was brand new technology. There was only a 25% chance that there would be a match in our immediate family. My twin sister and I were both matches! Unfortunately, Karen was not strong enough at that point to go through with the transplant. Eventually Karen got pneumonia, and the chemo weakened her so much that she could not hang on any longer. We were not able to do the bone marrow transplant, and we lost our sister, daughter, girlfriend, and friend — the beautiful, generous, and funny Karen Richardson on July 26th 1979. She was 18 years old.

Chapter 2
Sick and Tired of Being Sick and Tired

"Let go of your story so the Universe can write a new one for you."
— *Marianne Williamson*

AFTER GRADUATING FROM HIGH SCHOOL, I moved to Santa Barbara. I had been a grocery checker and was able to transfer to the city and still make the good union wages that supported me through my mid twenties. I would constantly marvel that I was living in such a beautiful city. Being on the ocean brought a new sense of awe and gratitude that washed over me even after years of living there, when I should have been used to it. It seemed so vast and mythical, and such a respite from worldly worries and concerns.

My community college was across the street from Leadbetter Beach, the perfect place to pretend to study while people-watching instead. On my more energetic days I would ride my bike to school along Cabrillo Blvd, which borders the ocean, watching people rollerblade, run, walk their dogs, and ride those rented bike carts for four. The beach path was lined with palm trees with green grass on one side and the beach sand on the other. People would have picnics on the grass, read books, or take a nap. I think this was my first experience in my life of truly living in gratitude.

Since I was born I had always been quick to get sick. I had bad skin allergies as a baby and toddler. I had many ear and sinus infections in my younger years and ended up on antibiotics often throughout my life. In grade school things seemed to level out for me with less illness, and I lived a rather active life of sports and even a brief stint at cheerleading in the sixth grade. Later that year I got the herpes virus with my first blister appearing on my lip. This is my first recollection of a blister on my lip.

My middle school years were very different and also difficult in many ways. In seventh grade I played sports and had fun with my friends until I came down with chicken pox for a couple weeks, followed immediately by bronchitis for another couple weeks, causing me to miss a full month of school. There was some concern that I wouldn't be able to finish seventh grade, but I did. My eighth grade year was much healthier for me, and I even learned to ski, which brought me so much joy with my friends for years to come. Things changed that spring, when my sister, Karen, was diagnosed with leukemia. This was devastating for our family and changed our lives forever.

It was the end of my freshman year of high school when we lost my sister Karen. That was a tumultuous year, with Karen going in and out of remission and trying different chemo drugs. The emotional stress of that year set me up for more healing challenges the remainder of my high school years. Right after Karen's death, when I was 15, I was at a hoedown for my church youth group, and a tailgate of a truck that was started while in gear without the clutch engaged shot back. The corner of the tailgate pinned my left femur bone to the barn door, almost breaking my leg. Luckily those 501 Levi's were in style, and I had a brand new thick pair on, which saved my leg from breaking. I later needed surgery to remove the cysts that formed in my leg where the damage happened.

That surgery was the physical fix for what happened, but recently at a class by Donna Eden I became aware of the energetic component to that accident. For those of you who do not know who Donna Eden is, I will share with you what an amazing and gifted energy healer Donna is. Since a very young age Donna has been able to see people's energy fields in and around their physical body. She can see dense energy that could be cancer, tumors, or cysts, and she can see if someone's energies in their meridians are running in the correct direction. Donna can see colors, chakras, meridians, life colors, auras, and many other forms of energy in the body. Her book *Energy*

Medicine and many YouTube videos show her practicing her craft and knowing things most of us can't know.

Donna was able to work with her husband, David Feinstein, Ph.D., to create a way for the rest of us who cannot see energies to assess the energy systems in the body for their vibrancy to enhance joy and prevent dis-ease in the body. Energy needs to move, and if stuck, it can cause pain, discomfort, exhaustion, and illness. Being able to affect how energies are moving or not moving in our body is a key component to health, wellness, and vibrancy. Donna is a pioneer in alternative healing and is a gift to all of us. When I first found out that I could relieve pain by restoring energy patterns to their original vibrancy, with my own hands and although I'm a regular person who doesn't see energy, I was hooked. I will be deeply grateful to Donna Eden and David Feinstein for the rest of my life for developing this training program that I have been able to use as the foundation in my own energy medicine practice.

While attending a recent Advanced Eden Method class, a colleague noticed that a couple of my meridians that run through my left hip were very under-energized. I was aware of one of them and had been working on it, but the other meridian that I am not able to energy test myself went undetected until I went to this class. I had been experiencing pain on and off in my left hip that was hurt when the truck hit me when I was 15, and I knew I would eventually figure it out. Donna Eden had me come up onto the stage during that class, and she put my hip back into the socket energetically. She did a couple more things, retested, and things were strong. As I was walking off the stage it hit me that my leg had been energetically disconnected from my body since that accident. The pain I had been feeling was gone. More about Donna's work and how integral it was in my healing in Chapters 9, 10, 11, 13, 18, 19, 20, and 21.

I remember having horrible menstrual cramps in high school, the kind that would paralyze me with pain, make me weak and nauseous to the point of throwing up. I was taking four Advil at a time, which was a strain on my liver, but I couldn't function at work or school without the edge of the pain being taken off.

While attending college in Santa Barbara, I had even more things happen. I was having so much 80's fun with my sister and friends in my bright red convertible Volkswagen bug, but it was time to get serious about my finances and school. This translated into me doing more than my body and spirit could handle. I was working two jobs — waitressing and grocery checking — and taking 12 units at college, so my health issues were in large part stress and diet related. I experienced spontaneous menstrual bleeding that was so bad I was off work for a few weeks. This was very stressful for me because I was supporting myself, and financial stress didn't help my situation.

I wasn't grounded, and that causes problems in your physical body.

If you are going through big stress right now, try this:

Go outside if possible for this, but inside works also. Take a deep breath in slowly and fully and when you exhale picture an energy-grounding pole going from up in the sky, through your body down into the Earth. Connect the grounding pole into the center of the Earth and feel the grounding energies coming up the energy pole, through your body and spraying out your crown chakra on the top of your head like a fountain. See these energies spraying out about three feet all the way around you. Set the intention to keep this going all the time, continuously keeping you grounded, your aura clear, and supporting you through a challenging time.

The solution the doctors came up with for me was to remove my uterus to stop the bleeding. Thank goodness I said "no thank you" to that! We want to trust our M.D.'s to come up with the best solution for us in whole, but they have been trained to fix the immediate problem, not the whole person solution. Had I made that decision to get my uterus removed, I wouldn't have had my two biological children and subsequently the child of my heart (my son's best friend since kindergarten, that we ended up becoming legal guardians of). When I think of how that decision could have drastically changed the course of my life and all of the joy that my three kids have given me, it's unfathomable. I am grateful for my strength and courage at the age of 21 to have said no to that solution.

No one ever suggested at that time that how I ate could help me with all of these symptoms and illnesses. I was essentially feeding viruses and bacteria in my body, creating an optimal environment for them to thrive. Stress would cause my adrenals to produce adrenaline almost constantly, which is not only toxic to our bodies but (according to Medical Medium) it's also a preferred fuel and food for viruses as well. Accidents and surgeries would weaken my immune system and jar the nesting viruses awake again. I didn't know that breathing deep would oxygenate my body, providing an environment that isn't virus friendly. Balance in my life was never mentioned either. There were times that I would change how I ate to eating more fruits and salads, and I would go through healthier times. Leading a busy and stressful life caused me to get intense comfort food cravings, and I would succumb to them, not knowing I was making myself exponentially worse by feeding the viruses and allowing dis-ease to flare up again in my body.

After living in Santa Barbara, I moved up north to beautiful San Luis Obispo to attend Cal Poly. I was in my early 20's. Again, I remember having what I call "gratitude attacks" when I would drive from my rental house in Los Osos along South Bay Blvd to work in Morro Bay. This road wound its way around the beautiful back-bay, and I would find myself driving with tears of gratitude in my eyes to have that beauty in my life while driving to work.

Around the time I turned 23, I had met the man I would marry at a college dance club, and I thought I was on top of the world. He had met my twin sister first in a community college class, and we always wondered if he thought I was Dana when we met. He is staying with his story that he knew I wasn't her! I was so in love, having fun adventures with other couples and friends camping, hiking, and mountain bike riding. Right after graduating from Cal Poly, I broke my ankle in a car accident. I was on crutches in a brand new full-time job with an upstairs office, an upstairs apartment, and a wedding to plan. Life was again extremely stressful, and I was feeling it. After getting married in 1990 at the age of 26, we decided to really buckle down working many hours plus buying and fixing up properties. I was the controller of a law firm in town, also doing the books on the side for another person and managing the books for my husband's construction business. We had a 10-year plan to build up a nest egg and then slow down and enjoy raising our family together and being available again to make fun life memories with our close friends.

Shortly after getting married and settling into the rigorous work lifestyle that we agreed upon, I started having night sweats with my menstrual cycle and decided that there was some significance there. I went to the doctor to find out what was wrong. When the nurse practitioner asked my OBGYN about my symptoms, he was loud in his response in the hallway outside my room, saying in an annoyed way that I was at the wrong doctor. He thought it sounded like I had lupus or lymphoma. Well, you probably have an idea how that made me feel…

At this point I was starting to realize that I was not like other people I knew in my life. I couldn't eat whatever I wanted or be in stressful situations for very long, or I would have big consequences with my health and energy. I decreased my work commitments for a little while and was able to manage the symptoms again until my late 20's, when we started trying to get pregnant. It took us a while to get pregnant, but eventually we were successful around the time I turned 30. Both of my pregnancies, in my 30's, were difficult. I was so sick I called it morning, noon, and night sickness. I could barely function. My twin sister had the same difficult time with pregnancy. I lost a close friend to breast cancer in 2002, and she had a difficult pregnancy as well before her diagnosis. Recovering from my pregnancies and the birth of my two babies was not easy for me either. It took time.

When my youngest son was about five months old, I hit what I felt like was my rock bottom. One morning in September of 1999 at the age of 35, I woke up completely exhausted after sleeping eight hours and feeling like I hadn't slept all night. I thought, "I need another eight hours of sleep after waking up from eight hours of sleep." I was so inflamed, bloated, and tired all of the time. I felt like I was constantly swimming against the current and uphill. My hair was falling out, and I was depressed. I called my mom, crying. I asked her to please come over and be with my three-year-old and my baby while I tried to figure out what was wrong with me. I sat on the couch holding my baby waiting for my mom while my three-year-old was being entertained by a Disney movie. I was zoning out and crying, and a thought went across my mind. I did not know at the time that this was going to end up being how I "know" things. Anyway, what floated across my mind was, "If I don't get my shit together, I'll end up with multiple sclerosis, in a wheelchair, divorced, and unable to raise my kids, who I love more than anything in this life." I remember this vividly to this day and will never forget that moment.

When my mom showed up, I showered her with gratitude, literally and figuratively. I cried again. I went to my home office and searched "chronic fatigue" on my computer. A lot came up, but what caught my attention was a book called *The Yeast Connection*. It explained that if you have an overgrowth of yeast throughout your body, you would be chronically exhausted. It also explained how in some severe cases the yeast could be systemic — so overgrown that it's in your bloodstream. I found out later that this was the case for me. I remember previously having a severe yeast infection during one of my pregnancies and being told that I had a yeast overgrowth.

It was a long process of elimination with many doctors chasing many symptoms for years. At one point I took Diflucan for 18 days straight. Diflucan is an antifungal that's prescribed safely only as a one-time dose for yeast infections. I had 18 one-time doses in a row recommended for me by my M.D. My pharmacist was concerned and suggested that I get my liver checked afterward to see if it was compromised. Fortunately, my liver survived within acceptable ranges even with dealing with the constant stress of the metals toxicity and other chemicals and toxins I had built up along the way. I now know that acceptable ranges are not optimal ranges, and my liver had been damaged. Fortunately livers can heal, but it can take a lot of support and time for them to heal, especially in this current toxic world. During my 30's I kept trying different things to regain my health and would flow in and out of feeling ok with occasional setbacks while still working for our family business and raising two kids.

Around the time I turned 40 I was the strongest I had ever been so far in my life. I had found a routine of riding my road bike in the mornings after I dropped my kids off at school and then get work done for 3-4 hours. Around 3pm I'd pick my kids up from school and start the rounds of sports practices or games and making dinner. A couple mornings a week I would train with weights. I found cycling to be a form of therapy and spent many morning hours on my bike by myself or with friends. I got strong, although when I look at myself in pictures from that time I see myself looking fit but very strained with gray energy around me. I modified my diet to more fruits and vegetables, although I was eating way too much meat at that time, drinking Diet Pepsi and other processed foods. It caught up to me.

Vibrant health continued to elude me no matter how hard I tried to eat better, exercise, and rest when I could, which wasn't often. I was slim, fit, had a beautiful house, three amazing kids, and friends who loved and supported me. We were around 15 years into our 10-year plan, had worked very hard and had been blessed to be very successful. Our company was growing, we had a good nest egg, great people to work with, and we could slow down. My husband was unable to work less than 60 hours a week and be comfortable, so we kept going. I was unhappy, and it showed in my health and wellness.

It wasn't until my early to mid 40's that I was finally diagnosed with adrenal burnout from chronic and extreme stress in my life. I had been chronically tired and using sugar, sodas, and caffeine in small amounts to help me with my energy levels. I knew they weren't good for me, so I tried to consume the smallest amounts I could and still get energy from them. My sleep was not good since giving birth to my first child and because of the roller coaster of those stimulants, so I started taking chips of Ambien to get what sleep I could. Before this time in my early 40's, I had gone on an antidepressant for my depression over being exhausted all of the time. I ended up without either highs or lows in my life, and I gained 10 pounds, which made me depressed, so I got off that antidepressant.

The chronic exhaustion eventually got me to delve deeper with an M.D. who was also an N.D. He finally came up with the adrenal burnout diagnosis. I had been seeing a chiropractor for ten years, and she felt I was getting worse despite all my efforts to get better. My massage therapist, whom I saw monthly, also said my body didn't feel right. She said it felt like it was hardening and that I needed to figure out what was going on. It was scary and frustrating to have two healthcare practitioners tell you that you were getting worse, and that they didn't know how to help you. Looking back, I interpret these comments as my metal levels in my body getting extremely toxic and my liver getting very congested and unable to do its job. I later had this experience with a client of mine who was getting worse, and it felt like her body was hardening. It's a scary thing to feel, especially when you care about your clients as much as my massage therapist did about me and as much as I do about my clients.

This prompting from my chiropractor and massage therapist also inspired me to go to a raw food and juice detox place called Optimum Health Institute (OHI) in San Diego. That weeklong detox was one of the most difficult things I have done in my life. I was so sick that week at OHI from detoxing that I threw up and could barely function. By the time I went home I had a fine rash all over my entire body and head. I was very weak and felt sick. My husband hugged me when I came home and said, "You smell like metal." We didn't think anything of that at the time, since that was before I was diagnosed with heavy metal toxicity.

When working with my adrenal burnout through rest, lower stress, vitamin supplements, and healthier eating and still not getting the results that I should have been seeing, I was finally given a big orange jug, a cup, and a provocation agent in the form of a supplement that told my body to dump metals from my tissues into my system so they could be eliminated through my urine. For six hours I drank water and collected my urine (I know how to have a good time!). This produced results that told me that my metal levels were very far beyond the concerning point.

With the help of the M.D./N.D., I started a chelation process and was able to bring my heavy metals levels down, but they were still outside the bracket and far beyond what's considered "safe," which now I know is no metals. I will share with you in chapter 12 how I was able to get the rest of the metals out of my body and brain by using Medical Medium's protocol for detoxing heavy metals.

Anthony William in his books confirms that all of us who experience mystery and chronic illness in this lifetime are not crazy. When we are going through our deepest and darkest times of our health challenges, we are certainly not making it up, it is not in our head like some people may have told us. There is a light at the end of the tunnel and a plan for us to follow to regain our health.

By the time Anthony's first book, *Medical Medium,* came into my life in 2016, I had been trying to heal myself for well over a decade and a half with the core problem still eluding me. Anthony and Spirit showed me a way to regain my health and become healthier and happier than I could ever have dreamed of. I am deeply and profoundly grateful for Anthony's information, guidance, kindness, and compassion. I am passionate about helping my clients in their healing through these protocols. I cannot conceive of a world without Anthony's books in it to guide us all on our healing journeys.

Chapter 3

What Does God Want For and From Us?

"I believe that the only true religion consists of having a good heart."
— *Dali Lama*

WHAT OR WHO IS GOD? No matter what your worldview, I think those of us who believe in a Creator believe that our Creator is Love. Love heals, love connects, love calms, and love frees us. When you are standing, being, and breathing in love, then you cannot be in Fear. Life is about contrast, and my truth is that ultimately there is Love and there is Fear. When you choose to be Love you are better able to be and feel peace, joy, appreciation, gratitude, and so on. Love is light, fear is the absence of light, the opposite of love. Fear is the need for control. Fear is shame, fear is judgment, fear is viciousness, fear is anger, fear is resentment. Fear is the darkness in life.

I was recently talking to a friend who said that he wanted to make sure he had done everything he could in his marriage before he could move on. I took a minute to contemplate his concerns and then asked if he wanted to hear what I believe. He said yes, that we were put together on this day in another state with no one else around for a reason, which made me laugh. I said, "If we take all religion out of the equation and just think about God and his son, Jesus — I think he was sent to us an example of how to live and be was a good place to start." My friend agreed with that, so I continued, "I think all religions and most God-believing people would agree that God and Jesus are Love and Compassion. They would want us all to be peaceful, joyous, compassionate, and to love and forgive each other. They want us to not judge each other but to help each other. They would say that we all came from God, and that we are all connected, and we are all the same in essence or spirit."

"Since we are all connected and connected to God and Jesus, they would want us to live in love, in peace, in joy, in compassion, and in service to each other. They want us to live in the light and to let our light shine. That may look like being the person who makes the very difficult decision to move on and release themselves and subsequently their partner from unhappiness and perhaps frustration, anger, and judgment and allows both people to move toward love for themselves and others. The more we can live in a space of love, the more that high frequency energy vibration is felt in the world."

I would never be an advocate to either stay in a marriage until death you do part, nor would I only advocate for leaving a marriage. Every situation is different and has its own unique set of variables that make it difficult for anyone outside of the situation to dictate what is right or wrong. I do know that it cannot be good for kids to have an unhappy home life with miserable parents just for the sake of keeping the family together. Everyone feels those toxic emotions, and that is not healthy and could never be a good environment for anyone no matter how accomplished of an actress and actor the parents are.

We cannot make our partner change their behaviors that may be causing disconnection in a marriage or partnership, just as they cannot force change on us if it is not in resonance with us and who we are. I now believe that we have karmic agreements with the father or mother of our children to bring them into this life together for all of the genetic, socio-economic, and various factors that help the kids to live the lessons that they have set up for this life. After those agreements have been met, then we are teaching each other lessons and giving each other opportunities for growth that can be extremely uncomfortable because some lessons and growth opportunities are downright more painful than others. Sometimes the lessons are to figure out how we are willing to be treated in friendships and relationships and to have boundaries around that.

Let me ask you this: who do you want to sit next to on a plane, at a movie, live with, or be around? Would it be the person with a scowl on their face and energy around them that does not feel pleasant to you? Or the person who appears to be judging how you look or what you are wearing? Would you prefer to sit next to the child coloring and singing softly, the woman with a dreamy look on her face and pleasant energy around her, or the kind man? I know where I would choose to sit and whom I'd want to be near. Let's look at ourselves now and decide if anyone would choose to sit next to us or if they would pick a different seat. Can you laugh at yourself in a positive way? Do you smile at strangers? You know this can be the difference in a person's life. Seeing a smile and the act of smiling shifts our energy into a more positive vibration, which helps us make better decisions about our lives.

Please hold no judgment about where you currently are. I was an overstressed and unhappy person for years, and now I am the opposite. I ran into a friend from my past recently, and she said, "Please don't take this personally, Melissa, but you were hard to be around before. I now know a little of what you were going through, and it makes sense but man, it was tough some days because you were so stressed and unhappy." That was not fun to hear, but it was true. I did not enjoy Me back then, and if we do not like our life or love ourselves then how can we expect or hope for someone else to? Sometimes you have to realize that you are in a situation that you cannot change and perhaps you have tried so many times that you are tired of banging yourself into the wall without any change for your efforts.

Radical change is sometimes needed for everyone to heal, and I believe God and Jesus do not judge us. They love and support us as they want us to do for each other. I also believe that we cannot change others, **but** we can change our perception of others, and that allows them to change and be their better selves. If both partners want to stay together and experience their own personal growth in and out of the relationship, then that is the best solution for the whole family. I will go into how to do this in more detail and give examples of how it has changed lives profoundly when I discuss clearing contracts, energies, vibrations in our field, and fractal repeating sequences in Chapter 16. We can heal and change, and this book is a framework to help you. I am living proof of this!

Back to my friend, after I asked him whom he would rather sit next to he laughed and said, "This was exactly what I needed right now and what I needed to hear." I said that this of course is what I believe, and I do not put my beliefs on anyone — I just choose to share my beliefs if I am asked. We professed our love and gratitude for our friendship. Spend time with and enjoy the people you resonate with. Appreciate the gift of sharing love and laughter with them. Recognize that we are placed with certain people at certain times for a reason.

Who do you want to be? Who do you choose to be? I choose love, lightness, laughter, joy, peace, gratitude, compassion, forgiveness, and service (it feels good!). Let's talk about compassion and forgiveness for a minute. Compassion and forgiveness start with you, *to* and *for* yourself. If you want loving, connected, accepting relationships in your life you have to be connected with yourself, love yourself, forgive yourself, and have compassion for yourself. In past years when feeling rather ragged, I would see myself in the mirror, smile, and say to my reflection "you are a good soul." I may have even pointed at my reflection and wiggled my finger at myself and really smiled or laughed, because I'd hear my longtime friend's voice in my head saying, "You're a good egg, Melissa." Who wouldn't smile or laugh about that! What the heck does that mean anyway? Hang out with people who make you laugh or smile.

Find people who accept you exactly how you are and who do not judge you or others. Spend time with people who see your beautiful soul. Break your drama addiction if you have one and stay away from people who have one. I recognize this is not easy, especially when drama-obsessed people are close to us or even part of our family. I found that once I decided I was done with drama in my life, it fell off around me. Friendships ended — some very painfully — but eventually it was a gift. This could be the best gift you give yourself.

If we do not judge and we do not feel judgment then we can be free to be our most authentic selves and be happy. Don't we all want that? Sing along with the Steve Miller Band ("Jungle Love" of course!) in a low voice in a store if you want to (I just did that, I couldn't help myself!). Most people enjoy happy people and being around them. It does "rub off," or more accurately they feel it because we are all connected. It allows them to be themselves and feel accepted and even appreciated, which is how we should all feel. We are all weird, which is freeing to accept that. I live by this; I try *really* hard not to judge, and I do not accept judgment of me. Even judgment of myself from myself! I believe we are usually our worst critics.

Being love. Living a life of love is sometimes not so easy to do. When you first commit to this, it's a matter of retraining your brain, thoughts, expectations, habits, and actions. It's a process and does not just miraculously happen overnight. We are creatures of habit for better or worse. We are here living an imperfect human experience, and some habits are harder to change than others. This is all growth, and growth can be uncomfortable. They say the contraction before the expansion is not always a comfortable place to be. I have learned about, and, I have also experienced the contractions and expansions, and it is truly freeing! We will have contractions in this lifetime, as we are here to grow, not stagnate. Recognize the contractions and know that we are being given yet another opportunity to heal, clear, and release things to become an even better version of ourselves.

We learn grace by living through situations that call for grace. The same goes with compassion, forgiveness, and the other soul lessons. We are born with a certain tendency toward being and having these abilities, but it is our life experiences, the threads in our tapestries that truly teach us to have grace, compassion, and forgiveness. Those don't necessarily come from happy situations either. You can have some compassion for the apparent pain of childbirth, but until you live through it you do not know its depth and texture to truly empathize about it.

We are all connected and come from our Creator, who is Love. This is why the vibration we have individually is also related to the vibration we have collectively. As each of us starts to remember how and why we came into this life and the true vibration of our essence, then our vibration increases, and therefore the vibration of everyone we touch or have contact with in our lives increases. This goes out to the rest of the world — the threads of connection between all of us.

Some days I experience a lower vibration than my normal. I ask myself if it is my "stuff, emotions, etc." that are causing my lower vibration.

If it's not my stuff, then I do the following:

I determine whom I'm connected to by getting quiet and listening to my higher self. I then ask Archangel Michael to please come and help me to disconnect from that person so that they can live their journey and I can live mine. I ask Archangel Raphael to infuse that space where the cord or connection was with divine, loving, healing light energy. I begin to pull out of the lower vibration soon after that.

When the shootings happened in Connecticut back in 2013, I was having a difficult day. I did not know why I was so down, but I did everything I could to shake it without being able to. I choose to let only a small amount of breaking news into my life, at controlled intervals, as I do not want to go to the lower vibration of fear. I hadn't heard about the shooting until that evening I was having some friends over to create vision boards, and they mentioned the news. That's when I realized what I had been feeling all day. This happens with big earthquakes, tsunamis, and any large-magnitude tragedy. We feel these crises from across the world. There is a scientific machine that correlates numbers and their frequencies in different locations around the world. The numbers changed right before 9/11 happened, so on some level we can even "know" right before catastrophic things happen.

If you are familiar with the field of study called Heart Math then you know that we all know what is going to happen before it actually happens. This is not with our eyes, it is not a prediction or a guess, it is the intelligence of our heart, which is the seat of our intuition. I first heard about Heart Math in Tom Shadyack's movie *Happy.* This is a great movie to watch periodically. In this life we do not have to be Mother Teresa, nor do we have to be famous or brilliant to really make a change in the world. Making a change to help the world is making a change in and for oneself first. If you want a higher vibration then pay attention to what you do, what you think, what you say, who you spend time with, and what you put in your body that makes you feel good or even joyful. That is the first step to making changes in the world.

There is a shift happening now with this new generation that are in their teens and 20's. Millennials and Gen Z are more sensitive and concerned about themselves, other people, animals, and the Earth. They are here to help us into this next level of higher vibration that we are moving into now. They want to be, receive, and give Love. They want the connections and the joy. They need balance. Simply put, they are not willing to do what my generation did, which was to simply put your head down and work for financial stability and commercial wealth.

We were programmed to put one foot in front of the other in this life until you retire. I compare that to road bike riders. I was an avid cyclist for years, and it was great for blowing all the yucky stuff out of my head. It was my therapy for a while, and it was a gift. If you are a serious road bike cyclist, you know that you don't ever get off your bike and push it or walk unless the tire is flat or the bike is broken — especially if you are wearing those very attractive tight clothes! Now that I am so happy, I just do not have it in me to push in that way anymore. The mountains I climb these days are different and happier. I am enjoying the scenery, noticing the smells, smiling more, and breathing deeply.

Chapter 4
We Are Guided

"There is a voice that doesn't use words. Listen."
— Rumi

MANY IF NOT MOST OF us in the U.S. grew up with a Christian worldview. Whether you went to church every Sunday, and whether you read the Bible or not, Christian references, holidays, and culture are prominent in our daily life. I grew up with parents who took us to First Baptist Church for services on Sundays, and us kids were also very active in the youth group functions. I was baptized eventually at Valley Bible Church, a non-denominational church where I grew up. After my marriage to a Catholic man in my mid 20's, I attended Mass and Catholic school activities for a couple decades honoring the beliefs of my husband. My views have evolved over the years to where there are a lot of details I'm not sure of with regard to Jesus, and what the "right" church might be, but I accept him as an example, powerful healer, and guide.

We all have our own spiritual and religious experiences. I respect everyone's choices and beliefs. I am sharing my beliefs merely as part of the unfolding of my story and the protocols that I will share with you for healing. Faith in a higher power isn't necessary for healing, but belief in the body's ability to heal is, as well as an awareness of how emotions affect the body's functioning. I believe that the emotional and spiritual parts of us are integral to healing and living in vibrant health.

I see Jesus as having been sent by our Creator (Heavenly Father in general Christian parlance) as an example of how to be "love." I've read a little of the New Testament, but from what I have read I marvel at Jesus's reactions to events. How did he find such generosity, such radically loving, overpowering, transcendent vision? He seems to have been the embodiment of love, peace, joy, compassion, kindness, forgiveness, non-judgment, and service. I see it as a challenge and a great opportunity in this life for me to try to become as generous and as loving as he was.

A friend reminded me the other night that Jesus was human when he was here, and he also got mad and even angry at the judgment of others and at various injustices. We are souls living a human emotional life experience, so we need to learn how to handle these emotions in the best way possible as Jesus did in his human experience. The end goal is not to be perfect but to be Love. We are here to learn, practice, grow, and "be" with as much love and grace as possible. We don't learn and grow without adversity and opportunities — my words for uncomfortable situations — that stretch and stress us into making change.

How can we be like Jesus if we are stressed out and fearful most of our life? How can we be free of limiting beliefs, resentments, fearful thoughts, and triggers that take us to places emotionally that are not happy and light? The good news is that we can clear, balance, and release these things so that we are able to grow and evolve to be more like Jesus and our best selves. It won't happen today or tomorrow and probably not in this current lifetime. It's called "work," but I believe it's the most valuable work you can do. It can take years, decades, a lifetime, or many lifetimes of work, but the more you release the things that stress, anger, sadden, and scare you, the happier and healthier you become in body, mind, and spirit.

You will also touch other people's lives, and that can heal them as well. Heal yourself — heal the world. That all-important principle: put the oxygen mask on yourself first. Do your healing work and then you will be able to help others heal. If you are outwardly focused, then you're not focused on healing yourself. This is a form of avoidance because healing old emotional wounds and traumas can be difficult, but the result… is amazing! The more spiritual work you do, the more you will feel so much better, lighter, and more joyful.

Every person's tapestry is unique and responds differently to the different methods of healing. These days many people are advocating a 100% raw vegan diet. Others swear by the opposite: a carnivore diet, consisting of meat, vegetables, and not much else. Ever tried a diet and then another, and another? Like different religions, there are many different beliefs about ideal diets.

There are many methods, teachings, and ways of clearing blocks, just as there are so many different ways to choose to eat. We have to know what's right for us, and at this particular time. For that we need guidance. Just as we have "chemistry" with a partner, we also feel attracted to or enthusiastic about different teachings that resonate with us. Pay attention to how your body reacts. If a diet or an energy clearing method is too restrictive, no matter what it promises, if you feel it "shuts you down" in anyway, it's probably not for you. Your energy needs to "sing," and despite being a small to moderate challenge, a plan needs to feel exciting and stimulating and resonate with you.

A beautiful place to start is to get quiet. Pray, ask for guidance, meditate, and then listen. Every spiritual tradition teaches us that we have helpers, angels, and well-wishers in the invisible realm who are here to guide us. It helps to be out in nature when getting grounded, centered, and quiet. This is not always possible, so setting up a meditation space where there are no distractions and it's only for this purpose can be very helpful.

When you are quiet, pay attention to anything that's brought into your awareness. If it is about daily things or your never-ending to-do list, just see it and watch it float away. It's normal to have these things interrupt our meditation, but the goal is to have them just float on by. You will know when you get your answer or guidance. It often comes not when we are most ardently asking for it (when we're in "asking mode") but when we least expect it — while out on a walk, talking to a friend, sleeping, or taking a shower or bath.

You may hear a voice or see words or just know it. We may sometimes get a feeling or goose bumps and feel like something or someone is there with us, helping and guiding us on this journey. Do not ever discount these feelings, as they are your intuition. You may have a strong thought that could be your answer, or you may be like me and hear a voice from time to time. This is your inner "knowing."

This is how I started to listen to my intuition and pay attention. In 2005 I was doing a construction project that was on a ridiculously short schedule set mostly by myself. During that time I received a couple books from my Mystery Book Club. As a member you got a small catalog in the mail and agreed to buy an initial seven books at a reduced rate. After those seven books that you picked and paid for, you were able to select the books that were sent to you a couple times a month with no more obligations. I opened the mystery book club box, and the book that was sent to me was by Sylvia Brown, the psychic medium: ***Conversations With the Other Side***. This was not a mystery book and certainly not any book I had ordered! I was pissed to say the least, because I thought Sylvia Brown was *crazy*, but this was a Mystery Book Club that you only get books that you order in the Mystery genre. This was a highly unusual situation. I proceeded to say the "F" word in a few different ways as I put the book back in the box and at the back of my bedside table. I was too stressed and busy to return it.

None of us are ever our better selves when we are stressed. After that construction project in 2005, during which I almost had a nervous breakdown, I pretty much crashed in every way. I had to make the choice to make changes and start to really take care of myself because I couldn't continue my life how it had been going. I believe this was a "nudge" from the universe for me to change. That Sylvia Brown book stayed there at the back of my bedside table until after I crashed on my road bike a year later.

Do you ever feel like life is throwing a lot of stress at you, and you're trying to slow down and manage things, but it keeps getting out of control? In 2006, at the age of 42, I crashed on my road bike. I broke my left collarbone, tore my left rotator cuff, and got a brand new dent in my left humeral head. This was another "nudge." I found out later that the breaking of a bone is like breaking the pattern of how we have been living. I thought I had slowed down and changed some things in my life after that project in 2005, but this got my attention, and I made more changes. I simply couldn't continue living my life as I had been.

Do you find yourself ever saying, "Ok, universe… I get it. I need to slow down"? I finally started being able to say no to things I had been saying yes to that were not making me happy, grounded, or balanced and that were keeping me from healing. Things were finally moving in the direction of healing and self-preservation for me. Because I was not in balance, I wasn't as good at the things I was doing anyway. I'm pretty sure I wasn't much fun to be around either. I was finally starting to put the oxygen mask on myself first. As a mother this is a very difficult thing to do because we are "on" all the time. But I started with the outside world first by saying no to things that did not directly support my healing. That was a huge change, one I implemented with trepidation but a deep knowing that it was necessary.

As I was recovering from my crash I had to change sides of the bed because of my broken collarbone. When I was finally able to move back to my side of the bed after two months, I decided to clean out my bedside table. That was when I found that box from my book club with the Sylvia Brown book in it. I was in a much humbler and calmer space. I still thought Sylvia might be crazy, but I finally believed there are no coincidences in this life.

I read the book, but I could only wrap my brain around 30 percent of it. The only major thing I could accept at that time was this: *if* we plan this life and other lives, then we can handle whatever happens, because **we planned this life**. Meaning, we choose where we are born, who our parents are, who our friends, siblings, lovers, partners, lessons are, so that we can learn the lessons we were meant to learn. This was comforting to me, and I thought at the very least if we all keep existing on some level and we keep coming back, then we were not losing our loved ones forever, and that made me feel much better. Having lost my sister Karen to leukemia, if we/she/us all planned our lives with Karen's death in it to learn and evolve, then we can handle it and she is ok, even better than ok. I took solace in these things and decided I would reread Sylvia's book in about a month. I read it two more times in the next year, and by then I could pretty much accept it all. What a gift that book was to me! I am very grateful to Sylvia Brown for writing it and to my guides for getting it to me.

Another time when I felt my guides brought something important to my attention was in the spring of 2012 at the Optimum Health Institute in San Diego, California. I was at the gift shop and I saw a book that I had seen two other times in my life recently. I thought, "Ok, universe, I see it and I hear you." I believed I was being nudged again by the universe and my guides, and I knew for certain I preferred the nudges rather than the karmic 2x4 upside the head, so I bought the book — *Introduction to Energy Medicine* by Donna Eden. I had seen it on someone's blog, and recently Amazon had suggested it to me. I went back to my room, climbed into bed, and started reading. Within ten minutes, I felt like my soul was singing! I thought, "I can't *not* do this training and work."

When I returned home I looked into taking the training and found out I had just missed it and that I would have to wait a year. I had to get creative. I looked for training in other states, and I had missed them all. I dug deeper and found out that I could miss one class per year but that I would need to self-teach it, take and pass a 12-page written exam, and then do a demo on a person in front of my teacher, whom I had never met, over Skype. That is the problem or gift of us souls who feel like there is nothing we cannot do. We do it, but we pay the price in stress and health.

Fortunately for me, energy medicine came pretty easily to me. I started to heal energetically, and everything flowed better in my life. It was very small at first because I was not as disciplined at doing my daily self care, but as I did it more and more I realized how beneficial it was in my overall wellbeing. If you are interested in energy medicine that goes much deeper than Reiki, complimenting Reiki, and also ties into acupressure then you may be interested in this training program, the Eden Method. In year one you learn how to work on yourself and your loved ones. Year two gets you ready to start your own practice as an energy medicine practitioner. Year three is a Clinical Practicum — you work on 100 clients throughout the year and are supervised by a mentor. Year four is by application only with proof that you have done your own extensive work on yourself so that you can take your work with clients to a deeper spiritual level. I cannot say enough great things about this program and all that I've learned to help my clients and myself. I believe this is the direction that medicine is going, and this program is a gift to us all. If you are interested you can go to Innersource.net to look into Eden Method training and certification. This is a certification program that also has a Code of Ethics and an Ethics Board, which I believe is integral to the healing industry.

Has it happened to you that in a moment, there's a shift in the atmosphere and you feel touched by a sense of grace? Recently my daughter asked me to go with her to Michael's, the craft store. I was in the passenger seat as she was driving my car, which was unusual. When we got there, I opened the car door and almost stepped on a brass coin. I picked it up and looked at it. It had an angel on both sides. I had been seeking answers that week on choices I had to make, and in that moment I felt like I wasn't alone, that there was compassion, wisdom, and love being expressed to me by guides who were very near and very loving.

We come into this world to learn, grow, and evolve. These lessons are ours forever. Growth is not easy or without struggle, so we inevitably end up with debris in the form of stuck energy and emotions that we need to release out of our body. We have help and guidance with this if we listen and pay attention. If I'm struggling with something, I open my heart and ask for help, then I pay attention to emails I get, articles and books I read, and conversations I have with people. If I read about something related to what I am currently struggling with, well, that is no coincidence. I take the guidance with gratitude, and I look into whatever it is and I continue to heal myself.

If you are struggling with something now try this:

Sit quietly and ask either your angels, God, Jesus, or your higher power to take a burden from you, releasing it to them. You can also ask for guidance and then sit and see what comes to you. If you are releasing something, you can ask Archangel Raphael to fill those spaces where that challenge was in your body or field with beautiful divine, loving, healing, light energy restoring it to its original vibrancy. If you are asking for guidance, it could come in the form of a thought, hearing a voice, a dream, something a stranger or friends says or gives to you.

A friend gave me a plain white business-card-sized card that says, "Expect miracles." That card had been on the dashboard of my car for several years. I gave it to the next person who needed it, and it will continue on helping us to remember to expect miracles, be grateful for them and they will happen. It is a great reminder that miracles are at our fingertips and can happen in a moment. We simply need to ask for them, be open to them and grateful for them.

Miracles can be great or small. I was reminded of that again after an ayurvedic consultation a few months ago. The practitioner recommended that I spray rose water into my eyes every morning upon waking. I intended to buy rose water at Whole Foods, but I kept forgetting. Two weeks later, I opened the door at my work to an energy medicine client, and she said, "Hi, I brought you some rose water!" I laughed and hugged her, thanking her and my angels.

Another example of feeling guided and receiving a reassuring message from the universe was when I was coming to the end of a 1031 Reverse Exchange on a property I was selling. This is a tax strategy and form of taxation strategy for investment properties. I had already purchased and remodeled the property I was exchanging into, and I was on a deadline to sell the original property that ended up needing to be fixed up to sell it. It was a very stressful time for me, and I had so much on my mind regarding the taxes I would have to pay if I was not able to get a buyer and close escrow in the next 45 days. I was asking for guidance and reassurance from my angels daily. One morning when I was bringing my trash and recycling cans up from the street, I saw a beautiful earring in the gutter next to the cans. I believed this was a message that I was supported financially in that situation. I was able to relax more around the situation and release much worry. Very soon after I found a buyer for my property, and everything closed and finalized with only a couple days to spare.

There are many ways to address the energies and emotions we have accumulated in this life and others. The emotion of worry and over-concern had been energetically getting in the way of that business transaction for me. With awareness and help from my angels and guides, I was able to recognize and acknowledge my over-worry and over-concern. These emotions had created a block to the energy of releasing that property to the next owner. By recognizing and acknowledging it, I was able to release those stuck emotions and create a pathway for that energy to move and the property to sell. We can release stuck emotions in many ways such as through hypnosis, regression, energy medicine, emotion code, sound healing, energy psychology, and other methods. I will go into great detail on how to release these emotions and blocks from our body in Chapter 18.

Ask your guides, even if you don't believe in guides or have a hard time visualizing them. If there were guardian angels with you, as so many spiritual traditions teach, how do they feel about you? It is my belief that they see our soul, love us unconditionally, and want to help us become lighter and better versions of ourselves. As we do this work we get lighter, brighter, and happier. Our vibration increases and consequently raises the collective vibration as we gradually heal each other and ourselves. As we get clearer and lighter by healing and releasing traumas and emotions from our bodies, we are able to get clearer guidance because we are not as weighted down or blocked by the traumas and stuck emotions. It is a simple practice but deeply transformational.

Chapter 5
Dreams and Intuition

"Dreams are today's answer to tomorrow's questions."
— *Edgar Cayce*

I FIND DREAMS TO BE very interesting. What I have learned and experienced is that they are our subconscious working out and processing what is currently going on in our lives and what happened recently. Dreams can also be about events from our past that are ready to be worked out and released. They can also be messages to us from our higher self, angels, God, or whatever is your belief of the origin. Some dreams can be prophetic, warning us of some event that is or could be about to happen. They are rarely direct and to the point and they are usually symbolic or an analogy.

I woke up this morning at 5:58 am after asking my guides and angels last night to have me wake up at 6am so I can have time to write. Right before I woke up I experienced the thought or voice in my head, in a dream, saying, "We are coming into a 576 or 676 frequency, and our physical body needs to come into a higher frequency to be able to function optimally or better in this new frequency." All-righty then! What does this message mean to me? My first thought was, that I need to be grounded, meditate more, breathe better or more mindfully, eat higher-vibration foods, and think and feel higher vibration thoughts and emotions to prepare for and thrive in this new frequency. I need to be balanced in my life. I also thought the specific numbers were given to me for a reason, so I looked them up in my *Angel Numbers 101* book by Doreen Virtue, and this is what it said: "576: Give any fear or doubts about changing your life to Heaven, as these changes will ease a lot of stress." "676: Have no worries, you are doing the right thing." As far as I was concerned these were both good messages, and I always listen and act on my guidance with gratitude.

There are words, thoughts, and emotions that are a higher frequency. Some of the higher vibrational emotions are love, joy, and gratitude. I believe to have a higher vibrational life you need to create a balance between your work and your play so that you can be in the vibration of the higher emotions as much as possible. This has been very out of balance for me in this lifetime, and to feel, think, experience, and be more of those higher vibration thoughts, feelings, and emotions I needed to make some changes. I know how to work hard and to self-care, but I have not been good about taking time to play or relax. I have also been drawing more angel cards recently with the same message. I guess I need to get this into my life sooner rather than later, as I am now getting dream messages.

My dream a couple nights ago and a little while after the number dream I just mentioned was in a park setting, and there were a lot of squirrels in it. I looked up what squirrels mean in the book *Animal-Speak Pocket Guide* by Ted Andrews: "Squirrel (work and play): Balance your work and play. Prepare for the future, but do not get lost in preparations. Find ways to gather and gift." There was also a pack of coyotes in the same dream. I was a little afraid of them in the park I was walking through in my dream, but they weren't after me. Here is what the book said: "Coyotes (wisdom & folly): Balance work and fun in your new endeavors. Trust all is happening according to plan. Do what is best — even if it is difficult." I have been sensing a theme in my messages, and it is loud and clear. If I choose to not only listen but to also implement change in my life, things will flow better for me. I am paying attention, and I am working on this.

This is the new frequency that we are coming into. It's a frequency of being more in tune with our guidance and following it. Not pushing but rather balancing, allowing, and healing. We still need to work but we should enjoy our work, find time for play or joy, have friendships, and take care of our physical, emotional, and spiritual bodies. This is how we will be healthier and happier. I'm finding that implementing this for me looks like I need to get to bed a lot earlier, say "yes" to more social invitations, and look into joyful activities.

I find it exhausting to be in all of my dreams. I wake up tired, and that's not good. I figure I need to rest while my subconscious works these things out, so that I can be my better self during the day. I generally have my most important message dreams right before I wake up in the morning. Every night at bedtime I say, "**I AM** sleeping deeply and restoratively, and **I AM** only remembering the dreams that are important messages." This works a lot of the time, but I find that I go through different phases where I am more active in my dreams than other times, and I figure this is part of my process of working things out while I sleep.

Dreams started getting my attention back in the early 2000's. I had a few repetitive dreams for years that make some sense now. Around November of 2011 my dreams started to change. I remember the first dream vividly. I was standing on a bridge. In the book *Cracking the Dream Code* by Lauri Quinn Lowenberg, the meaning of bridges is "transition — getting from point A to point B; crossing over into a new area of your life." In the dream I was just looking out at the horizon and being still, leaning on the railing of the bridge when I felt someone walk up behind me. I actually felt their energy, and it felt familiar and really, really nice to me. It was an energy that I would want to be in all of the time. It felt like love, lightness, home, peace, and yumminess. I turned around, and it was someone in my current life that I did not know very well at that time. I was surprised to say the least. I was about to go through a huge transition in my life and didn't know it yet. That person was a peripheral part of that transition in a positive and familiar way. I believe I was being shown how my life could be different being around people that had a wonderful vibration. This person continued to show up randomly in my dreams and life for several years and to give me messages from time to time in my dreams. I have lived many lives with this person and feel a deep love and connection to them. They helped me tremendously both in this life and in dreamtime, and they may not even know it.

I find it interesting that people come into our lives for a previously agreed upon and very specific time and purpose — to help us transition, to learn lessons, to guide us or support us, or many other reasons. Not all of these feel positive to us while we are learning these lessons, but they are all positive in that they are personal growth opportunities if we recognize that and allow it. When the purpose or agreement has been met then these people are not such a big part or even any part of your life or journey anymore. Lives move on as everyone is figuring out their own journey and moving through their own growth opportunities. There is always an energy recognition or attraction or soul recognition between you for that particular life but if your agreement is done then things move on or fade away. There is of course free will on our part, but we often have karmic agreements that come into play and opportunities present to us to fulfill these soul contracts or agreements to move forward on our soul's journey. The people we have agreements or contracts with have a very energetic attraction for us and to us. We are literally drawn to them or they to us so we can fulfill our agreements.

Not long after I moved into my new house in 2013, I had a dream. Again, it was the last dream right before I woke up in the morning. It was a man's voice that said, "I really like your new address." I woke up the second he said that. I then looked up the number of my address in my book *Angel Numbers 101* by Doreen Virtue: "God is ensuring that, as you devote your time and energy toward a spiritual focus, all of your material and financial needs are met." Well, I was around a year and a half into my education as an Eden Method Practitioner, which was turning out to be not only for the healing of the physical body, which was why I originally got into the program, but also about deep spiritual healing. I was happy with that dream message, as I was already committed heart and soul to this new profession that will help and has helped so many people heal their body-mind-spirit, including myself.

We spend time with other souls during our sleep. This is called astral travel. We know we have done this when we have dreams where we are in a car, boat, airplane, or other method of transportation with other people. I remember a lot of these dreams. What I've read from several authors is that our soul actually leaves our body at night and travels around. The soul is tethered to the physical body by an etheric cord so we always come back, so do not be concerned. I really like the idea that I can spend time with souls I'm connected to in dreamtime. I did, however, astral travel one time in a car with a former friend and her friend, who I did not care for. There was a message in that dream, and I was grateful for it upon awakening. You want to be careful and not get too into this travel time and subsequently not live vibrantly in this life, which is the important time spent on your journey.

When I was around nine years old, I shared a room with my identical twin sister. We had one of those 70's corner console tables that two twin beds connected to at the head of the bed in the corner of the bedroom so that each bed was against a wall. I remember having a very vivid dream that my sister was in with me, and it was weird. I woke up, propped up on my arm, looked over at her as she had just woken up as well and was looking at me. I said, "That was a really weird dream," and she replied, "Yes, it was." We chatted about it for a minute and then went back to sleep. Neither of us can remember the dream now, only that it was really vivid and weird, and that we both had the same dream.

I remember the first time I met Donna Eden. I had been in the Eden Method Certification Program for about a year and a half when I had a dream that some fellow classmates and faculty and I were going to a party. We knocked on the door of a condo, and the door opened and I saw Donna Eden at the eating bar in the kitchen with my instructor, Kim. They were talking to other people and eating snacks, and when we came in Donna and Kim turned to say hi, and their eyes locked on mine like lasers. In the dream my body lifted into the air and started spinning slowly like cartwheels. I felt like it was an initiation by them. When the spinning was done I woke up. That dream is still so vivid in my mind. I met Donna for the first time in person not long after that. She said she found my energies to be familiar when she first met me.

I learned from Donna that we come into this life with a primary life color or maybe two life colors. At that time, Donna could see four colors in my energy field, which she said was very unusual. I was told by an intuitive that I had brought in those other colors to help me in my transition. My life colors were purple-violet. I learned later about them in a class taught by Donna's daughter Titanya Dahlin, who is very good at life color readings and interpretations. I have included Titanya's contact information in the back of this book in case you are interested in a life color reading from her. I learned from Titanya that when you have a violet life color you are either a victim or you are a leader after being a victim. I had already done the victim thing, so now I was apparently off to learn to lead. I've reflected on what that might mean, and I suppose I am helping on a team of amazing, brave souls to lead the world in alternative healing modalities, especially Energy Medicine, Reconnective Healing, and Medical Medium's protocols. It takes courage to do this, and I am finding that I have an abundance of courage these days.

My other life color is purple, and I learned that people with a purple life color are typically healers and have been healers in many life times. Well this was not a surprise given that I am an Advanced Eden Method Practitioner and when I read Donna Eden's book for the first time I felt like my soul was singing. Purples also have the ability to easily dimensionally travel. This definitely helps in my work with clients, but it makes it hard for me to stay grounded. When the proverbial shit hits the fan in my life, the best way I can describe what happens is that my spirit pops out of my body and wants to go elsewhere.

When I am in stressful times I can in my mind's eye see a bridge in front of my body. I guess this bridge is metaphorically connected to other lives or dimensions, and there I am (in spirit) leaning against the railing looking at myself here saying, "How's the shit storm going for you?" This is yet another example of my spirit's sense of humor. I do not like it when this happens. I need all of me to handle whatever is going on in this life at that time. I know this is happening and that I am not grounded when I cannot get a deep breath. This is not a comfortable feeling. I immediately notice if I am holding my breath and most times I am. I start my 5 seconds in breath, hold for 5 seconds, and breathe out for 5 seconds while saying "I am grounded and 100% in this body, in this life, this time, in this moment, on this earth." This brings my spirit back completely in this body, grounding my body and helps with my fight, flight, or freeze, and then I can breathe deeply again. I also trace my stress meridian backward, saying that I am safe, which I will go into in greater detail about this in Chapter 7. I do my grounding visualizations throughout the day to keep me tethered and in my body. In my life color reading I was told that I would most likely be a full purple in my next life. I am good with that.

Pay attention to your dreams. They are guidance and messages for you on this journey. I've received many messages just before I have woken up that I honored, and I believe they saved me from a bunch of heartache and discord. I love my dream interpretation book, *Cracking the Dream Code,* and I also recommend a journal by your bed, especially if you are in a big transition. Be clear when you are going to bed about what you want guidance on and what you want your dream experience to be like. It may take up to two weeks to get an answer in a dream, but it will come if you continue to hold the intention for it and ask every night before going to sleep. I personally only want to remember the important messages and blissfully sleep the rest of the time. Sweet dreams!

Chapter 6
Pain Is Energy

"Forgive anyone who has caused you pain. Keep in mind that forgiving is not for others. It is for you. Forgiving is not forgetting. It is remembering without anger. It frees up your power, heals your body, mind and spirit. Forgiveness opens up a pathway to a new place of peace where you can persist despite what has happened to you."
— *Les Brown*

EVERYTHING IS ENERGY, AND ENERGY is everything. Our thoughts, beliefs, and emotions are all energy. What we eat, say, wear, drink, and sleep on are all energy but at different vibrations. Energy needs to move, otherwise it cannot be vibrant. Lack of vibrant energy in our physical body can lead to dis-ease. Pain of any type — whether emotional, physical, or mental — is trapped, frozen, blocked, or buried energy.

We all have a vibration starting out in the field around our body. Some people can see these energies, and some of us are able to physically feel these energies or just "know" them. I'm starting to see them myself from working with and in energy so much. I have been able to feel them for years now. Most people have felt these energies around other people when they say that they did not like a certain person's "vibe." You've likely felt residual energies in places such as buildings or homes. A bar feels different than a kindergarten, right? Even if there are no people present. If you are interested in doing space clearing, Denise Linn has a wonderful Elemental Space Clearing Certification course and has written many books on the subject. I have included her information in the references at the back of the book.

The energy out in our field around us is at a much higher vibration than the denser energy of our physical body. If we are energy and our thoughts are energy, then it's important to remember that when we are in a constant state of lower energy thoughts, emotions or beliefs. Others can feel the low vibration from those low vibration energy thoughts in our field. That lower energy state can even attract other similar frequency energies to us. These energies can get stuck in our physical body and block the movement of energy in our body. Disease in the physical body can and often does have an emotional or belief-based component. I will go into this more in Chapter 8.

We also can be in a higher vibration by eating clean and healthy food. Do you remember the saying "You are what you eat"? Such a true saying! If what we eat has no vibration or a low vibration, we will have a lower vibration. Just like being in a space of higher frequency vibrational thoughts, feelings or emotions of love, joy, and gratitude will bring our vibration up. This is the vibe that we all want to be around and attract to us. I "see" this vibration in and around people as bright and sparkly, and it feels really good to be around. This is how we came into this world and what we can get back to.

This makes me think of something my brother-in-law says to my sister. Whenever my sis would voice an opinion that would be critical of herself (lower energy), he'd simply say to her, "Hey, I don't like it when people talk bad about my wife." Her response was always a smile and her saying, "Good grief!" usually followed by a kiss between them. He is a very happy guy who has a rather sunny and hardy disposition. What a gift! Something as simple as that reminds us when our inner voice needs a more positive direction. Notice your inner voice. Is it positive, loving, encouraging, and supportive or is it belittling, judging, or hateful?

Other people can often feel when you hold feelings or beliefs about yourself or others in the form of anger, resentment, shame, loathing, or judgment. These lower energies can get stuck in your physical body where you may have experienced a physical trauma at the time of these deep emotions. The spot on my leg right on and around my shinbone where I got my skin cancer is where I banged my leg hard getting into my motorhome. The step into the motorhome was at a rather awkward height and was a perfect shin-banger if you were not paying attention. The emotions that were prevalent for me back then were anger, frustration, and resentment. I'm sure those emotions were being felt by my former spouse, which was not fun for either of us.

Try this experiment when you can:

The next person you come into contact with, look them in the eyes and think, "I love you," and see what their reaction is. I have startled a couple of people with this experiment — they would pause and their eyes would open wide looking at me — but it was worth knowing how our thoughts toward other people are felt by them.

Resentment was a biggie for me. I believe it was trapped in my shin and festered until the perfect storm happened and my immune system wasn't able to hold the cancer in my body in check anymore. Too many things in my life were out of balance. I will go into greater depth on this in my Chapter 8 about cancer, but I wanted to introduce you to how these energetic and emotional imbalances can be the start of dis-ease in our body.

Another place for these emotions to get stuck are in the various organs of your body. This goes back to ancient Chinese Medicine about meridians, elements, or rhythms tied to different organs in your physical body. A common organ/emotion relation is Liver and Gallbladder (Wood Element) being associated with repressed rage, anger, resentment (hello!) and/or frustration. I will list the different elements with their associated stress emotion for you to consider in your healing journey. When these elements are out of balance from lower-vibration thoughts, beliefs, or stress they will present with physical imbalances in the body. I "see" these emotions as being dark, gray, red, or black.

Water Element	Kidney and Bladder Meridians and organs are associated with **fear**.
Wood Element	Liver and Gallbladder Meridians and organs are associated with **rage, anger, resentment, shame, judgement, and frustration.**
Fire Element	Includes Small Intestine, Heart, Triple Warmer Meridians (Triple Warmer governs the flight, flight, or freeze response), and Circulation Sex Meridian (governs the pericardium around the heart for protection of the heart). This element and these meridians and organs are associated with **panic and anxiety.**
Earth Element	Spleen and Stomach Meridians and organs are associated with **over-worry and over-concern for self or others.**
Metal Element	Large Intestine and Lung Meridians and organs are associated with **grief (Lung) and not letting go (Large Intestine)**.

Looking at, honoring and releasing these emotions in the form of forgiveness of self and others back to source is not only freeing for you but for others as well. You are releasing them out of your physical and energetic bodies so that you can have a higher vibration and more vibrant health. Ease in your body is the natural flow of energy in your energy systems that feed and harmonize your physical body, including your organs, ligaments, and connective tissue. I will guide you through the clearing of these emotions from your organs in Chapter 18. I also included an addendum at the back of the book for this protocol for your reference.

It is my belief and experience that any energy blocks left long enough can lead to or contribute to chronic pain, diseases such as cancer, tumors, heart disease, lung conditions, kidney disease, gallbladder disease, stomach problems, liver cancer, or just about any other chronic condition. You cannot only treat the symptoms of the physical body. You must also address the cause or the root of the condition. Our body gives us messages, and we need to pay attention to these messages, honor them, and even be grateful for what they are telling us is out of balance. Then and only then can we fix the root challenge or issue and grow to be our better and healthier self.

I recently received guidance that the healing of my liver would happen much quicker if I would release emotions/energies from my liver with my pendulum. If you have a pendulum, this may be easy for you. If you do not own a pendulum then you can order one on Etsy or look at a gemstone store and pick the stone of the pendulum that feels perfect for you. I will help you to get started with a pendulum now and get back to how I cleared my liver later in this chapter.

When you get a new pendulum you want to clear it with any of these suggestions: selenite will clear it, smudge it with white sage (burn white sage next to it and the smoke will clear the energies), leave it in the sun for several hours, run it under cold water for a minute (check to make sure it will not dissolve — selenite should never touch water or it will dissolve). After you've cleared the pendulum then hold it in the palm of your hand, infusing it with your energy.

When you feel like you have done this, you are ready to attune it to your intentions for guidance. What I mean by that is you hold the intention that if it moves up and down like a nod of your head it is a "yes", and if it moves side to side it is a "no." You can take this further with a diagonal movement, but I will not go into that for these purposes. I need to mention that if you are going to use a pendulum for guidance with questions you need to be careful with your intentions and the wording of your questions. I always state that the answers will come from my higher self only and then ask the yes or no question or make a statement. The reason I say this is because we can move the pendulum however we want to with our mind or our eyes. Play with it and you will see.

As I mentioned previously, I received guidance to do a more in-depth clearing of the energies in and around my liver with my pendulum.

When I was ready to do the clearing, I held the intention that I would release any and all energies cellular or otherwise from this lifetime and other lifetimes that are ready to be released. I held my pendulum a couple inches above my liver (below your right breast), and my pendulum started to spin counterclockwise which is the direction of clearing or releasing. It did this for a while as I held my arm and hand very still. After a little while it started to slow down. I yawned, which is a release of energy and the body syncing to changes. I was done clearing. Then the pendulum came to the middle and bounced a couple times and then started spinning clockwise, filling up that space that was just cleared with new and fresh healing energy. That eventually stopped, and I was done.

Try this now if you have a pendulum:

Hold it very still over your liver with the intention of clearing energies, emotions, etc. from your liver and watch your pendulum spin counter clockwise for a bit. It should slow down and do a couple bounces before spinning clockwise, filling your liver with new energy. You may yawn or cough, which are messages that energy is moving, connecting, and clearing.

Sometimes when I do this I feel emotions coming to the surface, and I may cry and just let it out. You can do this anywhere on your body that you sense has energies that need to be cleared. I was also guided to do this on my shoulders, hips, and on the outside below my knees where I had been having recent pain. What I "saw" was a man being torn apart on a torture machine in a past life. A deep cry of pain, despair, and anguish came out of me while it was clearing. Then I felt extremely tired but so much lighter of spirit. You may not be successful with this but do not lose heart. Clearing often happens without us feeling it, especially at the beginning. There are many ways to clear these energies and emotions, which is why there are many different types of energy healing.

I had a client session where my client had been having pain on her left side — sacrum, hip, and thigh — from a bicycle accident six years ago. She is in the healing profession, so she had tried many different modalities that had helped her but had not gotten rid of the pain all the way. We determined that she had an energy cord in her left sacrum and hip from her sister. We removed it in its entirety, but there was more to be cleared from that area, so I went deeper, and we cleared emotions from both of them that were being stored in her hip. After clearing everything else that was ready to be cleared from that area and getting her energies to start moving in their original vibrant ways, we put healing energy back in. Two days later I received a text from that client that the pain that she had been dealing with for years was gone! She was so excited because she had tried so many different healing modalities and this was what finally worked. She was happy to tell me that she had just gone to her regular yoga class, and it was a whole new experience for her. She said it opened her up in yoga poses and that it was truly a miracle. I recently saw her and it has been around six months since that session, and she said she is still pain free in those areas that we cleared and balanced.

Before I started the clearing of my liver with my pendulum, I energy tested and got the answer that my liver was 40% healed. That was several years ago but it is a good marker of my progress in my healing. Energy testing is a way to see which energies are strong or weak in your body and for getting answers to questions for guidance. Now in the beginning of 2020 my physical liver energy tests at 89% healed. Energy testing can be done on oneself with practice and intention. I will teach you how to energy test with different methods in detail in Chapter 11. I had been supporting my liver in its healing through diet, supplements, and some energy medicine, but it was time to help it by clearing it emotionally and energetically. Since clearing the energies around my liver my body has been able to accelerate the healing of my liver. Keep in mind that I eat very clean to support the healing of my liver, I regularly go in a sauna to detox my liver and body, I get colonics that help my liver to release toxins, and I drink herbal tea blends that help to detox specific toxins from my body and liver. Stored emotions cause blocks and sluggishness in our organs and body. I will go into more depth on clearing even more from our organs in Chapter 18 for optimal health and energetic support.

By doing this work you are creating transparency in yourself. I've heard people advise others to tell their dark painful stuff to someone safe. Tell it or share it with someone safe that you trust. With their love, support, and acceptance you can really look at it, forgive it, and forgive your imperfect human self. This is humility, and it's the pathway to releasing emotional pain and healing. Having nothing to hide and living in integrity creates transparency.

I believe this is why so many people who have a big challenge are hugely successful and able to help other people with it. Helping others with it means relating to them and showing your vulnerability. I think this is why AA works. AA is designed to be a safe place to admit your challenge, be able to share it in a confidential environment, be supported and support others with similar challenges, do your work through the steps of the program, and heal. It's humbling to share with strangers that you are an alcoholic or an addict who has made some bad choices that most likely did harm. I believe these addictions happen sometimes because of harm that was done to them as children and not being able to process it out in a safe and positively supported way. I also believe there is a component to addiction of being highly sensitive and receiving too much input all of the time. In other words, not knowing how to handle being an empath. I will discuss empathy in greater detail in another chapter.

You cannot be happy, healthy, vibrant, and live in integrity with painful secrets stuck in you. Here is an analogy: form is energy. Look at us as glass for instance. We all have our imperfections. Clear glass with cloudy patches shows the resistance of transparency and hides the total beauty of the glass with the small imperfections in it. These imperfections are what make each glass (us) beautiful and original. The fear of exposure of these painful clouds in us is what keeps us in a shame cycle of emotional pain living in the lower vibration of being discovered, judged, and condemned. Humility clears the clouds, releases the pain, and creates shine in our glass (us). Humility, forgiving of self, and telling someone safe allows love into us. It allows us to be loved deeply and unconditionally and to love ourselves deeply and unconditionally. That openness to love releases the pain.

Blame shifting doesn't work to free these energies. You cannot do something that has the energy of shame, grief, remorse, or any other lower energy and try to give that to someone else through blaming them to feel less emotional pain your self. You may feel a little better on the surface, but the energy is still in *you,* and it continues to cloud your glass because it's still there deep down. One of the hardest things to do in life is to heart-felt apologize to someone with complete ownership of your actions. Afterward, however, it's amazing. Whether the person you apologize to is in a space to forgive you or not, you can forgive yourself on the premise that we are human and therefore very likely to mess things up, but *everything* is forgivable. And I say that because of my belief that we live multiple lives, and when we do we live out different life lessons.

We can be on both sides of these lessons. It's a great learning and growth opportunity to be on either side of these lessons, whether we are embezzled from or we embezzle from someone. If we are cheated on by our spouse or partner or we are the one who does the cheating. It's hard being a drug addict and also very hard being the loved one of an addict. Hard lessons and growth opportunities can be learned on both sides. All of these are opportunities for growth and becoming our better selves *if* we choose to do the work of really looking at it, forgiving, and releasing it.

I was listening to an Oprah and Deepak Chopra meditation when I was in an intense healing time several years ago. I believe it was Oprah who said, "You know you have healed when you can look back at the trauma that you went through, and it is no longer your story." That really stuck with me, because when I looked at it from an energetic point of view, it means that there is no longer energy or pain around that old yucky story, and it has been forgiven and released. Thank you Oprah for that and thank you to both Deepak Chopra and Oprah for giving these free meditation series to help and support all of us in our healing. What a gift! I have a friend who refers to that absence of energy charge regarding an emotional trauma as the "harmless passage through your thoughts or mind." *That* is the goal. Feeling a sense of neutrality about the story, event, or person. If not neutrality, then love or gratitude toward the story, event, or person is the ultimate goal, as well as gratitude for the lessons learned.

Please know that we are all on a journey and have wounds and pain of various origins. The lower energies of shame, anger, or loathing toward yourself only feed on themselves, dragging you down further. Please tell someone safe (a therapist, friend, partner, family member, or clergy) or people you consider safe until that hidden thing no longer has energy around it. Pray for that energy to be taken out of you and from you. Check out my clearing of emotions protocol in Chapter 18 and at the end of the book to help you release these emotional energies that are still in your energy field and are no longer serving you. The goal is to surround it in love and forgiveness, release it, and when thinking of it later, it's energetically neutral. Have compassion and love for yourself and what you have forgiven or released, as it's the more beautiful of the threads in the tapestry of our lives. When you're able to do this, you can help other people deal with their cloudiness by being that safe person to hear what they have to say. That is a gift to yourself and others. Be your most brilliant, sparkly transparent, non-judgmental, authentic self. Help others with what you have been challenged with. That is how you live a life of love, joy, and integrity.

In *The Biology of Belief* by Bruce Lipton, a former medical school professor, research scientist, and renowned cell biologist says something that ties into what I was just explaining about thoughts and emotions:

> "You can choose what to see. You can filter your life with rose-colored beliefs that will help your body grow or you can use a dark filter that turns everything black and makes your body/mind more susceptible to disease. You can live a life of fear or live a life of love. You have the choice! But I can tell you that if you choose to see a world full of love, your body will respond by growing in health. If you choose to believe that you live in a dark world full of fear, your body's health will be compromised as you physiologically close yourself down in a protection response."

Dr. Lipton wrote this book as a resource on the biochemical effects of how the brain functions and how all cells of your body are affected by your thoughts. Dr. Lipton discovers and shows us how the mind, body, and spirit are deeply interconnected. He discusses how it's widely recognized how DNA and genes do not control our biology, but rather, signals that come from outside of our cells do. His experiments and the experiments of other scientists are in his book. If you want the scientific proof of what I have experienced and am sharing with you, this will be a great read for you.

Chapter 7
Bike Crash, Broken Bone, Life Changes

"When you look deeply into your anger, you will see that the person you call your enemy is also suffering. As soon as you see that, the capacity for accepting and having compassion for them is there."
— *Thich Nhat Hanh*

WHILE WORKING ON A CONSTRUCTION project in 2005, I earned the name "ramrod" with regard to my scheduling of the phases of the project. This was not a compliment, although everyone appeared to like me and wanted to help me get this project done within my somewhat unrealistic expectations. Anyone who has done any construction will see where this is going. We started with rough framing mid June of 2005 right when my kids got out of school for the summer. My daughter was nine, and my son was six. They were too old for childcare and too young to be left by themselves. That left me with a babysitter two days a week for four hours each of those two days. The rest of the time they were with me.

I was the project manager, interior designer, and superintendent, and I did some labor as well. I did construction cleanup and helped unload heavy tiles off a lift. I helped get furniture up steep stairs, and I purchased and brought in everything to set up two houses — all the decorations and smaller furnishings for both units: bedding, fixtures, furniture, kitchen, and cooking supplies. I completely set up those two houses by myself on a crazy schedule with two kids in tow. Yikes.

At the same time, there was a commercial space on the bottom floor of a mixed-use project that was being completely renovated and restored as a small grocery store and deli. We had a project manager on that part of the project, so I was only needed to do small things like pick out electrical fixtures and set up soft water. I was exhausted all the time, and when I wasn't exhausted I was a bit manic to get everything done. Apparently, I had something to prove to my spouse and myself. I had a need and a drive to feel like I had worth and value in our business and partnership.

Of course, as promised, I managed to complete the whole project, and have the two beach vacation rentals fully furnished and ready to rent out the weekend after Labor Day, exactly three months from the start. All of it over the summer time with kids. Although I felt a huge sense of accomplishment, I ended up paying a big price.

How did I do it? I did the typical thing that we all do to get through stressful times. I had caffeine throughout the day: a latte for breakfast, Diet Pepsi after lunch, decaf latte in the afternoon around 3–4 pm, and semi-dark chocolate throughout the day. One of my go-to's were those big Ghirardelli chocolate chunk pieces wrapped in cellophane that I'd get at Trader Joe's. I figured it was healthy chocolate — antioxidants and everything. Embarrassingly, I'd gnaw on a big chunk of that semi-dark chocolate and always kept a supply in my car. I say "embarrassingly" because my twin sister would look at me sometimes and say, "Have you been gnawing on that chocolate again? You have some on your face, and you look like me — we are twins! You've got to stop it!"

My family ate a lot of takeout for dinner and Subway sandwiches for lunch for those three months. Not optimal healthy food by a long shot, but at the time I felt that I was getting the healthier of the takeout options. This may have gotten me through that period, but it contributed to my inevitable crash at the end of the project.

I would jokingly say that project about killed me. Well, I don't think that was a joke anymore. I was 41, and by the end of the project I was not doing good on any level — body, mind, or spirit. At one point close to the end of the project I felt like I was on the edge of a high cliff, spinning super fast, about to shatter into a million pieces and blow away in the wind. I thought that must be a sign of a nervous breakdown in the near future if things didn't get under control. I knew I was in a bad space and that it was not good for my health and well-being, but I was at a loss as to what I could do to fix it. Thinking about that time gives me a tight feeling in my solar plexus. I don't know how I also managed all my family responsibilities for a husband and kids (laundry, grocery shopping, meals) — all while managing rental properties we owned that always turned over the end of June, because they were college rentals. With so many balls in the air I know I had to have been dropping the ball somewhere. It turns out to have been my self-care and relationship nurturing. No one is fun to be around when they are in stress mode. I was stress mode on steroids.

The techniques I'm about to share with you will help your body manage the negative impact of the stress and the tightness in your body. It will help to get your body back to a more peaceful existence and out of the fight, flight, or freeze mode. The goal is that while you are in the midst of a stressful situation, you can avoid getting stuck in a stress response pattern that depletes other meridians and organs. If unchecked, this stress can lead to an autoimmune condition. Our stress meridian, Triple Warmer, will weaken our physical body over an extended period of time by pulling energy needed from everywhere else in the body, because fight, flight, or freeze mode is so energy-intensive to maintain.

I am going to share a calming exercise with you that I call the "chill pill." I learned it, or a close version of it, originally in my Eden Method training. Donna Eden calls it the Triple Warmer Smoothie. Besides managing stress, Triple Warmer is the "keeper of habits," and in extreme stress, it can save our life. When we are in chronic stress with periods of extreme stress we do not want our Triple Warmer Meridian to get stuck in a habit of a body stress response. If we do, we can end up depleted on many levels like I did, as the Triple Warmer Meridian goes to the other meridians in our body for energy in case we need to run, fight, or hide, therefore depleting the other meridians over time.

This exercise is what I have my clients in stress response do regularly until they are out of stress response and more balanced. This is also what I do once I'm safely stopped after I run a yellow light, get honked at in my car, or if I have a close call and I feel the stress in my body.

A quick way to soothe anxiety — Chill Pill/ Triple Warmer Smoothie:

Place fingers on temples and breathe in. On the exhale, drag fingers lightly around the top and back of your ears down the neck, and hang them off the muscles between your neck and shoulders. Inhale and exhale, drag fingers forward deeply, giving a good trapezius massage to yourself. On the next inhale, cross arms, placing fingers on the opposite trapezius and then sliding fingers down each arm and off the ring finger on the exhale. You can stop at the elbow and do one lower arm at a time and off the ring finger. Do this while repeating in your mind or saying out loud, "I am safe, I am well" or "I am perfect" — whatever you feel like saying that lets your body know that it is time to be peaceful. In order to see this to better understand, I would search "Donna Eden Triple Warmer Smoothie," and you will have some YouTube videos of it to choose from.

My kids still remember that summer of being hauled around on construction errands and stuck at the job site with me for long periods of time. I have apologized to my kids, and they now say they were somewhat traumatized but that they forgive me and are grateful for how hard their dad and I worked over the years.

I spent that next year, 2006, after the project ended working on regaining my health and energy. I was still managing many rentals, did a small upgrade to our family home, had a built-in pool and pool house put in at our house, volunteered at my kids' school a lot, and handled our family's busy life. It was becoming clearer that I had not yet learned, that in order to heal you need to stop **all** the extra things in your life.

On October 12, 2006, roughly a year after that big project, I was working on yet another big construction project. This time, unlike the previous project, I had a project manager and a superintendent, so my participation was less, though it was a much bigger project. I had built myself back up somewhat physically and was riding my road bike again to help manage the stress and to maintain a level of fitness. My riding partner and I were riding a 20-mile ride, but in the middle of the bike ride something happened and caused me to hit a construction delineator and crash into the road at around 14 mph. I took a direct hit to my left shoulder and right thumb. The good news is I wasn't hit by either the truck coming toward me or the truck behind me, which is a miracle, because my momentum sent me into the lane about 5 feet.

My injuries ended up being a very painful collarbone break (which I was told later was a clean break and did not require surgery), a dented humeral head and a torn rotator cuff. My right thumb knuckle was jammed pretty bad and is bigger than my left thumb knuckle and slightly bent to this day, although completely functional. There is nothing like a serious accident with multiple injuries to bring you to your knees. I spent three months feeling as I had the previous year, with the total exhaustion plus excruciating pain for the first three weeks. I was able to continue my life, work construction projects and responsibilities after a couple weeks, but I wasn't able to do all the things my spouse was used to having done by me, which caused more stress on our already tenuous relationship. After a few months and a lot of intentional and alternative healing, I was mostly healed, very humbled, and getting back into my full life and duties.

Yet again, I had been ignoring the karmic nudges from the universe, and my guides were apparently upping their game with me.

No coincidences in this beautiful, messy, and sometimes very painful life. On October 12, 2007, exactly a year to the day after my bike crash, I was given some news in my life that shattered me. The best way I can describe how I was feeling was that I felt like someone had skinned me alive, that all of my nerve endings were exposed, and it hurt to breathe. I was adrift and felt like I had no internal compass to follow. In the Eden Method training I later learned that my Assemblage Point had shattered from the severe emotional trauma. You can heal Assemblage Points by seeing an Eden Method practitioner, but back in 2007, I was not aware of that type of healing yet.

I had found out that my marriage wasn't what I had thought it had been for the previous ten years. Consequently, I felt like I didn't know what was or had been true in my life on any level anymore. The marriage I had been committed to for the past 20 years — and I thought for the rest of my life — was not something I understood or recognized anymore. Infidelity and loss of trust is a fierce and painful lesson.

Once again I found myself with total physical exhaustion, although this time it was from an emotional trauma. I had a new companion in my life called depression. I was trying to figure out how the bottom of my world just dropped out and how I was going to be alive again and be the mom I needed and wanted to be. I was a shell of a person. How do you keep going through these growth and healing opportunities? When you can see absolutely no light at all? When you have children in your life who need you and when you have not even a glimmer of life and hope in you? I'm crying as I write this feeling such compassion for that Melissa who endured that pain and challenge. I cried a river, and eventually I healed. Even though I felt weak, depleted, and vulnerable, I found that I was strong, resilient, and determined to figure this out and heal.

You get up, you make sure you eat a little bit, you get through the day, you accept the love and help from friends and family, and eventually you heal tiny bits at a time. I think I went somewhere else a lot of the time mentally, but I was able to function on a minimal level. A friend suggested an antidepressant to help ease the emotional pain that was my constant companion, but I knew that would just put off dealing with the emotions that needed to be processed and healed. You have to go through what you are going through, and I knew on some level that I needed to be present to feel it, live it, and eventually heal from it to move forward. I didn't want to ignore it or tuck it away and take a pill every day only to have to get off the antidepressant eventually and have to deal with it then.

It was such a dark time in my life. The beautiful tapestry of my life with all of the threads from my experiences, challenges, and painful lessons was becoming exquisite. I knew I would never be the same. A part of me had died, and I didn't know it at the time, but that means there is a rebirth to follow. My old life wasn't working anymore, so this was a karmic 2x4 that I needed to change, since I hadn't been able to make the necessary changes myself yet. This news was what finally stopped me and changed me forever. It was a healing opportunity and the sign to do my work and become a better version of my former self. Thank goodness nothing lasts forever, so the hell I was in didn't last either. Time heals, but we also need to do our work. I wouldn't have believed it at the time to see how my life unfolded from that point.

I'm grateful for the love, support, and humor from my closest friends and sister, who kept me going. In addition to these spiritual and emotional growth opportunities, my physical quest for health and wellness was ongoing. My biggest emotional healing opportunity was coming toward me in my future beginning in the year 2012.

I eventually quit seeing the M.D./N.D. and ended up with a good intuitive N.D. who helped me periodically for several years to try and balance my hormones, recover my adrenals from everything

I had gone through, and to get me off of thyroid medication. I was eventually successful after several years weaning off the thyroid medication. I got off it and onto natural supplements instead. I was very proud of this, because I had always heard that once you are on thyroid medication, it's for life. I was eating as healthy as I knew how at the time but nowhere near as healthy as I would learn to be.

In the spring of 2012, I was at Optimum Health Institute, as I mentioned earlier. There, I finally bought the Donna Eden energy medicine book and later started the training program. 2012 was a year of change, angst, and fear. Do you remember the angst and fear that last few months of 2012? Since 12/12/12 was the end of the Mayan calendar, many feared it was the end of life on Earth. Those anxieties caused an uncomfortable vibration of fear for us sensitive beings. It seemed like my twin sister and I kept having opportunities to say, "Good grief, what next?" a lot. It was the end of the Mayan calendar and the end of a way of life but not the end of the world, as many thought at that time. It was a death of an old patriarchal way of doing things, and the world was shifting into the new way of partnership and rebirth. We could either fight it or go along with it. It rang true for me in my life and in almost all of the lives around me. Major changes were taking place and our old ways were no longer viable.

October has proven to regularly be a rocky month for me. My twin sister and I called October 2012 "Roctober." The air was turning crisp, and the light was softening after the heat of summer. The days were getting shorter. I saw myself standing at the edge of the cliff of my life, and I decided I needed to fly. My current life was not working even after all of my work over the past five years and it was time to leap off the cliff and trust that I could fly.

My marriage had been under reconstruction the past five years, but things were going back to the old unhappy and unhealthy patterns. I wasn't willing to get the karmic 2x4 again (I was learning!), so I jumped, stepped, and tripped toward my new life, ending my

22-year marriage and a quarter of a century relationship. It was the hardest thing I had done in my life, but I knew I had to do it. Times were changing, and my old life was untenable.

I spent a lot of what free time I had the next few years on my outdoor couch being healed by the birds, old oak trees, wild turkeys, deer, and other sights and visitors nature brought me. I knew I needed to support my kids in their transition with the divorce by being my best self that I could during that challenging time, so that was my goal and highest priority. When I wasn't actively doing my healing on that couch in my backyard, I was moving, untangling my complicated old life, creating new and fun memories with my kids, studying to become an Energy Medicine Practitioner and setting up my new life. My heart was so happy when I was doing the energy work, helping myself and other people to heal and feel better. When you do what you are meant to do, it flows, but that doesn't necessarily mean that it will be easy.

Sometimes you look back on your life and you're amazed you were strong and courageous enough to do what you did. I don't feel sorry for the old Melissa. I feel gratitude for the lessons and the learning that made me into this much better version of myself. I'm grateful for the energy medicine protocols I learned, which were key to my healing during this huge transition. These protocols allowed me to experience a more graceful, compassionate, and loving presence through this painful growth opportunity. I also look at how it must be hell for the person who is teaching us these lessons, and that is where I find the compassion and forgiveness for them that we need for our own personal growth. I was and am a teacher of lessons as well as we are all here to teach each other and help each other to grow and evolve. None of us are perfect on this journey, or we wouldn't be here.

Chapter 8
Cancer Is an Opportunity

"Accept — then act. Whatever the present moment contains, accept it as if you had chosen it... This will miraculously transform your whole life."
— *Eckhart Tolle*

IF WE WERE TO GET a cancer diagnosis we would have several options. We could deny it, essentially sticking our heads in the sand. We could go the conventional treatment route where we may have surgery followed by either radiation and/or chemotherapy. We may choose to go the alternative route where we take a more holistic approach to healing the body-mind-spirit in the hopes of healing the root cause of the cancer. Or we may do a combination of conventional medicine with some complementary alternative holistic healing to support the side effects of the conventional treatment.

What if we consider the above quote by Eckhart Tolle and assume that we chose to have a cancer diagnosis as part of our plan for this lifetime? Wow. Why on earth would we do that!? There are many reasons I can think of. Perhaps we wanted to learn humility and suffering from this challenge and experience the opportunity for personal and soul-level growth. Maybe along with that, we are meant to heal ourselves from cancer and then share our story with the world to help others to heal from cancer. Perhaps, like my experience, I was meant to lose several loved ones to cancer so that I would be interested in figuring out how to heal from my own cancer opportunity in a more holistic way and then share my story with the world.

Whatever option you choose — own it and feel that it is going to work for you. Go into it fully, and make changes in your life that support healing no matter if you go holistic or conventional.

I have worked with clients who were doing chemotherapy. We were able to help their body to not react negatively to the drugs by balancing the meridian/organ that was being negatively impacted by the medication, and they felt much better taking it. They also supported their healing experience with healthy eating, which helps to minimize side effects as well.

Our immune system plays an integral part of a cancer journey. I believe that when our immune system can't keep up with all of the stressors in our lives and body, the cancer cells — ever the opportunists that they are — can take over. It is also my belief from my own cancer journey and from my energy medicine practice that sometimes, cancer cells will start at the site of a trauma or injury. These injury sites are where there is also stuck energy of the emotions at the time of the injury. Cancer or dis-ease can also be stuck emotions in organs, which I teach you how to clear and release in Chapter 18. In my healing work, I've seen that these stuck emotions can be carried forward from many lifetimes. Until these stuck emotions are addressed, released, and healed, they will continue on with us in our essence, as everything is energy, and energy always moves and continues. These emotional traumas are part of the essence and energy pattern of who we are, and they can fester until they cause dis-ease in our body. This is the energetic component of cancer.

The *New York Times* bestselling book *The Truth About Cancer*, by Ty M. Bollinger, explains that cancer isn't genetic — it's the result of immune failure: "Cancer, in essence, can be summed up as a *failure of the immune system* to eradicate abnormal cells before they take root and become full-blown cancer."[3] The book quotes Dr. Bita Badakhshan, M.D., an integrative Physician at the Center for New Medicine in Irvine, CA: "Our immune system's job is to get rid of all of those (cancer) cells — *if* your immune system is perfect, if you don't have a virus that it is already trying to fight, if you don't have too much chemical or other stuff going on in your body. If you do

---

[3] Bollinger, Ty. *The Truth About Cancer*. HayHouse, 2018, p. 102.

[have viruses and toxins] then [these malignant cells] keep growing and growing, increasing in number and then you get a tumor."

This validates my beliefs that I have acquired through living many years of health challenges that led to my cancer challenge and my opportunity for healing and greater health. I had so many things stressing my immune system all at once and chronically for years. Among my immune system stressors were systemic candida, herpes on my lips periodically since the sixth grade, bacteria (strep), and parasites. I had a high level of heavy metals and many other toxins in my body. Along with all of these that I just mentioned, my body and organs were overburdened by all of the emotions that were stuck/stored in my organs. My immune system was so challenged that it was recommended to me by my M.D. back then to get regular flu shots. I listened to that doctor and got my shots and ended up getting sicker and sicker. Adding yet more toxins to my system in the form of the preservatives and metals in the flu shots was not a good plan after all.

So back to the above quote by Eckhart Tolle, "accept — then act." Your body is giving you a big message in the form of cancer. Listen to that message and then get rid of viruses, toxins, yeast, and parasites. Quit feeding them what they want and need to replicate and instead feed your immune system what it wants and needs to be strong and help to get rid of those cancer-enabling things in our body. Support your immune system by reducing stress as well and finding balance in your life.

There are many ways to stress your immune system — other than the ones I just mentioned — thereby weakening it and allowing the opportunity for cancer to possibly rear its ugly head. The top stressors in life are: death of a spouse or child, separation or divorce, getting married, starting a new job, workplace stressors, financial problems, moving to a new home, chronic illness or injury, retirement, living in a toxic environment, transitioning to adulthood. (I believe graduations should be on this list as well.) We sometimes have 1 to 5 of these top 10 stressors happening in our lives at the same time.

When I had my cancer opportunity, I had several of the top 10 stressors going on in my life all at the same time, and I remember saying that I had no immune system back then. Life is busy, and it can be very stressful. Cancer is an opportunity for us to make changes in our life to get back into balance. Cancer is a symptom of dis-ease in our body-mind-spirit that is a message to us to take notice and make big changes. I had to make big changes in my life and get serious about my health when I received my diagnosis. I remember thinking, "I've got this, but I have to do the work and be willing to eat and drink only foods that nourish and heal my body." I had to put my oxygen mask on first, and I needed to do my emotional work as well. To this day I have not met a sad or miserable cancer survivor. They are all grateful to be alive and generally happier and healthier than they have ever been because they had to make big changes and do the work in order to LIVE. We can choose to live and heal, or we can choose to not make changes, be miserable, unhealthy, afraid, out of balance and possibly die.

Dr. Badakhshan — whom I mentioned previously in this chapter and who started off her career as a conventional doctor — says that many of the patients she sees at the Center for New Medicine suffer from immune suppression caused by persistent viruses such as herpes, HPV, EBV, and parasites. I found out through Anthony William's book *Medical Medium* that I also had been dealing with EBV for many years as well, so I was a prime candidate for cancer. Dr. Bakakhshan says that these are all common predictors of cancer and are conditions she has observed countless of times in conjunction with a cancer diagnosis.[4] When asked what parasites do to the body, she says that they suppress your immune system. Dr. Badakashan follows the theory of cancer that the true cause of cancer is rooted in mitochondrial dysfunction, which stems from inadequate oxygen

---

[4] Ibid. p. 103.

delivery to healthy cells. This results in a lack of ATP production, which, combined with the immune shutdown, creates the perfect environment for cancer to thrive.[5]

The Truth About Cancer says that "immune failure is at the root of what allows cancer to flourish and spread, and more often than not this destruction of natural immunity is a product of toxin overload." *The Truth About Cancer* talks about how in 2009 The President's Cancer Panel declared that the true burden of environmentally induced cancer has been grossly underestimated and added:

> The American people — even before they are born — are bombarded continually with myriad combinations of these dangerous exposures. The Panel urges you most strongly to use the power of your office to remove the carcinogens and other toxins from our food, water, and air that needlessly increase healthcare costs, cripple our nation's productivity, and devastate American lives.

The Truth About Cancer cites Dr. Rob Verkerk, Ph.D., executive director of the Alliance for Natural Health International, who offers insights regarding this major problem, stating that "the average city dweller is exposed to upwards of 20,000 industrial chemicals every single day."[6] He says that many of these chemicals are known carcinogens, and the majority of them emerged after World War II.[7]

The Truth About Cancer also mentions that the Pesticide Action Network of North America has been tracking the progression of chronic disease in conjunction with crop chemical use over many decades, and the data is sobering. "Chemicals can trigger cancer in a variety of ways, including disrupting hormones, damaging DNA, inflaming tissues, and turning genes off." It states that many

[5] Ibid. p. 104.
[6] Ibid. p. 105.
[7] Ibid. p. 106.

pesticides are known and probable carcinogens, and as the panel notes, exposure to these chemicals is widespread."[8] *The Truth About Cancer* goes on to say that children and pregnant mothers are most affected by these chemicals by inadvertently exposing fetuses and small children to these chemicals. It also mentions that farm workers exposed to pesticides on a regular basis have significantly higher rates of prostate, ovarian, and skin cancers.[9]

Another concern besides pesticides on our food is GMO's. Also according to *The Truth About Cancer*, "Despite their official status as "food," GMOs are essentially drugs that have been sneaked into the food supply without consent, and with mounds of independent research exposing them as a health disaster."[10] The American Academy of Environmental Medicine (AAEM) reports: "Several animal studies indicate serious health risks associated with GM food consumption including infertility, immune dysregulation, accelerated aging, dysregulation of genes associated with cholesterol synthesis, insulin regulation, cell signaling, protein formation and changes in the liver, kidney, spleen and gastrointestinal system."[11]

The good news is that when you eat organic, exercise regularly, avoid processed foods, alcohol, and sugar, your body is able to detox these chemicals. The other good news is that when a person's immune system is strong, it will destroy the cancer cells if they start to multiply. Cancer is an opportunist and is merely doing what it is here to do. Our best friend and biggest ally is our immune system, but we have to treat it with respect and appreciation by minimizing our toxin exposure, getting old toxins out of our body and eating a balanced and clean diet. I have been intentionally detoxing and eating clean for four years now. I never wear deodorant anymore, and I know when I need to get in my sauna and detox because I will smell

[8] Ibid. p. 108.
[9] Ibid. p. 108.
[10] Ibid. p. 109.
[11] Ibid. p. 109.

a little body odor when I am in downward facing dog pose in yoga. Usually it will only take one sauna session these days to get rid of the B.O. But if not, definitely two sessions have me smelling like my rose water spray once again! I'm grateful to not wear deodorant anymore, but I remember when I stopped using it I was very concerned about it. I started by just using a crystal stick and that works really well and is a great gradual step toward deodorant-free eventually. I dedicated a whole chapter (Chapter 14) to detoxing and will go into much more detail there.

An alternative way to heal from cancer that appears to have a good success rate is Hope4Cancer. According to their website, they have Seven Key Principles of Cancer Therapy:

Non-Toxic Cancer Therapies
Immuno Modulation
Full-Spectrum Nutrition
Detoxification
Oxygenation
Restore Microbiome
Emotional and Spiritual Healing

This sounds like what I did to reverse my cancer and more. This center believes that "in the process of killing cancer cells, traditional treatments often end up destroying healthy cells as well. Their non-toxic therapies target only cancer cells, keeping vital tissues and organs healthy while avoiding the debilitating side effects of chemotherapy and radiation."

Hope4Cancer conducted a study that tracked the survival rate of 365 patients from 2015 to 2017, representing 41 cancer types. Ninety-two percent of patients had a stage IV cancer at the start of their Hope4Cancer journey. This study used NCI (National Cancer Institute) SEER data as comparison data. The NCI SEER database has much larger percentages of early-stage cancers representing much more favorable average prognosis than the Hope4Cancer data, which is 92% stage IV cancers.

Based on this study Hope4Cancer had a 2-year survival rate of **78.9%**. They shared data from the NCI-SEER database that showed that survival rates drop from 69% (all stages, all cancer types) to only 25% for stage IV patients using conventional methods of chemotherapy, surgery and radiation.[12]

I found this data to be eye opening to say the least. Personally, I like the outcome of the Hope4Cancer with a 78.9% survival rate, and that is for 92% of the patients starting with a stage IV diagnosis. It is also a nontoxic and whole-person treatment, getting to the core of what the imbalances are. The data provided goes into much more detail according to specific types of cancers and survival rates and also quality of life aspects.

Do not be afraid if you have done surgery, radiation, or chemotherapy. Your body can heal from these as well as cancer through good nutrition, some supplements, mind and spirit healing, and with the help of good-quality organic herbal teas. I have done this and will continue throughout my life. I will also have more details and a reference to the teas that Anthony William recommends to get various toxins out of our body in Chapter 12.

So what feeds cancer? Anthony William says to avoid dairy, as it's high in sugar, and it feeds cancers, tumors, cysts, viruses, and bacteria in the body. He also says that eggs feed cancer, tumors, viruses, and cysts as well. Back when I was still drinking coffee but while reversing my cancer, I switched to organic unsweetened vanilla almond milk in my coffee. It was only a couple days of adjustment for me, and then I was good with it. I used a lot of almond milk with less coffee, and it helped to cut the acidity of the coffee, while still giving me that artificial, but much needed at the time, energy boost. Eventually, as I got less acidic, I couldn't handle drinking coffee anymore. It fell off for me, and I haven't had it in years. I enjoy a cup

---

[12] https://hope4cancer.com/about-us/hope4cancer-survival-rates/

periodically but never with cow's milk anymore. Just recently I tried to drink a few sips of a latte someone got for me with cow's milk in it, and I couldn't drink more than a couple sips of it. The milk in the latte upset my stomach, and the coffee felt acidic in my body.

I remember at the beginning of my cancer opportunity, the feeling of being open to any information that came to me and trusting that it was going to be for my highest and best good. I ran into a friend while I was doing a little much-needed clothes shopping at her boutique, and my cancer opportunity came up. She asked me if I had heard of the alkaline diet, where you cut out or decrease the acid in your diet.

Basically, that diet says that animal protein is acidic (I cannot verify this, but there are many benefits to healing by cutting out animal protein for a period of time) and unless you are careful, meat also has growth hormones, antibiotics, and parasites. These things are all especially harmful for people with cancer and anyone with a compromised liver, which is the case for so many of us. Medical Medium says that the fats in animal protein use a lot of energy for our livers to break down. Then our livers aren't able to process toxins, and our toxic burden increases. To support our bodies to heal, the Medical Medium recommends a plant-based organic diet while healing to help our liver and body to release toxins. He also advises avoiding fats, oils, and even nuts for a period of time. This was the same thing I learned at Optimum Health Institute, where healing miracles also happen.

Like viruses, cancer cells can mutate and become resistant to different chemotherapy drugs and radiation. Many times the first course of action in the medical world is to cut the cancer out of the body, but that often causes the cancer to spread. I found this to be true in my cancer opportunity. My doctor cut it out, and it grew back right next to the original site. The first chemotherapy injection appeared to stop the cancer from growing temporarily, but the second injection of the drug caused the cancer to start acting aggressive and irregular, according to my dermatologist.

That was when I decided that the conventional methods weren't going to work for me. I knew that in the beginning, but something inside me told me that I had to try the conventional method first. With that being said, I was not a stage 4 cancer, or I would have gone more aggressively and done an all-raw diet immediately or gone to Hope4Cancer. Ultimately, everyone has his or her own healing opportunity with his or her own unique set of circumstances to heal.

How anyone decides to treat his or her own cancer or the cancer of their children is a personal choice, and a difficult one. Any alternative treatments we add or substitute for conventional treatment must be undertaken after serious consideration. It's sad to see cases of children being taken away from their parents and made wards of the state when their parents do not want them to undergo chemotherapy.

There is no one cure for all people. We are all unique, and all available methods, information, and opportunities should be taken into consideration. If chemotherapy and radiation are so terrible, then how do people survive cancer after those treatments? I spoke to a naturopathic doctor recently and posed that exact question. She replied that even though she believes it is toxic she thinks in large part it's the belief in the treatment and the absence of fear. I then suggested that possibly it's also in large part due to the change of lifestyle, diet, and self-care to boost the immune system in conjunction with the short-term chemotherapy and belief system and emotional work that could play a big part as well. We were in total agreement.

This goes the other way as well — some people seem to do everything right the natural way but still do not survive. There are other forces at work for sure. I'd venture to say that would be the emotions, thoughts, beliefs, and fears that were in play. Or sometimes it's your plan for this lifetime and your time to go.

Chapter 9
My Cancer Victory

"Do not die with your music still in you."
— Dr. Wayne Dyer

I HAVE SHARED MY BELIEF that cancer is in all of us and that it waits for the perfect opportunity to rear its ugly head. If you are not balanced and taking care of your various bodies (emotional, physical, mental, and spiritual) then cancer or dis-ease can find the opportunity to arise more readily due to a weakened immune system. I am honestly very surprised cancer did not find me sooner than in 2012–13. I lived a life of chronic stress with periods of extreme stress. I was toxic with heavy metals and pesticides, and had many viruses and bacteria that made me crave foods that promoted an environment in my body that viruses, bacteria, and cancer thrive in. I self-soothed or self-medicated with sugar, carbohydrates, caffeine, processed food, and alcohol, though the alcohol was in moderation. By the time my personal storm intensified in 2012 during my stressful divorce, it became the perfect opportunity for cancer to show up for me.

There is nothing like hearing that six-letter word to scare you straight, bring you to your knees and hyper-focus your attention. I had been doing my body~mind~spirit work, or so I thought, and I still ended up in that 6-letter word space. I felt from the beginning that this was something for me to experience, overcome, and keep living so that I could help other people with it. I had to ramp up my efforts because even though I felt that way, I still had to make it happen. Cancer is a big motivator for shifting priorities if you are willing and able to do that. I quickly realized that even though I was being the "over-concerned mom" I was going to be of no value to my kids if I didn't start putting myself higher up on my priority list. I had to put my oxygen mask on first and keep it there and then help my kids. Everyone else at that time in my life was on their own. I had officially shifted my priorities and I was in healing mode, finally.

My cancer opportunity started as a bug bite on my right shinbone over the summer of 2012. I thought nothing of it and carried on with my life while dealing with the changes from the divorce and unwinding the complicated the life we had created together. There was so much going on that I didn't even notice that I kept shaving over the bug bite, and it kept growing in a not-so-attractive way.

I was doing a little self-care to help support myself during this stressful time by getting a massage once a month and seeing my chiropractor once a month as well. It was my friend and massage therapist who finally told me I had to quit ignoring the bug-bite-gone-bad and get in to see my dermatologist right away. She was the same massage therapist who several years before said that my body did not feel right and that I was getting worse. I listened to her again and I made my appointment for the dermatologist the following week.

My dermatologist was in his late 70s and has been practicing medicine for many decades. He's been around the skin cancer block, so to speak. He said it looked like cancer, and we decided we should have a biopsy done. He was going to try to get it all, if possible, for the biopsy. Get-er-done, right? There was not a whole lot of room to dig in, since the bug bite was right next to my shinbone, but he gave it a good effort and sent it to the lab. The results came back a week or so later: squamous cell carcinoma. We decided to wait and see if he had gotten all of it, rather than go in for more at that time. We were hopeful, and I was optimistic that we would be done with it. About a month and a half later, the cancer came back right next to the original bug bite spot on my leg. It definitely had our attention then!

After examining the new cancer growth, my doctor said he would like to inject the cancer with a chemotherapy drug to try and kill it directly and hopefully avoid further surgery on the site, since it was so close to my shinbone. I guess it was the look on my face when he suggested chemotherapy that had him saying, "I know how you feel about antibiotics and other medications that you feel are overprescribed. But I've had some success with this and strongly recommend this as the next step." In my mind what I heard was: "I know, crazy lady, that you don't want to have any medications ingested or injected at all, but this could save your life if you just ease up on your crazy this time."

I remember just looking at him and thinking that there was no way in hell I was going to let him inject those toxins into my body now or ever. This is my opinion and not medical advice. Sadly most of us have had some experience with cancer, whether it was ourselves or with loved ones. I mentioned previously that I lost my sister Karen in 1979 to leukemia when she was 18 and I was 14. The pain Karen had was horrific, but the side effects from the chemo were equally horrible and painful for everyone involved. It was so obvious to me at that time that the chemo drugs were killing Karen as well. I went through the grief and pain of watching more of my loved ones suffer and die again in 2002 with my dear friend Barbara, who was 39, and in 2015 with my dear friend Kat in her early 60's.

I felt helpless as I watched them take chemo treatments until their body simply could take no more of it. I thought to myself that I would never do that if I had that challenge. Yet here I was with a decision to make. I didn't know if I was going to end up with the cancer spreading to my bones like it did for my loved ones. It's a terrifying space to be in, and an important decision needed to be made. It's not my intention to compare my cancer and experiences with it in my life to anyone else's experience, pain, or situation. I'm just sharing my perspective and experience to present possibilities for alternative healing.

I asked my doctor if I could have a minute to tune in to myself and see what I needed to do. He said sure and graciously allowed me "to do my thing." I tuned in and what I heard from my guidance or inner knowing was that I needed to let him do this. I needed to go through with this for some reason, and I knew I would be fine. I gave him the go-ahead with "I can't believe it, but apparently I'm going to let you inject that poison into my leg." He nodded and proceeded to get everything ready.

As I was waiting for the injection I asked him if this was going to be quick because I had promised a couple of my girlfriends I would try Bikram yoga with them for my first time, and class was starting in 30 minutes. My doctor asked what that was, so I told him that Bikram Yoga is a series of 26 hatha yoga poses that are done in a room heated to over 100 degrees with a very high humidity. It's intended to detoxify your body, strengthen your muscles, and invigorate you. He replied that most of his patients have extreme pain with these injections and that they have to alternate Tylenol with Advil for around 24 hours. I was very familiar with that protocol, but I wasn't interested in the least in having any pain associated with this or in letting it stop me from trying Bikram Yoga with my friends. I thanked him for that information and voiced that I was not going to need to do that. I reassured him that I would be fine as long as I could leave his office in the next 5 minutes. He was shaking his head as I was hustling out the door five minutes later. I only experienced one minor twinge of pain during that yoga class and no more after that. The power of the mind is unbelievable!

My follow-up appointment had been set for 6 weeks, in which I experienced no pain and no change to the cancer. I went back in to my doctor, and he confirmed there was no change. He smiled when I said that yoga had gone well with only one small twinge of pain. I think he was softening toward me. My doctor then got serious and told me that sometimes he had seen some stubborn cancers that required a second injection of chemotherapy drugs to get their attention and knock them back. He suggested that it could be beneficial do another injection into my cancer. He said, "I know you have to do that thing you do, so I'll give you a minute." He crossed his arms and sat back as I tuned in to my inner guidance again.

I was surprised that what I got was that I needed to let him inject my leg again, and I told him that exact thing. We chit chatted while he was getting the injection ready, and he inquired if I was planning to do something extreme after this visit as well with a smile on his face. I told him that I had nothing new or exciting planned and I was bummed about doing this again. I felt like we were building a personal connection, and I was grateful for that. My follow-up appointment was scheduled for two weeks this time. I did not question how it was so much sooner than the previous appointment, but was very grateful for it when the time came for that next appointment.

This next appointment I had brought my son with me for a double appointment to get his very dark moles looked at. My son went first and then wanted to stay in the room with me. Then it was my turn to hop on the table and have my leg looked at. My doctor got serious real quick and said that my cancer had officially gone "aggressive and irregular." In other words (my words) it was pissed off. Our next step now was to schedule a Mohs surgery, where a pathologist is there to make sure that all the borders of the cancer that is removed are clear of any active cancer cells. It was at this time my doctor got very personal. He asked what type of birth control I was on. I was quiet and processing this question while looking over at my 13-year-old son to see if he was paying attention to any of this. I told my son to cover his ears really tight (he did), and I said that due to my divorce, school, and my kids, I didn't have time or energy for a relationship, so birth control wasn't necessary at that time or in the near future.

At this point I was very curious why my doctor needed to know this about me and in front of my son, so I asked if it was because of the hormones and any change affecting cancer growth. I had previously read something about hormones stimulating cancer growth. Well that wasn't where he was going at all. He said that if the Mohs surgery didn't work (they examine each tissue sample to make sure that all of the cancer cells are removed) then the chemotherapy drug that I would need to take orally would cause severe birth defects to my baby if I were to get pregnant. WTF?!?! I calmly said to him, "I'm pretty sure that I will not be putting that in my body anyway, so this surgery is going to work." I gathered my son and I went up front to make that surgery appointment.

My surgery was set for four weeks into the future. My son was picked-up and heading to his Dad's house, and I was off to host a baby shower for a coworker. Needless to say I'm not sure how I pulled that off with my head filled with all of this stuff. After all the girls left with the cute pink baby things, I cleaned up and finally had time to really examine everything that was going on with me. The next day I made time to really explore this challenge I was currently going through. What I came up with was that I acknowledged all of the changes I had made in my life toward healing myself and doing my emotional work but that I had to *seriously* ramp up my efforts now. I was going to make changes and beat this thing. At the very least, I had the back-up plan of the surgery but I immediately came up with some big changes to my diet. I realized that I had not trusted what I believed in while going through this cancer and divorce experience, so I resolved to change that right away. **I cut out the following five things immediately and completely: alcohol, sugar, dairy, animal protein, and gluten.** I kept my coffee because I was so exhausted at the time, and I felt like I needed it to even "do" life.

This was not easy. I kept my heart open and paid attention to any information that was brought to my awareness as I was going through this. I was told about drinking alkaline water because cancer can't live in an alkaline environment, so I got that. I was also told about the magic of lemons and how outside of your body they appear to be acidic, yet inside your body they are very alkalizing, antibacterial and much more. I was told to eat the whole lemon except for the seeds, so I added that to my diet as well. I then eliminated eggs, as I was told they are acidic as well. This was about 3 years before I found Anthony William, the Medical Medium, so I was unaware at that time that eggs actually feed cancer.

A friend in my exercise class mentioned essential oils to me. She said that she had great results from putting frankincense oil on her skin cancers, so I bought some frankincense oil and got that on my cancer at least two times a day. I started being extra careful of what I put in my body and on my body, even though I had slowly been moving in that direction already. If I couldn't put a facial cream on my tongue, then it didn't go on my body. Our skin is our single largest organ and absorbent of toxins that we put on it. I had already switched to a hair salon that was green certified and much less toxic than other beauty salons. The hair color product they use is a soybean oil base instead of chemical base, so that helped.

My cancer scare and shift in daily habits, use of cleaner products, and even better food choices was all happening in the spring of 2013. Also happening at the same time was that 5 months previously I had left my 22-year marriage; I was in school for my Eden Method Energy Medicine Practitioner Certification, looking to buy a house, selling a property, and navigating my first 1031 reverse exchange with two small construction projects on the two properties. I needed to navigate all of that stress but in a better way.

I immediately shifted this health challenge to being my highest priority for the next 4 weeks and minimized as much as I could of all of that other stuff. I mentally released the other obligations, giving them only minimal effort. I prayed and intended that everything would be fine, and it was. I began clearing the energies around my cancer with a technique I learned in my energy training. As I got more into it, I realized I needed to clear the emotions around my cancer, and I bought Louise Hay's book *Heal Your Body: The Mental Causes for Physical Illness*.

I looked up cancer in the book, and it's about forgiveness and releasing resentment and anger. I remember that an intuitive in my family had asked me just a short time before if I had any injuries on my shin in the spot of the cancer. That got me thinking, and I remembered hitting my shin really hard on the running board of our motorhome while getting ready for a family trip. I was most likely feeling anger, frustration, and resentment, and all those emotions were charged and stuck in my cancer site. I got focused and committed to finally releasing and healing these things. What I realized about forgiveness was that it has to extend to everyone, including you. The woulda-shoulda-coulda's needed to go, and soon.

Any stories that are being held onto from or about the past need to be released so that they are no longer your story. The goal is to acknowledge that it's not your story anymore. Mentally and emotionally take yourself to a place of neutrality and allow no energy charge around any stories or people. This is not easy by any means. It falls into the category of work, but it's possible. With intention, practice and focus, it will be successful.

I set aside time several times each day to put my frankincense oil on my cancer and to clear the energies around my cancer with my hands while reciting forgiveness affirmations and positive affirmations. I could have done this with a pendulum, but I didn't know that at that time.

If you have an injury anywhere on your body and a pendulum (or even a necklace with a crystal on it that can be used as a pendulum) try this now:

Hold your pendulum or necklace very still over the injury with the intention of clearing the injury and watch your pendulum start to spin counterclockwise clearing the energies from the injured site. Make sure you are holding your hand very still and allow the pendulum to slow down if it starts to. It may bounce a couple times in the middle and then spin clockwise after it has cleared the energies going counterclockwise. Spinning clockwise brings new healing energy in the injury site after the injury energy is cleared.

One day after doing this for a week, I realized I had an energy pattern around these emotions with someone from this life and previous lives together who is my greatest teacher in this lifetime. I began working on forgiving all those previous lives with them also. All of those lives had a similar theme of abandonment and infidelity. No one in my life went unforgiven, not even me for any part I played or contributed. I think the forgiving of myself really helped to release the story that was causing pain, grief, anger, or fear in the current time.

When you decide that painful story is not serving you in heading to a happier you, the story no longer has as much power over you. I realize this may seem oversimplified, but it's the truth. However, it's **very** difficult to do and it simply takes practice and time in letting it go. There is no shortcut. But I am here (thank you!) to tell you that it's worth the work. Whenever my mind would go to my painful story, I would picture it flowing like a raging river through a gorge, under a bridge, and into a sinkhole. Did you get the "rage" in raging river?! Eventually I didn't need to visualize that anymore because it was no longer my story. The rage was gone, and now I see a lazy river instead. The energy to it had been neutralized. Visualizations are a powerful tool for healing. With the help of my guides I have come up with an even quicker way to address these emotions in our field, and I will go into more detail on that in chapter 16.

After a couple weeks, things really started to change with my cancer and also with me. I was much more peaceful. I had been putting mostly good stuff on me and in me, and I was setting aside time to do forgiveness work and positive affirmations. By week three it was apparent that my cancer was rapidly going away, so I called my doctor's office to tell them and let them know that they could give my surgery time to someone who needed it more than me. I was told that they do not do that and that I needed to come the following week no matter what.

Leading up to my surgery date I kept up my daily energy work, forgiveness work, rest, and healthy eating. My doctor came in and took a look at the cancer and proceeded to wheel his stool away from me, pushed his glasses up onto his head, and crossed his arms across his chest. He looked at me and said, "I do not know what you have done since I saw you last time, but this looks nothing like it did four weeks ago. I can't begin to imagine what you have been doing but I think if I send you home and have you continue doing what you have been doing and come back in two weeks it will be completely gone. In fact, I am willing to send the pathologist home now without any charge to you because I have never seen anything like this in all of my years as a dermatologist."

I was so happy! I requested that he go ahead and cut the last little bit out so that I could tell my daughter in particular that I had "clear borders" and that it was all gone. I had just found out from my sister that my daughter had confided in her that she had been really having a hard time with the divorce and her mom having cancer. I felt like it was time to just be done with it and give my daughter some peace of mind. He did a very small biopsy, and ten minutes later I was told it was clear borders. Wooohoo! After that my doctor said that he wanted to meet with me when I had my healing and wellness retreat center open (something I've dreamed about doing and felt compelled to do), so he can give his patients another option to try when they ask for it.

I haven't mentioned the wellness retreat center to you yet. It came to me in a meditation a year or so before my big life change. I really wanted to co-create a wellness retreat center where people can come to heal their body~mind~spirit. A place that would have all the alternative wellness modalities that helped me with my healing opportunities and a large focus on energy medicine and the Medical

Medium protocols. Now that I have experienced great success with healing my cancer, I'm even more excited about this healing retreat center and plan to dedicate all of the proceeds from the sale of this book to fund this healing retreat center.

I experienced a huge cancer success and was deeply grateful. What I didn't know at that time was that I hadn't addressed the underlying challenge completely that would help to keep cancer from rearing its ugly head again. I noticed how much better I felt eating in this new, healthier way. So I continued that diet for the most part going forward. This in turn helped support my body and immune system to keep the cancer at bay. I was still at risk for more cancer opportunities if big stress came my way again or as I accumulated more toxins in my body. We all need to be diligent in protecting our bodies from toxin exposure and also in detoxing toxins from our body.

This is my cancer story. I will go into greater detail in Chapter 19 on how I would eat now to beat cancer. I will list the supplements recommended to manage viruses and to stay cancer free. I am committed to being here for my loved ones and my clients and to do the things that I am compelled to do in this lifetime.

Chapter 10
What's Wrong With Me Now?

"Be kind, for everyone you meet is fighting a hard battle."
— Plato

SINCE MY CANCER EXPERIENCE I had been eating healthy, as healthy as I knew how. I had also been exercising and becoming more and more peaceful and happy all the time. I was continuing to get the heavy metals and toxins out of my body by going in an infrared sauna a couple times a week when possible. I felt like I was continuing to get stronger, healthier, and happier. It appeared that I was reverse aging, and I was looking and feeling the best I had in years. I had also been learning amazing information in my energy medicine program. In 2014 I opened my energy medicine practice out of my home. Finally, I had a combination of a daily energy routine that I was doing, along with my healthy eating and exercise that was really working. I was thoroughly enjoying seeing clients and helping them to become healthier and happier.

By the end of March 2016, three months after I experienced a really silly slip and fall on a hike in which I bumped my head, I saw a photo of myself and thought, "What is wrong with me?" I could tell that I was slowly losing my vibrancy — again. I sense and "see" vibrancy in others and myself now that I work as an advanced energy medicine practitioner. It's the same with colors. I see and sense the colors red, black, gray, and sparkly light. I generally would see sparkly light around myself in recent years, but it was fading.

A friend mentioned that I hadn't been the same since that fall in January when I hit my head. He didn't mean that my personality had changed in any way, but more of my overall health and stamina had decreased since then. I had not connected the fall with what I was going through later, because what I was experiencing on a hike in March 2016 was dizziness, nausea, ringing in my ears, weakness, and lost strength. I had also started having a twitch in my left shoulder. That didn't freak me out because I've had trauma release from my body through the shaking of my shoulders. I felt like that was a piece of it, but I found out later that it was much more than that. I should have been freaked out…

I am a person who does everything possible to be healthy and feel good. I was doing everything I knew to do to get healthy, but I felt like I was getting worse. When I tuned into myself I felt like my vibration or life force was decreasing. I was a strong, hard-working, get er' done, high-energy spirit in a body that was losing its vitality. Something had to change. I was thinking "what now?" Good grief. I reversed my cancer; I was eating as well as I knew how (which was pretty darn good compared to most people). I had gone to Optimum Health Institute for a deep detox 5 times by then. I worked out regularly and was pretty good with my daily energy routine. I was baffled.

What the heck was going on with my body and energy levels being lower? I had been eating eggs most mornings, adding in spinach, kale, mushrooms, garlic, and anything else healthy believing that I was supporting my body in health. I had read somewhere that if you are a woman and want to lose belly fat then you need to eat eggs for breakfast and not eat bananas. I thought eating eggs for breakfast every day would be healthy for me because I was no longer fighting cancer, and I felt like I had a fairly alkaline environment in my body at that time. I now know that this thought process is very far from the truth of what's good for me and why we get belly fat.

My sister had told me about a book called ***Medical Medium*** by Anthony William. By the 3rd time I was told about that book I finally bought it. I started on Part II of the book — The Hidden Epidemic. Chapter 3 was titled "Mystery and Chronic Illness: Epstein-Barr Virus, Chronic Fatigue Syndrome, and Fibromyalgia." The chapter started saying that the Epstein-Barr virus (EBV) has created a secret epidemic and that most of us have it in one version or another. I'm not going to rewrite the book here, but I will say that by the end of that chapter I knew that I finally had the answers to what I had been dealing with most of my life.

It explained everything I had gone through *and* what I was currently experiencing. I was so relieved to finally have answers! I decided that buying this book was the best $20.00 I had spent in my life. I was and still am so grateful to Anthony William for writing it. He has since written four more amazing books. *Liver Rescue* explains why we get belly fat *and* it is not from healthy carbs! It's about supporting and healing your liver, which we all need to do. Anthony just released his latest book *Celery Juice* and I am enjoying reading about all of the medicinal benefits of celery, which I learned is actually a herb not a vegetable. He is currently working on a book about how to safely cleanse your body and I am very excited about it. I know it will be information about safe ways for everyone to detox and cleanse the body.

Chapter 3 of the Medical Medium book described all of the diagnoses I had accumulated over the years as if Anthony William had my medical history. The book outlined a plan based on fruits, vegetables, herbs, and supplements to finally kill off the viruses that had been causing so many health challenges for me for the past 3 decades. I felt like I had a new lease on life and was determined to follow his protocols 100% and finally get my life back. With any health-based program, it really is an all-or-nothing plan to truly push the reset button and allow change to happen in your body.

All-or-nothing is not easy to follow for a long period of time. But what I realized is that some version of this is how I need to eat and live for the rest of my life to truly be healthy, happy, and vibrant. It will also enable me to be the best energy medicine practitioner I can be. Previously, I would choose fish and chips, alcohol, chips and salsa, gelato, nachos, hamburgers, etc. But the reality set in that when

I choose those "comfort" foods there was, in fact, a price to pay. It wasn't just gaining a few pounds here and there. More importantly, it was costing me my health and vibrancy.

One of the most important things I learned from the *Medical Medium* book is that eggs are amazing nutritionally. So much so that cancers, tumors, cysts, viruses, and bacteria love them also. So, when I fell in January 2016 during that hike, I jarred the EBV awake in my body, and it got active again. I was feeding it regularly on eggs, canola oil, citric acid, corn products, MSG, and heavy metals in my liver and body. The foods I just mentioned are some of the foods on the "Foods to Stay Away From List" in the *Medical Medium* book.

According to Anthony William, there are around 60 different strains of the EBV. Some are more aggressive than others and show up when we are at a younger age as the underlying cause of some serious illnesses in children and teens. Others are not quite as aggressive but start causing health challenges in your 20's, which was my experience. This virus plus the addition of toxins can cause breast cancer and other cancers. There are some strains of EBV that are not as aggressive and do not really cause as many problems (prostate cancer in men) until in your 60's. Almost all of us have it. I just read an article[13] that Western Medicine is saying that 90% of the current population has EBV. According to Anthony William we got it from someone who was in stage 2 (mononucleosis). This is the very contagious stage of the virus. Some people navigate stage 2 with more ease and think they just have a bad cold or the flu. These are people with a better immune system in place due to less inherited and acquired toxins. When they get rest, eat well, and drink fluids their immune system kicks in and knocks the virus back, so they feel better.

I will briefly tell you about the stages of EBV how they were presented in the *Medical Medium* book. This is a loose recap, so please consider getting the book — it's a wonderful resource, a

[13] https://www.sciencedirect.com/topics/neuroscience/epstein-barr-virus

lifesaver, and a game changer. You will finally be in control of your health when you have this information.

Stage 1 you get infected with the virus, and it comes into your bloodstream and replicates. It then waits for an opportunity to attack, which is when you get run down, stressed out, are in an accident, have surgery, or get pregnant. It loves heavy metals, dioxides (carbon dioxide, chlorine dioxide, nitrogen dioxide), and hormones. So if you have some hereditary metals in your body or an accumulation of a high amount of metals from this life, you will have more EBV challenges than others. When you get pregnant the levels of hormones in your body increase, and the EBV feeds off the excess hormones and replicates, causing more challenges. Both my twin sister and I had very difficult pregnancies. We were very nauseous and exhausted the whole time.

Stage 2 is when you actually get run down, stressed out, and are not able to take care of yourself with adequate water, good food, and rest, and the EBV attacks. Sounds like typical high school and college students, right? If you get tested in this stage you will come back positive for mononucleosis with antibodies of the EBV being present. The Medical Medium (Anthony William) says that there is not a definitive medical test yet for EBV and there will not be one for another ten years (another 5 years by now). At this stage the EBV heads for your organs — either the liver, reproductive organs, and/or the spleen. EBV has a best friend or cofactor in the form of streptococcus. The benefit to the virus in this relationship is that your body is not only dealing with a virus but also with a bacterium, and this confuses the immune system and allows the virus to elude your immune system. It's tricky like that, but now we have the knowledge available to take charge of it.

After you are able to rest and boost your immune system the EBV "nests" or hides in your organs. In my case it was definitely my liver. I know this because my liver has always been challenged, and especially when I detoxed. I also couldn't ever handle alcohol as well as any of my friends could. I always felt terrible the next day, even though I would consume less than other people. To my liver's credit, it was continually dealing with the heavy metals, DDT, other toxins, and all of my repressed emotions of anger, frustration, and resentment that were energetically stuck in it. I've been told it was congested, blocked, or just not functioning to its potential. It also had those mega doses of Diflucan for my chronic yeast infections that harmed it back in my 30's.

In Stage 3 the EBV will drill into your thyroid and cause you to get a diagnosis such as hypothyroid, Hashimoto's, or thyroid cancer. The virus is feeding off toxins, toxic by-products, along with the die-off waste from the virus that causes thyroid cells to die off. This is a terrible cycle but it can be stopped. Anthony William wrote a book, *Thyroid Healing,* that goes into great detail about the thyroid and the healing process.

Stage 4 is the end game of the virus. It's when the virus attacks the central nervous system. This can be seen in the form of M.S. and other central nervous system diseases. *Thyroid Healing* goes into a much deeper explanation. EBV is a very intelligent virus that does everything it can to go undetected by the immune system. We need the information in Anthony's books so we can get rid of this virus and finally heal.

At the end of March 2016, I knew something was really wrong with me. I realized it was time to up my game, so before I even read the *Medical Medium* book, I started drinking green juice for breakfast, a fruit and veggie smoothie for lunch, and a mostly vegan dinner. I had snacks of dried fruit and nuts. Everything was organic, of course. This immediately threw my body into detox crisis, which feels a lot like the flu. What this told me is that my liver was very congested, my detox pathways were not open enough for the amount of toxins I was trying to release, and I felt terrible. I needed to slow my detox down a little with some cooked vegetables. What I was doing was a start, but after reading the *Medical Medium* book I had a plan to actually stop what was happening to me and get rid of it once and for all. This was powerful knowledge that I now had to not only heal myself but to keep myself healthy for the rest of my life. What a gift!

I admit it was extremely overwhelming at first, because it is so much information, plus most people reading about it are pretty sick and not feeling very smart at that point in their lives. I know because I was that person. When you are that sick, you're also desperate to figure out what has been wrong with you. I truly believe and I am proof that Anthony William has provided the answers.

After reading the chapter about mystery illness and EBV, I figured out the EBV had made it to stage 3 in me years ago, because I had been on thyroid medicine for hypothyroidism since my 30's. I also had figured out in my early 40's that I was toxic for heavy metals. But the scariest and most concerning thing I learned from that chapter was that the shoulder twitch that I recently developed was a central nervous system dysfunction due to EBV. The virus had made it to stage 4 in me! That was frightening especially since I had that realization (or message) years ago that if I didn't get my healing act together, I would end up with multiple sclerosis, be divorced, and have to be in a wheelchair and unable to participate in my children's lives. I was not interested in EBV doing any more damage to my body, and it was no longer welcome in my body. I finally knew what was wrong with me, and I was ready to do the Medical Medium protocols and to kick some EBV ass!

Chapter 11
Energy and Muscle Testing

"Curiosity only does one thing, and that is to give. And what it gives you are clues on the incredible scavenger hunt of your life."
— *Elizabeth Gilbert*

ENERGY TESTING OR MUSCLE TESTING is a way of seeing how our body reacts to food or substances. If you have a strong basic energy test, it means that the substance either strengthens your body or at least it's neutral and not harmful. If the energy is interrupted or weakened (a weak energy test) then your body is not supported by the food or substance, and it's not beneficial. I've practiced energy testing for many years now and have been able to take the Medical Medium protocols and fine-tune them for which supplements were going to be most effective for me and also for my clients when requested. Through energy testing, my client's body shows me what it wants or needs for their healing. I can also assess my own energy systems to see what needs boosting, balancing, or releasing. This is not a way to diagnose illnesses or prescribe supplements for my clients, as I am not an M.D. or N.D. If my client requests for me to energy test their body for what it wants or needs, I am happy to help facilitate that.

Energy testing can be a wonderful tool for getting yes or no answers to questions and receiving guidance for what to eat or which supplements to take. Our body has wisdom that we do not have in our brain, which likes to be "in charge." I energy test my clients by having them hold their arm out in front of them at shoulder height, and I apply pressure while they hold their arm up strong. If their arm stays strong, that is a "yes" answer, and if it goes down or weak, that's a "no" answer. I can test myself in the same way, and there are several different ways to do it. When you are self-testing you always want to hold the intention that you are getting the answers *from your higher self only*. Your mind needs to be neutral to the outcome so that you can get a reliable outcome.

There are a few ways that I teach my clients to self–energy test. The first way is to use your body as a pendulum.

Try this now:

From a neutral position, while holding the supplement in front of your stomach, see if your body sways forward toward the supplement for a strong or "yes," or if it sways backward away from the supplement for a weak or "no." Set the intention before you do this that forward is a yes and backward is a no. You can think of it as your body is going toward what it wants or away from what it doesn't want or need. If your body does neither then it's neutral for your body. This can be done in a supplement store fairly easily if you are not readily distracted or embarrassed.

Another way to self-test is to fill a jug or pitcher of water about ½ to ¾ full, depending on what is going to be the best for you. You don't want it to be too light or too heavy. The goal is to be able to hold it at shoulder height for up to 10-20 seconds without hurting yourself or straining. Put the pitcher or jug on a table or dresser that is around shoulder height. Hold the supplement in one hand at your stomach and try to hold the jug up at shoulder height with the other hand. If you are strong and can do it no problem, then that's a yes or neutral answer. If you can't hold it up, then that's a no.

If you are curious what a yes or a no feels like before you start testing supplements, you can experiment with holding your cell phone near your stomach and the water jug in the other hand and see how well you can hold the jug up. This should be weak or a no. Try this also with your body as a pendulum. Then put your phone away from you and try saying out loud "my name is (say your name)" and then hold the jug up. This should be strong or a yes. These should give you accurate answers, and then you can start using this method with supplements. This eventually can be done at home as you get better at it by holding the picture or thought in your mind of the supplement you are wondering about and then getting the answer of whether your body wants it from the test. These are beginner testing methods and will give you a "neutral or positive" with a strong test and a "no" with a weak test. I will teach you a more advanced method later in this chapter that will help you to determine if a supplement actually strengthens your body or weakens it. It takes the neutral reading out of the equation and saves you money on supplements that don't strengthen your body.

Another way that I find helpful to test foods that I should or shouldn't eat and as a general energy test is the *leg energy test*. Sit down in a chair and lift your right (or left) leg off the floor. Think or say what food you are testing and then apply a good amount of pressure to push that leg down right above the knee. If the leg goes weak then your body doesn't want that food. If the leg stays strong then your body is ok with that food, or at least the food does not weaken your body. This is particularly handy at restaurants. You can easily do this under the table while looking at the menu and no one would know. My kids call this "hiding my weird." Whatever! I did this just last night at a Thai restaurant and got a "no" on Tom Kah soup. I was very bummed because I love that soup! I had recently been reading about my dosha in an Auyrvedic cookbook and read that I shouldn't eat mushrooms because of my dosha. This soup has quite a few mushrooms in it and I suspect something else I'm not aware of that would weaken me. I ended up testing strong for pumpkin curry and grilled veggie salad, and they were delicious. I felt good afterward, and that's the goal.

In Chinese Medicine, Spleen Meridian is in charge of metabolizing everything; food, supplements, medicines, thoughts, emotions, and toxins. The ***Spleen Meridian energy test*** in my opinion is the best test for foods and supplements, but it's not as easy as the previous tests that I just shared with you. The body as a pendulum test, the jug of water test, and leg test give you a strong response if something is good for you (yes) and also if something is neutral for you and doesn't weaken you. They will give a weak response if something weakens you (no). **What these first 3 tests don't do is differentiate between something that's beneficial for you and something that's neutral with no benefit but does not weaken you.** *The Spleen muscle meridian test will show if a food or substance will energetically strengthen you and is worth spending the money on the supplement.* I can't begin to even imagine how much money I've spent on supplements that were most likely neutral and of no benefit to my body. I learned this test in my Eden Method training and it has most likely saved me hundreds of dollars.

The Spleen muscle meridian test is not an easy test to master — it takes time and practice to build intuition and confidence. This test helps you avoid spending money on herbs and supplements that are neutral for you. With that in mind, I will share it with you but I will also share some spleen strengthening exercises for you to do as well with the intention that you will acquire a new beneficial tool that can save you money on supplements and can offer great healing benefits.

Because of this beautifully busy and stressful world we live in, many people's Spleen Meridians are weak from all of the stress. Our spleens are also weak from all of the over-worry and over-concern we hold in them on behalf of our selves, our loved ones, our ancestors, friends, clients, pets or the world. *Everyone needs to do emotion clearing of his or her Spleen (and all other organs eventually) before you can get an accurate spleen muscle meridian test.* ***Refer to the Releasing Stored Emotions from your Body and Organs Addendum at the back of this book to help you to clear your Spleen.*** I also explain this protocol in detail in Chapter 18.

After clearing the emotions from your Spleen you can assess your spleen muscle meridian test. Stand with your right arm hugged close to the side of your body with your hand perpendicular or sidewise to your body with your thumb against your body. Hold your right arm in tight and strong to your body with your right thumb only touching your right side and reach over with your left hand and slide the back of your left hand between the right side of your body and your right arm above the wrist. With your left hand/fingers try to pull or push your right arm above the wrist away from your body while you try and hold it tight against your body. This is awkward, and confusing so I will describe it again; slide your left hand between your body and right arm just above the wrist and using leverage and your left fingers, try and move your right arm away from the right side of your body. If you are unable to do this yourself you can always get someone else to test you but make sure that they understand that they need to pull just above your wrist with about 2 pounds of pressure, not yank your arm.

If it's hard to push/pull away from your body, then your spleen is strong. If you cannot hold it against your body, then it is weak. I would venture to guess that a lot of people have a weak spleen test before the over worry and over concern that is being stored in it is cleared. I find this quite often to be the case with my clients when they first come to me. I find a weak Spleen Meridian test also if my clients are sick a lot, have lived a stressful life, are a sensitive empath, or have been diagnosed with an autoimmune health challenge.

If your test was strong you can skip to **Spleen Muscle Meridian Test for Supplements** below. If it was weak test then release the stored emotions from your Spleen (Chapter 18 or use the addendum at the back of book) then retest your Spleen Meridian again, and if it is still weak then do the following.

Your Spleen Meridian starts at the outside bottom corner of the big toenail. That's the Spleen 1 acupuncture point. It runs up the inside of your leg and then up your torso and next to the outside of your breast and back down the outside of your breast on the side of your body almost to the bottom of your ribs.

Meridians are like energy highways. Some energy systems in your body can move outside of their energy pattern but not the meridians. They all have a specific pathway that they stay in, although there are some minor variances in the pathways. Each meridian is associated with an organ and also with a tooth. When you have dental pain in a tooth, it's beneficial to see which organ it is attached to and investigate what needs to be done to support that organ energetically and physically. This has cured many toothaches, abscesses, and even cavities. Meridians are on both sides of the body (left and right), mirroring the other, except for Central and Governing. Central runs on the front of the body, and Governing runs on the back of the body.

Now I am going to have you trace the Spleen Meridian backward with your hands slowly. With your hand on your body or just above your body, looking at the diagram, start at the bottom of your rib cage 6 inches below the armpit at the side of your breast and slowly follow the meridian line up the side of your rib cage to above the nipple. Then go down your body and off your big toe on the outside bottom corner. Do this on both sides. This releases old and stagnant energies from that meridian. Now we are going to fill the meridian with new fresh energy by tracing it forward 3 times on both sides of the body. Start with your hand at the Spleen 1 point, which is at the outside of your big toe, and trace up your body three times total. **So, to flush**

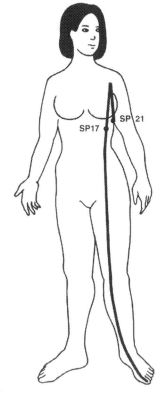

SP 21

SP17

Spleen Meridian, you trace it down *one time* and follow that with tracing it up *three times*.

After you've done that I would like you to tap Spleen 17 (below the breasts in alignment with the nipple) with your fingers bunched together. You can do this on both sides at the same time. Then tap Spleen 21 (the end point – see diagram) for about 10 seconds as well. Next thump your thymus (in the middle of your chest/sternum) at the same time as thumping Spleen 21. This is an immune system reset. Do both sides of Spleen 21. It's time to repeat the spleen test and see if it is strong now. If it's still weak or wobbly then hold Spleen 1 and Spleen 21 with your fingers at the same time on the same side for about 2-3 minutes then switch sides and hold for 2-3 minutes.

Now try the spleen muscle test again. It should be strong now when you try to push/pull the right arm away from your body. If it's still weak, repeat what you just did but only tracing the meridian up your body and very slowly. Hold the beginning and end points again, tap Spleen 17 (in alignment with nipple approximately 1 rib below breast) for 10 seconds and Spleen 21 at the same time tapping your thymus for 10 seconds and repeat until you get a strong test.

Spleen Muscle Meridian Test for Supplements

Once you get your Spleen Meridian strong, you are ready to do some deeper energy testing for supplements. Here is the thought process. If you have a Spleen Meridian that is going good and is generally strong and good at metabolizing food, supplements, and emotions then it can tell you if any of these things are good for you if they strengthen your Spleen Meridian. Now that we have your Spleen Meridian strong, we are going to weaken it and then strengthen it again to give us accurate answers.

To weaken your Spleen Meridian you need to waive or flutter your right hand in front of where your spleen is in your body. The spleen is below your left breast. Hold your right hand there with your palm facing your spleen and flutter your fingers together back and forth in front of your spleen, weakening it. Then try the muscle test again. Hold your right arm snug against the right side of body, back of left hand against the right side of your body between right arm above wrist and then push/pull to bring right arm away from the body. This should be easy to do now and very difficult for you to hold the right arm against the body now because the energy has been interrupted. This is a **weak** spleen energy test. To do a quick reset of the Spleen Meridian you can move your right hand in the air in front of your spleen (below left breast) in a slow figure eight pattern a few times, retest, and you should have a strong spleen energy test again.

You are now ready to test some supplements! How you do this is to have your supplement that you want to test near you on a table. You need to weaken your Spleen Meridian. (I know you just spent time getting your Spleen Meridian strong!) Remember you do this by waiving/fluttering your fingers on your right hand in the air back and forth above where your spleen is in your body. Your spleen is located just below your left breast.

After you do this, you then quickly put the supplement in your shirt or bra, tucked into your waistband of your pants, so it's on your body (you get the picture). Then do the spleen energy test with the back of your left hand against the right side of your body trying to push/pull the right arm away from the right side of your body while holding it into your body.

If it's easy to pull your right arm away, then the substance/supplement does not strengthen your spleen and it's not beneficial for you in your healing. ***If your spleen test is strong now after you weakened your spleen*** *but added the supplement to your body, then the supplement strengthens your body, and it is beneficial in your healing.*

It's not easy to grasp this test at first. It takes practice, patience, and trusting of your own intuition and your body's intelligence. Keep practicing and you'll get it. It's a tool that can fine-tune your healing process, speed it up, and save you a bunch of money on supplements. Find a friend who is interested in healing and assessing supplements and practice on each other. It's much easier to test someone else and be tested by someone else than to self-test at first. It will help to get a more accurate test if you and your testing partner hold the intention that you will get accurate tests and answers from your higher selves to help you. Don't give up on this. Look at it with curiosity. Play with it until you have it mastered and then you can help your friends and family with it. We can all be grateful to Donna Eden and applied kinesiology for this protocol. What a gift to be able to do this for yourself and others. I have this in the addendum section as well for your easy reference.

Chapter 12
Medical Medium Healing Came Into My Life

"Compassion is the radicalism of our time."
— *Dalai Lama*

THE NEXT CRUCIAL INFORMATION I read in the *Medical Medium* book was about heavy metals. In April of 2016 I had figured out that even though I had done a heavy metals chelation with the M.D./ N.D. about 6-7 years previously, I felt like I hadn't been able to do that process the best that I could have. I attribute it to my situation of a busy life, work, small children, and a spouse who worked 60-hour weeks. I knew I still needed to get even more heavy metals out of my body because I did another test after the first chelation, and my mercury levels were still well past the dangerous zone. I also knew I had to get to the root of my challenges. After reading the *Medical Medium* book it was clear to me that I needed to do the Heavy Metals Detox Protocol in order to not feed the EBV anymore.

Many of my clients choose to put the five ingredients to get metals out into a smoothie and drink it every day. This is the easiest way to get all five things in your diet every day. There is a recipe for the Heavy Metal Detox Smoothie that you can get at www. medicalmedium.com or do a Google search for it.

Anthony William says the 5 key foods/supplements that pull the heavy metals out are:

Hawaiian Spirulina — comes in either tablets or powder. Some people like the taste of it, but I don't, because I think it has a strong algae taste to it. I prefer to swallow 6 tablets per day instead of the recommended amount of 1 tsp a day in a smoothie.

Wild frozen blueberries — I was making a smoothie every day with one to two cups of wild blueberries from Maine. Two cups per day is recommended. The company Vimergy sells a wild blueberry powder that you can use when you travel.

Barley grass juice powder — I put 1 tsp of this in my smoothie. I bought it from Vimergy. They now have the powder in capsules if you prefer that — I know I do!

Cilantro — I would put as close to a cup in my salad as I could almost every day. This was hard for me, as I didn't love cilantro. Now that I have the metals out I like cilantro! There are cilantro drops that could be added to a smoothie instead or taken in water to make it easier, but I have found through energy testing that they do not work as well as the live cilantro. I didn't know about the drops until several months into the protocol. You can get the dosing amount from your N.D. or muscle test yourself for how much of the cilantro drops to take if you are unable to use the fresh organic cilantro.

Atlantic dulse flakes — I would also put 1–2 tbsp in my salad every day. They have a salty flavor, and when you add the juice of a lemon or a lime as your dressing it's quite tasty.

The first four items I mentioned pull heavy metals out from various places in your body and brain. It is like taking the trash to the curb according to Medical Medium. The dulse then comes along like the trash collection truck and takes all of the trash/heavy metals out of your body. The dulse packaging may have a warning on it that says that it may contain mercury. It probably does but the thing about dulse I learned is that it does not ever let go of the mercury or metals, and then it is all eliminated from your body.

I ordered the Hawaiian spirulina, barley grass juice powder, and the Atlantic dulse flakes from the Medical Medium.com/

supplements list. The list is in alphabetical order, and it takes you mostly to Amazon.com, which makes it an easy process. The dulse comes in large pieces or in small flakes. I prefer the small flakes.

I also add some the following (all organic) to make it taste better and for their healing properties:

Organic coconut water (Costco — there is better out there but this is what I did)
Bananas (I peel and freeze my bananas when they are perfect or very ripe)
Mango (frozen organic, Costco)
Cherries (frozen organic, Costco)
Pineapple (frozen organic, Costco)
Dates (organic, Costco)

In May of 2016 my N.D. energy tested me for a chelation product called Detoximine, which is a heavy metal chelating glycerine suppository. I tested strong for it with regard to my kidneys and liver and then tested to use one every four days. This is not in the Medical Medium protocol but because my body tested strong for it, I trusted the wisdom of my body and my N.D. and decided to do it.

In July I could tell I was finally pulling the metals out of my brain. I could tell this because I was losing thoughts, words, names, and ideas. After about 4 seconds I would laugh and move on. I was not scared. I knew it was a temporary phase and that I was making progress. I also had been having a bad runny nose for the past 3 to 4 months since I started the heavy metal detox protocol. I finally bought handkerchiefs because I was going through so many tissues. My sense of smell is still a little wonky, but it is normalizing more and more.

When I came out of my version of the 30-day all raw-food cleanse, I started adding in some lightly cooked vegetables here and there and wild caught salmon once a week. I was getting better at avoiding the foods not to eat and will continue to avoid them for the rest of my life. I was able to add in a very small amount of beans and grains at that time and continued to pull the heavy metals out by consuming the five things that I talked about previously. I was getting most of my protein from soaked raw nuts, dark leafy greens, pea and hemp powder, and spirulina.

I had noticed after reading the chapter on chronic and mystery illnesses in the Medical Medium book that there is some overlap in the heavy metal detox ingredients and in the EBV (anti-viral) protocol. Being the efficiency expert that I am, I decided that while pulling the heavy metals out of my body and brain, I was also going to take some herbs and supplements that kill off the EBV. My body was doing double duty for me that spring of 2016. Not only was I pulling the heavy metals out, I was also killing off the EBV and detoxing dead virus and the debris from the virus. I was no longer interested in feeding EBV or any other virus in my body. I also started drinking lemon water first thing in the morning to help my liver to release what it was detoxing overnight.

Over several months on these protocols, I experienced severe body aches, total exhaustion and temporary brain challenges. But I was able to release 12 pounds of inflammation, toxins (heavy metals and more), and viral by-product. It was such a humbling yet fascinating journey for me to experience and to feel the chemistry of my body changing. Even though I was so ragged, I could feel the vibration of my body increasing, and it was amazing! During this process, I would look at myself in the mirror with only love and awe that I was courageous enough to do this.

It was hard and uncomfortable, and I observed that I looked like something the cat had drug home, but I would smile at my ragged self in the mirror, and I would say, "I am kicking EBV ass!" I would do the muscle flexing motions while saying "grrrrr" and laughing. That told my immune system to go after the EBV, and it did! On the more positive side, I would say, "I am toxin and virus free" and still do something silly so that I would smile and feel a positive energy while saying it. I knew there was no going back to that lower-vibration state that I had been in. I was taking lots of salt baths for detoxing and soothing of my aching body. I was able to only do restorative yoga and gentle Hatha yoga after those few months, but I noticed a direct correlation between less toxins and more flexibility.

To help me release more toxins from my body I would sit in my infrared sauna at high temperatures for 30 to 40 minutes 2 to 3 times a week. The sauna company told me that the higher temperatures help with releasing heavy metals and other toxins from our organs on a deeper level. I was told that the lower temperatures are for detoxing the skin (approximately 120-130 degrees). The medium temperatures are good for detoxing the joints (130-140 degrees), and the high temperatures help to get the heavy metals out (140 degrees and above). My sauna only goes up to 145 degrees and I make sure I am very hydrated the day before, the day of and afterward. I also would energy test to see what would be the highest and best amount of time for me each time I went in it. It was usually around 35 to 40 minutes each time but sometimes 30 minutes.

Always be very careful with this process and get some guidance from a healing professional to set up your best program. If you are looking to buy a sauna like I did, it's important to get one that has no EMF's in it. EMF's are electromagnetic frequencies that have been proven to be detrimental for our health. I put Himalayan salt in my sauna to help with the EMF's and to alkalize and purify the air in there. I had a Himalayan salt candleholder that I was not using because candles can be very toxic, so I put it in my sauna. The brand of sauna I purchased is Sunlighten and they are third-party tested for EMF's.

My youngest son also decided that he wanted to get the heavy metals out of his body, so I was doing the following; juicing for 2 of us, shopping for 4 of us, and providing the food and supplements for whoever wanted to take them. I was also preparing 2 different dinners because not all my kids were interested in following my new dietary protocols. I was single parenting fulltime during this time, and although it was hard with the extra work, I believe it was a gift because I was able to be an example to my kids of doing something so hard but so important to heal myself. I was able to model self-care and eating healthy. My kids were 17, 17, and 20 at the time, so they were able to help juice sometimes and to grocery shop when I was completely exhausted.

Very quickly after starting the detox protocols I realized that I could not see any clients because of my extreme fatigue. April and May 2016 were rough, and I had to take them off from my energy medicine practice. In June I could only see clients with urgent cases. By July 2016, I was able to start seeing my regular clients but didn't take on new clients until August. I have to be at the top of my game to be an Energy Medicine Practitioner. I didn't have a desk job, but the trade-off is that I didn't have to work 8 hours a day. I have the utmost compassion for people who have to work full-time, have small children, and heal from major illness. I know they do it (very slowly), and I think they are true warriors.

During those few months I wasn't bringing in money from my business, and I had extra expenses for my kids being with me full-time and for all of the extra supplements for myself and any of my kids who would take them. I'm blessed to have savings and some passive income, so I figured this was as good of a time as any to use savings, because what good would it be if I didn't get better? I would have done anything to get better and would have figured it out even if it meant selling and downsizing or living with family or friends for a while.

We have nothing if we do not have our health. Sometimes we need to face the fact that we need a break — a couple months (and in some cases more) to stop the madness and allow our bodies to heal. I recognize that not everyone has these options, and I want to give love, recognition, and blessings to those folks. You could look into internship programs at healing retreats to see if that could work for you. Optimum Health Institute has a 3-month internship/missionary program both in San Diego, CA, and in Austin, TX, where you work 18 hours a week in exchange for room and board. The food is all organic and raw, so it's an opportunity to be supported in your healing journey.

Figuring out a new healthy lifestyle and healing was a part-time job. The eventual benefits of being more healthy and happy were a no-brainer for me. So I set out to do this healing as efficiently as I possibly could. In the *Medical Medium* book it said it could take 3–12 months to get the metals out. I did it in 4 months. After the first couple months I was able to start seeing some clients and work on my website. I knew I had to heal myself first and then I would be able to help others to heal. My healing went pretty fast because I was able to combine the support of Eden Method Energy Medicine with the Medical Medium physical body healing. This created a doubly powerful protocol and support for me. The combination of these two methods is what I offer in this book. They are powerful and both are complementary healing methods, especially to each other.

In early August 2016 I told my twin sister that I was really happy, because I had finally removed all the heavy metals from my body and brain, but that now what I was dealing with was healing the pockets in my brain where the metals had oxidized. I knew this because I had energy tested myself and that was the answer I got. My sister had also been pulling the heavy metals out of her body and brain, and needless to say she was very happy for me. We figured out I had more metals than she did, because of the well water I had been drinking for years with cadmium, aluminum, arsenic, etc. in it, plus I found out when I needed to have a root canal tooth pulled that my endo dentist had filled my root canal with mercury. Of course there was an infection underneath all of that. Who can be well when they have that going on?

That root canal needed to be fixed, especially because of the infection underneath it, but the Medical Medium doesn't necessarily recommend getting all your mercury fillings out. Sometimes they are better left alone he says in his book, as long as they are not cracked or leaching metals. In my case it was many years before I found out about the Medical Medium, so I had them all removed by a dentist who specializes in that procedure and does it in phases and very carefully. My M.D./N.D. was also helping by monitoring this and having me take chelating supplements at the same time. In hindsight, knowing what I now know, I would have been on the Medical Medium heavy metals detox for several months first and then I would have done the replacements one every two months, and only if they were cracked and it was necessary. I ended up with a titanium implant instead of that root canal tooth, and yes that is metal and not great, but my body is not having too a bad of a reaction to it.

There are always impacts to things like having metal in your body. Energy is interrupted by metal and that tooth where I have the titanium implant is connected to my Kidney Meridian and my kidneys. The Kidney Meridian is our life force, and I had been extra tired for years. My identical twin sister has an implant in the same tooth and has experienced chronic fatigue periodically in her life as well. I support my Kidney Meridian energetically to help with this. If I needed an implant now I wouldn't get another one. Please consider going to a biological dentist if you need dental help and listen to the Medical Medium podcast on SoundCloud about dental health. It is a wealth of great information and can help you to make an informed decision for your highest and best good. I did not know biological dentists existed at the time, or I would have definitely gone to one of them.

In July of 2016 I received an email from the Medical Medium. In the email he said he wasn't able to help all of the sick people in the world. He had 25,000 people on his waiting list for 30-minute phone appointments with him. He was looking to create a Health Practitioner Medical Medium Support Network for people in the healing profession who wanted to learn more and be supported by Medical Medium staff to help our friends, family and clients with his protocols. This way he could help more people by helping us understand his protocols on a deeper level and then we all could help more people. I thought about applying while I continued to work on healing myself. I was getting smarter (finally!) and felt more energetic and overall more vibrant every day. I decided to apply and was accepted. This was not a school or a certification program. It's only a support network of other practitioners that was supported by Medical Medium staff. We were able to delve deeper into the healing information from Anthony William and to support each other with any questions we had.

The M.D.'s, N.D.'s, chiropractors, energy healers, colon hydrotherapists, nutritionists, R.N.'s, acupuncturists, dieticians, and other therapists in the group were able to submit questions to Anthony William and listen to him answer all the questions we submitted. With all the experienced healing professionals in this network, we had access to very technical, complicated, and extremely important questions and answers from Anthony William. This was a huge amount of information for us and so helpful. We are all still continually learning from each other and supporting each other with questions and concerns.

Part of being admitted to the Practitioner Support Network was that we were all able to get a thirty-minute phone session with Anthony William. Mine was scheduled for a couple days after my birthday in August 2016. This was just a week and a half after I told my sister I had gotten all of the heavy metals out of my body and brain and that I was then working on healing the spaces in my brain where the metals oxidized.

I was excited and nervous for my appointment, but Anthony put me at ease, as he is an absolutely sweet and caring guy. He is what my daughter would call "adorkable." (This is the highest compliment by the way!) Anthony William said he had good news and bad news.

The bad news was that I have a long lineage of high amounts of heavy metals in my ancestry. I chuckled and said that I had already figured that out and he said great and that explains the good news. He said the good news was really good and that I had gotten all of the heavy metals out of my body and brain! He then told me that now what I was dealing with is the places in my brain where the metals had oxidized. I laughed when Anthony said that, and he asked why I was laughing, and I told him that I had just told my twin sister those exact words the week before. He was delighted!

He was pleased that I had been using energy testing, energy medicine, and my intuition in managing my protocols in an efficient manner. The other thing he told me was that my liver looked pretty beat up and battered. This was no surprise to me after all the Diflucan I had taken in the past for yeast challenges and the various toxins, viruses, and bacteria that had been hurting my liver for my whole life. He said it can take up to 7 years to really heal the liver and that is fine by me except I was determined to heal mine in less time than that! I love my liver and am so grateful for all it has done and tried to do for me. Healing my liver means no or low animal protein, fats, oils and alcohol. I also believe it means dealing with old anger, rage, resentment and frustration that is being held onto whether we realize it or not. I knew eating to heal my liver was how I feel the best anyway, so I eat as clean as I can, and my liver and I are happy.

Try this now:

Take a moment now to put both of your hands below your right breast on your liver area. Infuse your liver with love, light, gratitude, and healing energy from your hands, thanking it for all of its hard work on your behalf.

To sum all of this up, I was eating mostly raw from April to September 2016. I was avoiding the foods and additives that harm us and feed viruses as best as I could, while getting better at recognizing where they are hidden in foods as time went on. Here are the foods to avoid that I read about in the Medical Medium book and what I remember about why we should avoid them:

Corn — all corn even organic — has all been GMO'd at this point.

Soy — same story as corn, sadly.

Eggs — are great, ***but*** they feed viruses, tumors, cysts, bacteria, and cancers.

Natural flavors — means hidden chemical additives and usually MSG.

Gluten — avoid this to heal faster.

Sugar —Most sugar is corn-derived or genetically modified. Honey and fruits are not considered sugars and are beneficial to eat.

MSG — is a neurotoxin that kills brain cells.

Farmed fish — are given antibiotics, and the water has chemicals in it.

Citric acid — is a preservative and is bad for the gut.

Dairy — feeds cancers, etc. and is very inflammatory.

Pork — super high fat, which is a stress on the liver.

Canola oil — almost all canola oil is GMO.

Artificial sweeteners — are neurotoxins that cause terrible damage to the brain and are proven to cause cancer.

There is much more depth and detail about these in Anthony's first book, *Medical Medium,* and it's worth the time reading about why they are so harmful to us. When you read these details you will be very motivated to avoid them. These are the big ones, and like I said I did the best I could at avoiding them and I got better and better at it as time passed. If I accidentally had some of those foods my body started letting me know by stomach cramps, gas, or bloating. These are all messages if we choose to pay attention to them. Keep in mind that by avoiding these foods you will be eating a more plant-based organic diet, mostly cooked at home, and your body will be able to start detoxing and healing.

By the middle of August my website was up, and I was ready to accept new clients and work more. It had been 4 ½ months since I started the Medical Medium protocols, and I was feeling more energy, clearer in my head, and more focused than ever. By September 2016 I had been heavy metals free for a month and was well on my way of healing from that damage. I had also killed off most of the EBV in my body (around 91%) and had been detoxing the debris from it. My body decided at that time to present me with symptoms of SIBO (Small Intestine Bacterial Overgrowth). I found out SIBO is strep in the gut. I was having an unusual amount of gas, uncomfortable bloating, and stomach cramping that were getting in the way of my life. So I looked into what it could be. I remembered Anthony William saying that strep is a cofactor with EBV and heavy metals, and I remembered that I had experienced many cases of strep in my life. I figured this was my next step in my total healing, and I started the Medical Medium strep/SIBO protocol. I added a few more supplements to my current antiviral protocol, and I only had to remove grains from my current diet. This was hard, but I knew it was only for 3 to 4 months and that I could do it. I did on rare occasions have a small amount of grains, and I was still able to heal, but this may not work for everyone. The big part of the strep protocol, besides the diet is taking goldenseal - which is a natural antibiotic, and a few other supplements such as olive leaf extract, oil of oregano and colodial silver. You can find this information and the rest of the strep protocol in great detail in the *Medical Medium* book in the chapter on gut health. That chapter is a must-read for everyone.

Along with the antiviral and antibacterial supplement protocols (strep is a bacteria) I was incorporating foods into my diet that specifically helped to heal me from viruses and bacteria. I was also still healing my brain from the oxidized metals, so I was eating foods that support that healing. You can read about these foods and get recipes from Anthony William's second book, *Life-Changing Foods*. I particularly love this book because you can look up what you are challenged with health-wise in the back of the book and it will give you the pages where you can find information on different foods to eat to support the healing of what you are going through. What a concept, we can heal ourselves with food!

By February 2017, ten months after starting the Medical Medium protocols, my body was free of heavy metals and 90% free of EBV and 90% free of strep. I know this because I energy tested to verify it and because I felt like a new person. I was still healing my central nervous system from the damage caused by EBV, but I knew that was not for much longer.

As my body got stronger it started "cleaning house." In theory this is great and what we want — right? In reality this house-cleaning process can be humbling and teach us to surrender as it goes to a much deeper level in our body. In March 2017 I went snow skiing with my family and had a great time. I skied all day and felt strong, joyful, and energetic the entire day. I stayed on the intermediate runs and was happy with how great I was doing in every way, especially since I hadn't skied in many years. I did get some sun damage to the lower half of my face but it wasn't bad. I also ate gluten and had a small reaction to it, further weakening the skin around my mouth. The following day back at home I felt like I might be getting a herpes blister on my upper lip from the sun, the cabin environment, and from eating some things that may have weakened my system. The cabin we stayed in had an abundance of plug-in air fresheners, which are very toxic. Add in the lack of fresh cold air and the wood smoke from the fire, and it was terrible air that we were breathing in the cabin. All of these were a strain on my immune system. I was still doing the antiviral protocol supplements to support my body, so I wasn't overly concerned. Of course I unplugged the air fresheners and put them outside as soon as I figured that out but I was breathing in those toxins for a few hours before then.

What would have been a blister on my lip turned into an opportunity for my body to push the herpes virus out of my body in the nerves above and on my entire upper lip. I also had a couple blisters on my nose as well. This was a nightmare and a war. My body was pushing and fighting hard, and I was as low as I had possibly ever felt. I was down for the count and off work yet again for over a month. It took me a little while to realize that my body was literally pushing that virus out of those nerve bundles. When I mentioned it to my N.D. she said that she agreed with me and validated it by energy testing me. It goes against everything we are told and what was taught to her in medical school, but it happened to me, and she was able to experience it with me. In my Medical Medium group we learned that the body has "flares" of the viruses that we are killing off that can be very difficult and painful to deal with. They are generally a deeper level of healing and in the long run a good thing. When you are going through the most painful part of a flare it may be hard to believe it's a good thing, but just hang in there. It will get better.

I learned in the Medical Medium book that there are many more herpes virus strains than we have heard about. Previously, I only knew about what we were told — if the virus presents above the waist, it's Herpes 1. If the virus presents below the waist it is Herpes 2. This is not accurate. Apparently there are over 12 different strains of the herpes virus. One of the strains, HHV 6 (Human Herpes Virus) in particular attacks the heart and is lethal for many people. Anthony William goes into this in great detail in the *Medical Medium* book and it's very enlightening.

I was getting energy work done during this war on herpes on my lip by my N.D. She was clearing energy in the sinus region under my left eye and working energetically on the nerve bundle that starts below the eye and on the nerve bundle that starts over by the ear, as both of these were involved in what was going on. I told her that I could feel a spot where she was working on me that had some clogged energy that needed to be released and possibly more virus pushed out.

She said for me to do it later and to go slow with it. I went home and continued to work with it, released it, and got more of the virus out. I was ok with that, as I was already housebound and in "the thick of it," to quote my dad. I was committed to getting it completely out and gone forever.

This was a deep healing crisis for me. It was an opportunity to surrender, be humble, grow, and learn. In any healing crisis, especially the ones that take you to your knees and guide you to surrender, there is always a silver lining. I have had many silver linings that I'm deeply grateful for. In this case I was able to finally take an online course by Jeffrey Allen. It was a great class, and I've been able to help my clients and myself with what I learned. My lip healed and looks great, as if it never happened. I had healed at a deeper level and released more of that virus. My kids got to experience something really epic with me, which brought us closer.

This was yet another example and opportunity for my kids and myself to be more compassionate to others and our selves. My son needed to tour a college in another state and wanted me to go with him. This was less than a week into this virus hell I was in, and I felt like I had nothing in me. This battle had taken me to my knees in every way. My face and body hurt, and I looked like I had a botched plastic surgery on my lip and above it, or that I had been in a very bad car accident that left me with a mangled upper lip. It was hard to look at for me and everyone else.

We already had our airline tickets for the college tour, and everything was set up. My twin sister did not think I should go. I talked to my N.D. who was helping me through this. She energy tested me and got that I could do it if I was careful. I told my son that I did not want to embarrass him with how bad I looked. He looked me straight in the eyes and said, "I can handle it Mom, can you?" What a stinker.

So I went, and it was very difficult. It was hard for me to look at my face, and I didn't want to put other people through that as well. I wore a mask the first day on the flights and that made everything worse. After that I had to just let the world see it. That was an interesting social experience. I met some deeply compassionate people. Most people just looked at it and then quickly looked away. I completely understand. Being an empath, I was able to feel their pity for me, but mostly people were kind. My sister says she is still a little scarred from seeing it. I, of course, sent her pictures every day showing her the progression of the blisters, and it was horrific. She was so concerned for me through the whole humbling experience. It was good for my son to share this with me as well. We are both more caring and compassionate from it. All my kids had to share the grocery shopping and family errands for a month and witness me going through that hell with trust and as much grace as I could muster. Speaking of grace, I was supposed to co-teach a class during that time, and my teaching partner was the epitome of grace and love as he taught the class without me and held a healing space for me throughout my experience.

My body fought so hard against that virus that it took me months to recover on some levels. I had been off my thyroid supplement before this happened. Afterwards, I needed to be on it again for around 10 months. That gives you an idea of how hard my body fought for me to get that virus out and what a strain it was to my system. My adrenals took a huge hit as well. I had to take supplements to support them again and I also worked on my adrenals energetically daily for those 10 months. I will be teaching you how to do this in chapter 20. I also knew being back on these supplements for my thyroid and my adrenals would not last forever. The tapestry of my life is richer for this experience, and I'm definitely more compassionate and better for having gone through it. I am blessed. If I have another deep healing crisis, then so be it. I know I will come out better, more compassionate, and even stronger on the other side.

Chapter 13

My Daily Energy Routine and Life Habits

*"With everything that has happened to you, you can
either feel sorry for yourself or treat what has happened as
a gift. Everything is either an opportunity to grow or an
obstacle to keep you from growing. You get to choose."*
— Dr. Wayne Dyer

WHEN HEALTH BECOMES YOUR FOCUS, you realize what a difference it makes when you prepare yourself mentally and physically in the morning for the day ahead. I was tired a lot of the time but didn't have the sheer exhaustion I had been battling for a decade or more. Physical healing was well on its way, but I needed to get a daily energy routine that was easy to do each day, that I could do while lying down in bed, and that would help me in all the ways that I needed.

We are used to brushing our teeth, getting medical checkups, trimming our nails — caring for our physical body. The energetic body needs care and attention as well. If we do not care for our energy body it too will start to fall apart. Then we end up with pain, exhaustion, depression, and/or anxiety.

I decided I needed to set my inner alarm or my physical alarm for 5 minutes earlier each morning so I could prepare myself for my day before I even rolled out of bed. I know this will seem daunting at first, especially when you're getting up in the 5am time range, but the nice part is you can do it all lying down in bed. It's the best and most loving way you can wake up. The first thing I do before getting out of bed and getting distracted by so many other things is my daily grounding visualization followed by my quick energy tapping. This routine has been hugely transformational for my loved ones, my clients, and me.

In the morning all of this can be done in bed.

Grounding — take a deep breath and on the exhale gently close your eyes. See an energy pole coming from your root chakra down into the center of the earth. When you get to the center of the earth, attach your energy-grounding pole. Picture the earth energy that will nourish and support you on your physical journey coming up that energy pole and spraying out your crown chakra like a big fountain clearing all of the stuff out of your aura that is not yours and is not serving you. See that stuff washing down into the earth to be transmuted. See yourself keeping that energy and fountain cycling at all times.

Celestial energy — **see** that energy pole going up through the center of your body, out your crown chakra, and up into the sky and stars. See it connecting to your soul star. Your soul star is your higher self — it provides you with guidance on your spiritual journey. See that celestial energy coming from your soul star, down the energy pole and into your crown chakra. See the celestial energy going down the energy pole through your body mixing with the earth energies that are coming up. Take these mixed energies and push them out from your body as far out as your fingertips around your entire body. Keep this energy flowing at all times and out at your fingertips. This will keep your aura clear, keep you grounded and connected and will establish your space so that you don't hang onto other people's "stuff" in your aura.

Octahedron — **bring** your attention to the top of your head and see the top of an octahedron connected to your energy pole above your crown chakra and coming down to the four points mid body in front, behind, and to both sides at arm's length. Then see those points go down to the point right below your feet connected to your energy grounding pole. Picture your body inside the octahedron.

When you use the geometric shape of an octahedron around your body, you are energetically reinforcing your connection between heaven and earth. It creates a feeling of grounding and connection, and it creates and keeps a personal energetic space around you. I have found this to 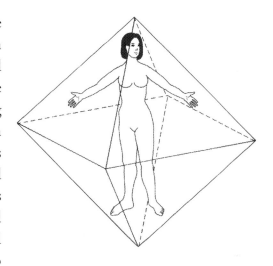 work better than all the other methods I've tried over the years to keep my energies in and other people's energies out. In combination with pushing the earth and celestial energies out to my fingertips, it unscrambles my energies and it keeps my aura out to my fingertips (with arms outstretched) unless I choose to expand my energy out further.

Energy tapping — this sequence is from Donna Eden's Daily Energy Routine with a couple minor changes from me. On the tapping parts you can use your fingertips to tap on most points, but I prefer to use my flat fist to thump my thymus. I also like to start at the top of my body and make my way down in order:

Crown Pull — put fingers from both hands at the middle of the forehead and gently slide-pull them apart toward the temples. Continue pulling apart along the midline of the head, opening the top of the head, all the way down to the neck, stretching the back of the neck open. (This improves circulation and can help with headaches and fuzzy brain.)

Tapping cheekbones — this is very grounding. Tap your fingers on your cheekbones about an inch down from the pupils of your eyes for about 10 seconds, or until you yawn or sigh.

Neck/thyroid stretch — gently put the fingers of both hands in the middle of neck together and stretch them apart, up and down, at the front of the neck, similar to the Crown Pull. Continue doing this around the front of the neck. You can do this in all directions, including the diagonals. This brings healing energy to your thyroid. I believe doing this was part of what helped me to get off my thyroid prescription and eventually thyroid supplements.

Tap K-27's — these two points are below the collarbone, about an inch down and an inch towards the armpit from the clavicle notch. Tapping these points tells the energy in all of your meridians to move forward in the right direction.

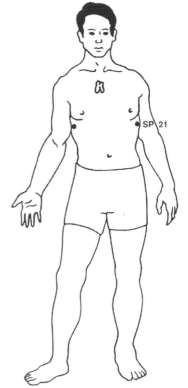

Tap thymus *(Tarzan thump– bump in middle of chest)* — this stimulates the thymus to produce T-Cells, which kill cancer.

And at the same time:

Tap spleen points — one side at a time while thumping your thymus. These points are on the "side seam" of the body — Spleen 21 (4-6 inches down from the armpit — it should be a tender spot!) on both sides of the body. Tapping these points will help to boost the immune system.

Connect head with body *(Hook Up)* — place the middle finger of one hand in the belly button, gently pulling up. The middle finger of the other hand is on the Third Eye — in-between and slightly above the eyebrows gently pulling up. Hold about 1-3 minutes or until you sigh or yawn. This connects head and torso and gives you a great sense of protection and connection to your body. It also helps to get you "out of your head."

Triple Warmer Smoothie *(Chill Pill)* — do this daily when you are in a stress response mode. Lay fingers gently on temples. Take a deep breath in, and on your exhale trace your fingers around the top and back of your ears and down the side of your neck to your shoulders. At your shoulders, switch your arms (left hand on right shoulder and right hand on left shoulder) and continue tracing your fingers down your arms to your wrists and then one at a time trace them off your ring fingers. This traces your stress meridian backwards, relaxing you and helping you to get out of the stress response.

Some days I do some light lymphatic massage under my collarbones, around the sides of my breasts, and down my arm seam.

After this I'm ready to get out of bed and start my day. I start by scraping my tongue with my copper tongue scraper. I do this before I drink any water or juice because I want to get rid of any toxins my body pushed out and onto the back of my tongue while I was sleeping. Next I splash cold water on my face and in my eyes, followed with a spray of rose water into my eyes and around my body, energizing my eyes and aura. I put Frankincense essential oil on my face and any other spots on my skin that I want to prevent from becoming cancerous. This is magic for your skin. I used it on my skin cancer and I believe it helped in reversing the skin cancer. I use it straight now, but you may want to start by mixing it in coconut oil as your skin may peel at first. It also helps with age spots and skin cancers. It will also dissolve bumps and skin tags.

Then I head to my kitchen and grab my 16 ounces of celery juice most mornings followed 30-40 minutes later with 16-32 ounces of lemon water. I prefer the lemon water to be slightly warm, but it can be room temperature as well. You can treat the lemon water as a flush by drinking it rather rapidly instead of sipping on it for a long period of time. Rinse your mouth with regular water after to get the lemon off your teeth to preserve the enamel.

For the daily celery juice, if you use a cold press juicer like I do you can make 4 servings (for 4 days) at a time as long as you drink one right away. You then have 72 hours (3 days) to drink the other 3 juices to receive the benefits of the juice before they diminish. It takes me roughly 30 minutes with my cold press juicer to do a batch for 4 days. Celery juice has amazing healing properties that can benefit everyone. Anthony William talks about a lot of the healing benefits of celery juice in his *Liver Rescue* book and in his latest book, *Celery Juice: The Most Powerful Medicine of Our Time Healing Millions Worldwide.*

The goal is to get to know your body and to learn how to communicate with it for what support it needs from time to time. The ultimate healing goal is to get all, or most, nutritional support from the food we eat if possible.

Wait at least 15 minutes after finishing your lemon water before you have breakfast. I generally have a smoothie in the warmer months. In the colder months this is my favorite — it is a variation of a recipe I got from my Ayurveda consultant although it is not recommended during your intense healing time as it has fats and oils in it that according to Medical Medium will slow down your liver in healing. Here is my version of the recipe:

Crust-Free Pie Breakfast

½ red apple cut into small chunks (I love Braeburn or Fuji)
½ pear (I love Bartlett) cut into small chunks
10 raw soaked walnuts chopped
¼ tsp cardamom
¼ tsp cinnamon

¼ tsp ginger
1 tbs coconut oil
Drizzle of local honey

I heat the coconut oil in a pan, add the spices and mix them together. Then add the pears, apples, and walnuts that have been diced and cook for a few minutes until they are soft. Put into a bowl and add any of the following; shredded coconut, ground flax, chia seeds and drizzle a little honey on the top. Enjoy!

I also like the following for breakfast in the winter months and not during intense healing periods:

Cooked quinoa with almond milk, raw soaked walnut pieces, berries, and honey.

Banana-oat pancakes — smash a ripe banana together with gluten-free oats and cook in coconut oil until formed and slightly browned. Serve with raw honey drizzled on them and enjoy.

I generally try to be fat free until noon or 1pm as much as possible so that I am continuing to support my liver in detoxing. Anthony William recommends this in his *Liver Rescue* book. But when I need to eat something for breakfast these are my "go to's."

For a snack I eat a red-skinned apple with a couple medjool dates or drink fresh juice.

Lunch is often a salad or a smoothie with fruit and veggies and either pumpkin seed protein powder or hemp seed protein powder. I like to add flax powder, as well as barley grass juice powder occasionally. I try to mix up the smoothies and rotate 4–5 different combinations to get more nutrition in me. For convenience, though, I will make a double batch, so I'm only making smoothies every other day. I love to have the wild blueberries when I can because of how amazing they are at pulling out heavy metals. They also have antiviral and antibacterial properties. During the Winter I struggle with the cold and instead of a smoothie I have a salad with a warm veggie burger pattie, warm sweet potato cut up or warm quinoa on it.

Often times I make curry or soup. Dinner is something similar. Recently my body has been testing strong for small amounts of turkey meat, lamb, and certain wild-caught fish. I feel really good eating like this occasionally. When I'm working on detoxing my liver I omit all animal protein, fats, and oils from my diet and stay mostly raw for a period of time. Mostly, when I have those fats I eat them in the afternoon so my liver can continue to cleanse and heal throughout the morning and into the afternoon.

I've been doing some version of this for around three years now. I did burn out a little and started eating out more, but I tried to be smart about it. The best food you are going to eat is at your home or at the home of friends who eat like you. Restaurants still use canola oil, MSG, and lots of butter, and they use oil at high temperatures, often frying in the same vat of oil long past that being healthy. Most are not organic. Your body may be able to handle it occasionally, but that's a slippery slope. I found that I would quickly get back in the habit of eating out too much. What happened when I did that? I got inflamed and started feeling and looking nowhere near as good as I had been. When you get inflamed, you gain and retain weight (inflammation.) You feel puffy and sluggish. Your vibration decreases. It's a function of the liver not being able to handle all it's being asked to handle.

When you eat out, make sure it is a restaurant that doesn't use MSG. Some Thai food restaurants can be a good option. Stick with veggie soups (no tofu or tempeh because they are soy products and according to Anthony William most if not all of the soy has been gmo'd) or curries. I love pumpkin curry the best, but it's best to switch it up. If you prefer to stay home to eat it is the healthiest option. The Medical Medium has many delicious and nutritious healing recipes in his books as well. My favorite breakfast that I mentioned above is like having crust free pie for breakfast. Make it fun and involve your family and friends so you have something to share along with good health, which is the best gift of all.

I have finally been able to incorporate yoga into my daily routine on a regular basis. I've found that the morning is the best time for me. I like yoga for its support through breath work, stretching, and strengthening/lengthening of muscles. In the beginning of my recent healing journey, I wasn't able to do anything for a long period of time. Then I started with restorative yoga and gentle stretching. Those were incredibly painful for me for a while. I'm now able to do Barre (combination of yoga, ballet, and pilates) 1–2 days a week along with 2–3 days of yoga. I add in hikes when I can. It's good for the soul to be out in nature, and the cardiovascular training strengthens the heart, moves lymph, and flushes toxins.

To help to get the toxins out of my body I dry brush before I bathe, bounce on my rebounder for 5 minutes daily, go in my infrared sauna 1 to 2 days a week if possible, and do some self-massage of my lymphatics.

I also try to drink at least one cup of detox tea per day and energy test for which one my body wants. Anthony William has come up with mixtures of herbs that will specifically detox certain chemicals from the body. These teas are:

Anti-chlorine and anti-fluoride
Anti-pesticide and anti-fungicide
Anti-radiation
Anti-cleaning solvents
Anti-plastics

These all contain the combination of around 4–5 different herbs plus some kelp and seaweed in the anti-radiation tea. Go to www.medicalmedium.com for the ingredients of these teas. I was able to find an organic tea company near me that was willing to create these teas for my clients and me to order online. You can check them out at www.wilwandteaco.com. They are in the detox teas section. I have them listed in the references section in the back of the book for your easy reference as well.

In the kitchen I've found Green Bags to be very helpful in keeping my produce fresh for much longer periods of time. I rarely have to throw away unused produce anymore when life gets too busy. I freeze peeled bananas and other fruits and vegetables that won't get eaten in time. I also juice or blend any veggies or fruits instead of throwing them out.

I got rid of all of my old nonstick cookware and only use ceramic now. I use parchment paper when baking food on metal pans to keep my food from touching metal of any kind. I will never cook food on a metal pan again unless there is parchment paper between the metal and the food. No more aluminum foil touching my food as well. I haven't used my barbecue grill for several years now. I drink my filtered water from a glass bottle and only use glass storage containers. No plastic.

I love to get good Thai food to go, but they put hot food in plastic containers. I just picture those toxins being leached into my food and I simply cannot eat it. I've been somewhat successful in taking my own containers, but most restaurants don't like that. The best way I found is to show up with the containers and then order so the containers can be taken to the kitchen along with the order. I use quart mason jars for soups, and if I have to use glass containers with plastic tops I have a piece of parchment paper to go in between so the hot food isn't close to or touching the plastic directly. This is a labor of love for my loved ones and me. I've been the recipient of lots of teasing and have been the butt of many jokes by my loved ones, but I stand strong in my health champion role. They are starting to read about the things I have been telling them for years and are now finally validating what I have been telling them and modeling in my life.

Even with all these good health habits in place I experienced a setback after purchasing a new electric car and started having flu symptoms. I knew when I bought the car that I'd have to be very mindful with the off gassing of the toxic plastics and solvents. I was careful, but it still got my body into an immune reaction. I started to feel inflamed again, and it took me a while to get my strength back. I would wipe down all of the surfaces in the car as much as possible with a vinegar and water spray, and I always kept the windows down when it was parked. I purchased a used air filter that plugs into the CLA, and it runs all the time. Before I got the air filter I drove with the windows down several inches, and you can imagine that wasn't fun in November even in California. I've read that the worst off gassing is over in about 6 months, and I am past that point now. The smell has been gone for a while, but I will continue with my air filter.

As of today in January 2020, almost 4 years since I started on my Medical Medium healing journey, I have healed tremendously. This healing happened fast for me as I incorporated clearing the old emotional energies out of my organs that were getting in the way of the physical healing. I discuss those and the protocol to clear them in detail in Chapter 18.

Three and a half years ago Anthony William had told me that my liver was very beat up and battered, which didn't surprise me at all. He said it can take up to 7 years to really heal your liver in general, but I decided I was going to do it a lot quicker. I'm committed to supporting my liver after I heal it for the rest of my life. We are never really done, because we live in such a compromised and toxic world, where our best health interests are not a priority to anyone but us.

It has been interesting to watch the layers of healing I've experienced and realize that sometimes we do feel worse before we can feel better. I haven't missed the irony of how when we feel terribly sick it's easier to stick with the healthy protocols, and yet when we start to feel better it's easier to reach for those foods that do not support us in health.

This is not a journey to perfection but a journey of supporting this physical body I was given. I want to use it to be joyful in the moment, live life to its fullest, and to give back and help others. We are not able to do that if we feel terrible. We all have those days where we just want something that we can eat that is both salty and crunchy, then followed by sweet. I feel like if you deny yourself you are not going to be in a happy vibration so find the best option to satisfy your need. Be happy about it and enjoy it every once in a while. I found Forager pressed greens chips that I think are very good, and I have organic guacamole and organic salsa. If I need a sweet I reach for fruit or make banana ice cream or chocolate vegan avocado ice cream. I'm not perfect and I will on the rare occasion buy coconut ice cream or cashew ice cream. They are not perfect, but they are much better than regular ice cream. Are these choices ideal nutrition? No, but they are not terribly detrimental, and I choose to be joyful when I have them, bless them, and be grateful for them.

Chapter 14

Detoxing

"Hardships often prepare ordinary people for an extraordinary destiny."
— *C.S. Lewis*

I'VE TOUCHED ON DETOXING IN previous chapters, but in this chapter I will go deeper into the process and what I know about it now that I have done so many years of it in many different ways. I am very excited to have just found out that Anthony William is currently writing a book specifically about cleansing. That will be a must read for everyone interested in cleansing in a safe way.

Your body is made to detox. It will naturally detox, primarily while we are sleeping, since it can put most of its energy toward that instead of supporting us with all that we demand of it during the day. This is another reason to get good sleep and eat a primarily plant-based diet, as plants are easier to digest than animal protein. Eating a large meal high in fats consisting of animal protein, shellfish, or both can keep your liver working to digest that for hours. Add in alcohol, and that is a recipe for an overburdened liver, especially if this is a regular occurrence. Your body is forced to focus on digesting instead of detoxing and healing, which is so necessary in our toxic world.

A lot of the healing work is done from 1–3am during Liver Meridian time, largely because our liver is made specifically for this job. Before this is Gallbladder from 11pm–1am. So if you have a dinner full of fats, which is what our gallbladder and liver work on, then they will be busy doing that work instead of doing healing work. Liver Meridian is a common time (1-3am) for people to wake up during the night because their body/liver is working extra hard to detox or process what we have consumed the evening before. I remember waking up earlier in my life drenched in sweat between the hours of 1–3 am after drinking too much alcohol the night before, especially when I drank wine. I now recognize that it was an obvious sign of my liver not functioning well and struggling to process and heal.

You may have heard people talk about detox pathways. They are talking about the liver, lungs, lymph system, skin, kidneys, and the colon. There may be more, but these are the most crucial from my experience. What I've learned is that you need to support these pathways so that they can handle the toxins processed and released by your body. These all need to be supported in body-mind-spirit. In chapter 6 I talked about emotions being energy. You have most likely met people who have current and repressed anger in and around them. This will physically impact their liver and gallbladder on a body level over time if they do not address it and release it. This can look like cancer of the liver, gallstones, or gallbladder disease. The same will happen with the lungs (grief) being susceptible to bronchitis/pneumonia and the large intestine (letting go) constipation, intestinal disorders such as Crohn's, leaky gut, etc.

Those dis-eases aren't only caused and cured energetically. What I am saying is that I believe there is an energetic predisposition to them and that diet and emotions play a big role in our organs wellbeing. I will go into greater detail in Chapter 18 about how emotions can affect our physical body negatively and how you can clear them so you can heal quicker. Spleen (immune system) and Stomach (over worrying) can show up as autoimmune for Spleen and ulcers for Stomach. Kidneys and Bladder (fear) could show up as chronic bladder infections or urgency to pee, and Kidneys can show up in the form of stones or even eventually needing dialysis. Small intestine and heart (panic and anxiety) can show up as SIBO for small intestine and A Fib for heart. These are just some of the possibilities of how dis-ease in the emotional/energetic body can show up in the physical body over time.

I am not going in depth on this, rather, just giving some examples of how these emotional energetic imbalances can present in our physical body if left alone for too long. These can be cleared many different ways. With energy medicine, a practitioner can assist in the releasing of stored excess emotions that are causing dis-ease in the physical body or with the protocol I outline in Chapter 18, you will be able to do this yourself. I have found this protocol to be the quickest and most profoundly effective way (from an energetic and physical perspective) to support the organs in healing and detoxing.

These emotions that you have been storing on behalf of yourself, your loved ones, ancestors, pets, friends, clients, colleagues or the world have been shrouding or clogging the healthy energy flow to, from, and within your organs. Be sure and read Chapter 18 and do the protocol so your detox pathways can be more open to releasing toxins from your physical body and healing. This is foundational in your healing of your physical body. I am so blessed and grateful to witness the huge transformations of my clients, loved ones and myself by doing this protocol.

Liver

Your liver is your first concern when it comes to detoxing because that's your liver's job. If your liver is congested then the toxins will not be able to come out easily, and you will feel terrible. If you are detoxing too much too fast and your liver can't handle it, the toxins will find a way out, and that could be through your skin. You don't want that to happen. What that was like for me was an ugly rash on my arms and my legs. They itched badly at first, and they took a *very* long time to go away. The rash on my arms went away after about a month, but my legs took much longer than that, around 4–5 months. Lucky for me, it started in late September and was done by springtime. I was ready for tank tops and shorts again.

If the liver is congested and you are not pushing the toxins out, then you are most likely reabsorbing them. We always want results for our efforts, and if we are willing to go through the discomfort of a detox, then we need to get those toxins out in an effective way and not through the skin. Start with clearing the emotions from your liver and gallbladder with my protocol and then read Anthony William's book *Liver Rescue,* which goes into great detail about detoxing your liver with what you eat. In my opinion that book is the way to detox your liver most effectively with food and juices in combination with clearing the emotions in all of your organs. This combination is the recipe for a faster and more thorough, deep, healing.

What can we do to support the liver? Energetically, you need to clear the rage, anger, shame, judgment, frustration, and resentment that you have been holding onto in your liver and gallbladder for yourself, your loved ones, your ancestors, the world, etc. Use the addendum **Releasing Stored Emotions from Your Body and Organs** at the back of the book after you read Chapter 18 to clear the excess emotions from all of your organs **before** you start on your physical body detox. One of the first things we can do to support our liver is to drink 16 ounces of fresh celery juice first thing in the morning on a completely empty stomach. Try to drink it fast so it fills up your stomach all the way. You then wait 30 minutes and then drink 16–32oz of good filtered water with the juice of half to a whole lemon. The celery juice will help your body to create hydrochloric acid, which breaks down food and supports your digestion. It's also a major detoxifier, supplier of minerals, and healer of the liver. As I mentioned before, our body's energy is focused on detoxing the liver from 1–3am. The lemon water will then flush out what the liver has worked so hard to process for us overnight.

What else can we do? We can eat a diet rich in fruits and vegetables for a long enough period of time for your liver to truly heal. The Medical Medium, Anthony William, recommends from his *Life Changing Foods* book to eat the following daily for your liver if you can: berries, cherries (small amount daily), mangos, papaya, pears, melons, artichokes, asparagus, cabbage, sprouts, cucumbers, cilantro, and garlic. Turmeric and ginger root are helpful as well. Eating this way is not only healing to your body but it also relieves the overburden on your liver from a higher-fat diet. When we consume a diet high in animal protein, fried foods, processed oils and fats that overburden the liver, it makes the liver sluggish and unable to do its job properly (and in some extreme cases not at all). When you have a liver that is already burdened with excess emotions, heavy metals, viruses, and the toxins that viruses love to eat, you have a sluggish liver. Sometimes in my energy work I feel like the liver is hot on some clients and not doing good at all. And when poor diet choices are added, things are going nowhere good very quickly. Anthony William says that even a lean piece of meat can have as much as a tablespoon of fats in it for your liver to process. You need to be gentle with yourself because this can take anywhere from 3 months to 3 years or longer to really heal. You will feel so much better after the first few months of intentionally eating well and supporting your liver. I know this because I did.

Lungs

Our lungs are designed to help us to detox or expel airborne toxins and pollutants with our breath. We need to breathe deeply and exercise to help us to move toxins out of the bottoms of our lungs. Most of us when not being mindful of it just surface breathe, using only the top half of our lungs most of the time. Having air-purifying plants in your home and office will help to clean the air, supporting healthy lung function. Good air filters and purifiers help as well. There are some herbs and supplements that will also help support your lungs so they can detox and also maintain healthy function.

Lungs overburdened with grief cannot function optimally. Again, after reading chapter 18 please refer to the **Releasing Stored Emotions** Protocol in the back of the book to release the excess grief you are holding in your chest and lungs and then address the physical support of your lungs.

I have found yoga to be very beneficial in opening up and deepening my breathing. It not only does that but it allows breath to flow through your body releasing stuck energy. Every time you expel a deep breath you are cleansing your lungs of toxins in them. Lung as a meridian is high energy and healing from 3–5am every morning. An early morning yoga or meditation practice with deep breathing can really help to move out those toxins the lungs were working to detox in the early morning.

Lymphatics

Our lymph system also moves toxins out of the body. The lymph system does not have breath to move it like the lungs do, nor does it have a pump, the way the blood has the heart to move it. So lymph needs some help from us. What can we do for the lymph system to help it? First of all, as with all of the pathways, we need to be hydrated. Our body and brain are made up of mostly water, so we need to keep good water coming into our body and brain so that they can function properly. With a properly hydrated body we can exercise and sweat to move and release toxins from the lymph system. Massage can release toxins from the lymph system as well. I am self-massaging most mornings as part of my daily self-care. I massage under my collar bones, the connection seam where my arm connects to my body, down the center of my chest, under and around my breasts to that oh so tender outside of my breasts which can be *so* painful when you first start doing it. Keep doing it though, and the toxins will move out and it won't hurt anymore.

Here is a fun experiment:

Slowly bend at the waist and see how close your fingers get to your toes or the floor. Make a mental note and then slowly rise back up. Next, put your hands between your legs at the top inside of your legs. Squeeze the inside of your legs hard and keep doing that as you move down your inside of your legs to your knees. What you are doing is massaging your Small Intestine Meridian lymphatic points, releasing toxins from them. Then come up to your diaphragm and massage up under your ribs hard, releasing those lymphatic points as well. These are probably extremely tight and hard to get to under the rib cage, but do your best, and it will get easier. After you feel like you have painfully released those toxins, try to touch your toes again and see how much further you can bend. Usually, you can get another 1 to 2 inches closer to your toes or the ground. It shows you how stuck our physical bodies are with toxins. Drink plenty of water after doing this to help move the toxins out of your body. A walk or exercise would be beneficial as well.

Dry brushing is another way to help the lymph system to move and release toxins. This is also very beneficial for your skin. I dry brush before I get in the bath or shower. I start at my fingers and brush in upward strokes up my arm toward my heart. Always brush up toward your heart. I do the same with my feet. I start at my toes and do light and then firm strokes up my legs, abdomen and back toward my heart. I am then ready to wash off the dead skin and my lymphatic's have had stimulation to help them to move toxins out. I read a long time ago that dry brushing is a beauty enhancer helping to get rid of cellulite, although I do it for the health benefits. Anthony William says that cellulite is a byproduct of a congested liver, so it makes sense that if you are dry brushing you are aware of eating a better diet, which helps the liver to heal, then cellulite will improve naturally. Speaking of beauty, I tell my kids that healthy is beautiful, and it really is. Healthy of body, mind, and spirit. Happy is beautiful. Being Love is beautiful!

Exercising and sweating helps to move toxins out of the lymph system as well. Move your body every day for at least 10 minutes. I know firsthand how difficult this is when you are detoxing and feel terrible, but do the best you can. For sweating, a warm salt bath is good and detoxifying, plus it really helps with the aches and pains. An infrared sauna causes you to sweat and release toxins from an even deeper level. Whether you choose to purchase a home sauna or use a public sauna, please make sure you purchase or use one that has extremely low or no EMF's (electromagnetic frequencies). There is no reason to spend that money for health reasons to end up with different bad electronic toxins.

I've recently purchased a rebounder and have committed to rebounding for 5 minutes each day. This is very beneficial for helping to move the lymphatics. A rebounder is a mini trampoline that you jump or bounce on daily. There are so many ways to help move your lymph, so it's up to you to discern the best methods for you and just do them.

Colon

Our intestines are meant to absorb nutrients to nourish our body, but how can it do that if it's all gummed up? Think of a pipe or an artery lined with thick and sticky sludge. When I first went to the M.D. who was an N.D., he did some testing on me with the supplements I was taking, and it showed that I was not absorbing any of it. What a waste of money and time taking all those supplements and then not even being able to absorb them. Shortly after that I went to Optimum Health Institute for the first time and did the raw food, juice detox for a week. There I was introduced to colon cleansing. If your colon is coated with old fecal matter or fecal matter is stuck in pockets of your colon (diverticulosis), you will not be able to get healthy. If you are detoxing and not getting the toxins all the way out of your colon then you will reabsorb everything back into your body.

Detox is not fun, so I'm always committed to getting the best results for my efforts and especially about feeling better. There have been times where I have felt so sick from detox and then after getting a colonic or doing an enema, I would feel so much better. Getting the toxins out of my colon and liver really helped me to feel better quicker and to heal quicker. A colon gummed up with waste will manifest as longer and thinner bowel movements.

I learned how to do enemas at Optimum Health Institute and how important it is to get your colon cleaned on a regular basis if you are going through health challenges. It is not easy (it wasn't for me!) to do enemas at first, but you do get used to it and you feel great after you get the toxins out. Wayne Dyer was very vocal about how he took his coffee. What he meant by that is that he was a huge fan of coffee enemas. He said at one point that he would do a coffee enema every day. So, why coffee enemas vs. water enemas? The caffeine in the coffee when held in your colon will stimulate your liver to dump toxins. That is the goal right? It is, but in the book *Liver Rescue*, Anthony William talks about how dumping too many toxins at once from using coffee can cause really bad outcomes and lead to reabsorption of what you intended to release. Anthony recommends using lemon water instead of coffee. It stimulates a release from the liver as well, but in a gentler, less extreme way.

Colonics are also referred to as colon hydrotherapy. I have been a big proponent of colonics, though I recognize they are not for everyone. Some people cannot do them at all, or it could be very harmful. If you are wondering if you could benefit from them, ask your N.D. and make sure you go to a certified colon hydro therapist who keeps up their certification and equipment current. *This is very important.* They will be professionals who are doing their continued education, keeping their machine in optimal working condition and can give you the best supported colonic. First colonics can be very uncomfortable because of having impacted fecal matter from a lifetime of constipation but if you are called to do them and have a doctor's approval hang in there because they do get easier and much better. I've had friends and family say to me that they were concerned I would get dependent on colonics and not be able to do my big potty (mom talk!) on my own. That is not the case. It helps you with constipation and hydration of the colon, so the opposite is true. Really educate yourself on it and then tune into your own internal guidance to see if it is the right thing for you. It has been around for hundreds of years. When I came back from the Optimum Health Institute, I was retested for my supplements, and I was finally starting to absorb them! I had been doing enemas and colonics that week to help remove the toxins my body was dumping, releasing old fecal matter that was toxic to me and I was able to cleanse my colon so it would be able to absorb the supplements and nutrition I was ingesting. I would say that the proof is in my before and after photos…

Recently my N.D. told me that she was getting an intuitive hit that I needed to get a colonoscopy. She prefaced it with, "You are not going to want to hear this, Melissa, but…" She was right. That was the last thing I wanted to hear. I do not concern myself with medical tests. I take care of myself instead. I unfortunately got the same message when I energy tested myself, so I got a colonoscopy. This is what I mean by listening to your body: I did not take the prescription Miralax, which made my energy test go weak. Instead, with the guidance of my N.D., I chose to do high doses of vitamin C and Calm magnesium formula. I did this with the guidance of my N.D., and I asked after the procedure if I was all cleaned out and they said yes and that it had gone great.

They said everything looked good and that I have a very long colon with lots of twists and turns. That was a cause of some old diverticulosis that they saw, which are the pockets in your colon that food can get stuck, fester, and become infected. I knew there was a reason that colonics had been so beneficial for me. I was glad to hear that I did not have inflammation because of my diet and regular colon cleansing. I know, TMI, but I share this so that some of you can heal from this as well. When I was looking into natural ways to prep for a colonoscopy, I found there are doctors who have their patients get a colonic the day before the procedure.

Mind

I cannot ignore the truth that you can eat everything perfectly, cleanse your physical body, and still not get well if you are having toxic thoughts or feelings about yourself or others or if you are full of emotions that you are carrying for yourself or others that are hindering your healing. Our experience in this school of life here on Earth is not always easy, mentally and emotionally.

I've found judgment to be an especially big challenge for me and just about everyone I know. Judgment in its lowest form is actually people watching and categorizing or labeling. I work on this still. When I catch myself doing it (especially when I'm driving), I ask my angels to take these thoughts from me and help me to only see love or to only see people in their truest and purest beautiful form. I also do this about myself. When we see something in someone that we are judging, it's probably something we do not like about ourselves.

I believe we are our own biggest critics and that we need to give the most grace to ourselves first. Then giving it to others will come naturally. This takes practice. I call it the loop of thoughts. Our inner voice and thoughts repeat in a loop. Learn to recognize this and to stop the negative or judgmental loop. This is a great start to creating new and better thought habits. When I first realized this and started recognizing it, I was redirecting my thoughts constantly. It was almost comical to me how much I was redirecting. I felt like all I did for a long time was redirect, redirect, redirect, all day long, over and over and over again.

If you are going to have thoughts over and over again, then make them count. Instead of "I look chubby," cancel that shit quick! We have 10 seconds to cancel a lower-energy thought. So I was thinking or saying, "cancel-cancel" a lot back then. Think or say "I am love" or "I am perfect" "I am vibrantly healthy" or "I am bitchin." Say it, think it, feel it, and then you can BE it. And it will trickle out from you to others. Our soul or essence is all of those things (depending on your definition of bitchin…:). In our human form we are meant to be imperfect. I laugh a lot over my beautiful imperfections these days. This life is messy, but we can make it a whole lot lighter and brighter by not taking it or anyone too seriously. Love and support yourself and others. We are all truly in this together. Redirect your loop thoughts and choose to be happy and healthy.

Chapter 15

Environmental Toxins

"Stay close to anything that makes you glad you are alive."
— *Hafiz*

Water

THIS WORLD WE LIVE IN can be toxic due to the efficiencies we have created around us and how we have treated our natural resources. I will break down these different toxins so that you can address or research further for your environment and what is best for you and your loved ones.

Water is critically important to us because our physical body is made of 60–70 percent water. The adult human body is comprised of 60 percent water, the brain and heart are 73 percent water, and the lungs are around 83 percent water.[14] Being dehydrated does not feel good, and if severe it can lead to death. When we are hydrated we are smarter and have more energy. A general rule of thumb for daily water intake is to take your weight, divide that in half, and that is the number of ounces of water you are recommended to drink each day. This would increase if you are in very hot weather, use a sauna, or if you exercise and engage in strenuous activity that makes you sweat a fair amount.

Water in our body has so many functions. It is a cushion for our brain and spinal column. It helps to deliver oxygen throughout the body, lubricates joints, flushes body waste, helps in digestion, and it allows the body's cells to grow, reproduce, and survive. These are all things I'm not willing to compromise by not drinking enough

---

[14] water.usgs.gov

water. I will not drink just any water anymore though. Fox News Health published an article[15] saying more than 24,500 chemicals are found in bottled water. These chemicals mimic the effects of potent pharmaceuticals inside your body. The article says that drinking tap water may be a safer option with regard to hormone receptor interference from the chemicals. Tap water may be worse in other ways due to fluoride (toxic when ingested) and chloride/chlorine (used to make cleaning products that is also toxic when ingested). I understand that municipalities need to add these chemicals so we don't get sick, but I decided to get a water filtration system that filters out the chlorine and fluoride before the water comes into my house. This has worked really well for supporting my family's health.

I committed to not buying plastic water bottles several years ago. This was hard at first — really hard, as it's the quickest and easiest way to get your water in you and in your kids, who forget to pack water. We also want to believe what the water companies are telling us — that it's good water. We don't know how the bottled water has been handled. It has most likely at some point sat in the sun, a hot warehouse, or a hot truck, allowing the chemicals from the plastic to be leached into the water.

I bought a couple glass water bottles from Bed Bath and Beyond using a 20 percent off coupon and saved $5.00 on each bottle. I like these in particular because they have a rubber casing, and the lid is an easy flip top rather than a straw. Pick a top that fits tight so if the bottle tips over you don't have a spill. I don't like the straw tops, as I don't feel like they get very clean. Each bottle was $20.00 after the coupon, and with the cost of plastic water bottles this is not only better for you economically, it's also better for your health. It's also not adding to that big island of plastic in the ocean so it is better for the environment as well. For refills I keep quart mason jars in my car and refill my bottle with them. Since I do not drink from the jars I

---

[15] Landa, Jennifer. "More than 24,500 Chemicals Found in Bottled Water." Fox News, January 13, 2014.

can easily refill them without having to wash them every time. Also since they are made of glass, I do not need to be concerned about them being left in my car in the heat. If you do this, be sure to get a box of replacement lids as the lids will start to rust after a while. Also change out the water periodically. These are habits that we need to practice. I got to the point that I notice if I'm not carrying my water bottle, my purse, and cell phone.

When I travel I take my Seychelle Water Filter Bottle. It is plastic (no BPA's) with a hard-to-suck top, but it's better than the alternative. I only have to use it during travel. The filter says it can even filter the contaminants from lake water. I have not tested this myself, as I use it for airport, restaurant, and hotel room water only so far. There are a couple more websites to look at water filter options: cerrawater.com and multipure.com. Do your research and see what feels right for you and your situation. The Medical Medium recommends Berkey filters.

I believe part of my metals toxicity and my health opportunity is from the well water I drank from 1993 until 2012. I believe this because I have an identical twin sister who did not drink that water for those 19 years except when she visited and she had better health than I did. We finally had our well water tested and it had arsenic, cadmium, mercury, aluminum, and a list of pesticides and chemicals leaching into our water table from the agriculture fields around us. Supposedly they were at concerning but safe levels according to the test, but is there really any safe levels of those for our body? No!

My sister and I would talk a lot about how I had so many health challenges that she didn't have. She always said it had to be the well water I was drinking. Unlike her, I was also exposed to pesticides when we would have the exterior of our home sprayed for ants monthly for around two years. We were told it was safe, and I trusted that. We had apparently built our new house on a huge ant civilization and had the worst ant problem the pest control people had ever seen.

The whole-house water filtration system I put in my current home is a Hague Water system. The water I have now is at an alkaline pH. It is tested and the filters changed every 18 months. I can't say that this is the most beneficial water system, because I haven't tested them all, but it's worked well for me. I'm getting the biggest negative health impacting chemicals out of it (metals, chlorine, and fluoride). This has made a big impact on my hair, which was the most noticeable benefit besides my continued healing and more vibrant health. If it's hurting my hair, I cringe to think how it was impacting me internally. My kids unplugged our system a couple years ago not knowing what the plug was for, and after a couple months my orchid plants weren't blooming anymore, my other houseplants were looking stressed, and my hair had become dull, dry, and frizzy (which is never good). I was feeling and looking dull and less vibrant as well. Fortunately it was time for our testing and filter change after only 2 months of this, and I'm happy to say that I'm back to having great hair and my orchids are continually in bloom without any fertilizer ever. My vibrancy increased as well, and within a couple of weeks we seemed back to normal. I'm a firm believer in the benefits of healthy water on our bodies, energy, and overall health.

There have been studies about how human consciousness has an effect on the molecular structure of water.[16] Happy feelings about your water and blessing it according to these studies can go a long way. Dr. Emoto has a 3-minute long YouTube video that describes some experiments and the findings if you are interested.[17]

One last thing about being hydrated. I was playing wallyball (volleyball in a racquetball court) once while I was on a juice cleanse. I was drinking so much juice that one day I forgot to drink much water. At wallyball my brain simply was not working very well. My teammate finally said, "You've never returned a serve with a set for as long as you have been playing with us [4 months], and in this

---

[16] www.thewellnessenterprise.com/emoto/
[17] "Water, Consciousness & Intent: Dr. Masaru Emoto" on YouTube.

one game alone you've done it 3 times!" This is not a good thing, as you are not allowed to return a serve with a set in wallyball. He was extremely frustrated with me which was not fun for either of us. When I came home my N.D. and friend who was staying with me and doing the juice feast with me said, "You're dehydrated." Duh! Clearly, my brain does not function well on only 20 ounces of water in a day. I like being my best self and not disappointing my wallyball teammates, so that will not happen again.

Dirty Electricity

Dirty electricity has been thought to contribute to many different health issues such as sleeping disorders, depression, headaches, memory loss, joint pain, migraines, seizures, ear ringing, rashes, cancer, and skin irritations. In her book **Zapped**, Dr. Ann Louise Gittleman not only presents her findings in a logical and scientific format, but she also gives solutions to living in this highly electric world. Dr. Gittleman has learned from her sensitivities and how she overcame them and also from engineers and researchers who study electromagnetic pollution. The findings are incredible. Not everyone is electromagnetically sensitive, but if you are, this information can be life changing.

I believe that if we are indoors a lot and around too much electricity, then there are most likely a combination of factors including dirty electricity that cause these disorders. It is recommended that we get around 10–15 minutes of sunlight per day. Sunlight is the full spectrum of colors, which is the best light for us. I will explain about other types of light and why they are not so good for us and what our best options are.

Fluorescent light has always made me not feel very well after a while. I read that is because it produces inconsistent frequencies that we can feel on some level, but it also lacks red and yellow in the light that we also need optimally. I also learned that dimmer switches are a big cause of dirty electricity, because they also produce an inconsistent frequency as well which does not resonate with us for very long. Some of us more sensitive types will notice it long before the less sensitive people. Not to worry, if you have dimmer switches in your house like I do, you can have them changed to regular on and off switches fairly easily.

So what kind of bulbs should you use in your house? What I've learned is to go back to the basics and back in time to incandescent bulbs. CFL bulbs (the ones that look like a twisted rope) have mercury in their bases and are very toxic if broken and come in contact with you, or if you breathe them in. It's not worth the risk. Plus they produce dirty electricity.

Let's look at sunglasses and melatonin production. Exposing our eyes to sunlight (not directly, of course) prompts our body to produce melatonin, which leads to better sleep at night. That got me thinking about a friend of mine who very rarely wears sunglasses, and he is the best sleeper of everyone I know. Is it related? I don't know, but I have been sunglass free for about 3 years now, and I've been sleeping better. Of course if I go skiing or am on or near the water, I will definitely wear sunglasses. Everyone's eyes are different. Some people who have had eye surgery are more sensitive to light and must wear sunglasses.

Electromagnetic Frequencies — EMF's

EMF's are electromagnetic frequencies that are emitted from electrical appliances, wireless devices, cell towers, phones, electric and gas smart meters, printers, and any other electric appliance. We are having these frequencies run through our body 24/7, and it can take a toll on us physically, mentally, and spiritually. EMF exposure has been linked to brain tumors, memory loss, cardiac disruption, dementia, cell damage, brain wave changes and various types of cancers. Humans are their own bioelectrical system. Our brain and our hearts are run by electric stimuli and signals. EMF's can interrupt or disrupt our own system, resulting in a loss of well-being and a plethora of symptoms. Check out www.bioinitiative.org.

There is a new and even bigger threat to our health these days and that is the 5G wireless system that is being implemented without our permission. This new frequency will be better, faster and all of that but how that happens is that 5G satellites will and have already been launched transmitting to mini cell tower antennas that will be mounted on every 2 to 3 light poles in our neighborhoods and all around towns increasing our EMF exposure exponentially 24/7. This is being planned and pushed through by Telecom and the government (FCC) without our approval. The health implications are epic. The Telecom companies are already promoting it as the newest, sexiest, fast network out there. They are starting to build interest and it is frightening! As an advanced energy medicine practitioner, many, if not most of my clients are dealing with depression, anxiety and many other physical challenges. The exposure I am getting to people who are thinking about or have recently thought about suicide is more frequent. Depression and anxiety from an energetic perspective can be from the constant onslaught of energies we are bombarded with daily either willingly or unwillingly. This is too much for our energy system and it starts to slow down and shut down and we lose our vibrancy and ability to cope and be healthy.

There are also serious physical-body health concerns with this new wireless radiation exposure, which I mentioned in the first paragraph. Cancer rates are on the rise and very concerning. Here is a link to a YouTube video by Dr. Ronald Melnick who explains the report. He is a retired Senior Toxicologist from the National Institute of Environmental Health Sciences. He explains the health study of the old wireless exposure and touches on the new 5G. Please take the 15 minutes to watch this so that you can be more informed and help to hold the government accountable for implementing this harmful technology without warning us.[18]

---

[18] "The NTP Cell Phone Study Explained — with Dr. Ron Melnick" on YouTube.

They put warnings on packaging about tobacco smoke and lead now therefore we should also have warnings about these mini cell towers taking over our neighborhoods. The study showed that fetuses and children are more susceptible to these toxic exposures and they plan to put them in neighborhoods!

What have I done after learning all this? I got rid of my wireless house phone and got the old-fashioned plug-in phone that is not readily available these days. I make sure my wireless printer and computer are turned off at bedtime, and I put my cell phone on airplane mode so my phone is not continuously trying to connect to a cell tower and Wi-Fi router. I also called my electricity company and had them turn off and lock my smart meter. I pay $10.00 per month to have my meter read by a person so I'm not getting those EMF's through my body. I read somewhere (I think on the bio initiative site) that a smart meter is the radiation equivalent of a small cell tower. Not good. Recently I bought an electric and EMF meter, and I think that my electricity company has since activated my meter again because of the intermittent spikes of the readings I got with my EMF meter around my electric meter. I decided to purchase a cover for my electric meter from smartmetercovers.com for it, which says it blocks 98% of the harmful EMF's.

To counteract EMF's I have salt lamps in my home and at work, black tourmaline crystals, shungite mineral stones, and various orgonite pyramids. These all help to counteract EMF's and protect from lower or EMF energies. I also have selenite towers throughout my home and work. Selenite is a clearing and light crystal. It will clear spaces and other crystals, and it never needs to be cleared. Don't ever get water on selenite, as it will dissolve.

Another great tool for neutralizing EMFs and electrosmog is BioGeometry (look up "Hemberg Swiss Project on Reuters" on YouTube). BioGeometry uses geometric shapes to neutralize electromagnetic waves and gridlines and to introduce highly beneficial, healing frequencies into a space. I continuously get feedback, comments, and compliments about how great the energy feels in my home and in my treatment room.

Please read up on 5G and use your vote to keep you and your loved ones protected. The side effects of living near cell towers are cancer, tumors, and general dis-ease in the physical body. We are not meant to be exposed to or living in that frequency. Doing your daily energy routine and spending more time in nature will help you to handle the 5G with more energetic stability, which supports your overall health.

Makeup, Lotions, Shampoo, Sunscreen

If you can't eat it, do not wear it on your skin! Don't even swish it. Mouth wash, toothpaste, shampoo, deodorant, and all of the products we use daily are very toxic. I learned at Optimum Health Institute that our skin is our single largest organ, and it is constantly taking in toxins from everything we touch or that touches us.

What do I put on my skin? I take my makeup off with organic coconut oil or I use Arbonne cleanser. I use coconut oil to moisturize my body and BOOM by Cindy Joseph, which is all natural. I wash my face with either BOOM or Arbonne cleansers and my body with natural soap. For makeup I use BOOM. I use Arbonne mascara and liner because they do care what you put on your skin. Is there better makeup out there with regard to being healthy and nontoxic? I do not know for sure. Maybe. Probably. It is about baby steps, and I give grace and acknowledgement to any and all improvements that I make, recognizing that I keep moving forward to healthier products each day. There are more and more companies that are conscious of their ingredients; therefore we are finding more options. Environmental Working Group (EWG) has a free app called Healthy Living that you can use to see if a product is nontoxic. You can scan the product's barcode and see if it is good for you. This is a great resource. Do your research because you are worth it.

Now that you have read the chapter about energy testing try this:

Take one of your body care products and hold the container on your body somewhere; bra, pants or shirt pocket or waistband of your pants. Now energy test yourself with your favorite method from Chapter 11 holding the intention that you will receive guidance from your higher self only if this product is safe to use. If you get a weak test then it is not what your body wants. If you get a strong test then it is good for your body or at least not harmful.

I use coconut oil for my sunscreen along with Badger sunscreen with zinc or All Good sunscreen if I will be having a big sun exposure. I also use clothing and hats as sunscreens for long days and hikes in the sun. All of this can feel expensive and a bit overwhelming at times, but what's more important than health? The expense of getting our health back is much more costly than preventative health measures. We are worth the effort and expense. There is the quality of life component as well.

For hair products I use Davines and according the EWG (Environmental Working Group) it has a rating of 4, which is a low/moderate concern rate. They aren't completely nontoxic, but they are less toxic. Again, baby steps and continued detoxification and heading toward more and more safe products. I don't know if there is a safe nontoxic hair color out there except henna or something called Hairprint, which are botanical based. I recently decided that I was done with coloring my hair because of the chemical exposure. Instead, I had them do some highlights with my natural color but with no skin exposure to help my gray hair to come in more gracefully. I read that gray hairs will not normally be covered up by henna, unless you add coffee to it, but will take on more of a naturally highlighted look. Henna should last 4 to 6 weeks. Recently when I got out of my sauna my sweat towel had a strong smell of ammonia. I remembered getting my hair permed several times in the 80's and early 90's and looked up the main ingredients for perm solutions and found out the active ingredient is ammonium thioglycolate which is an ammonia salt of mercaptoacetic acid. When I looked it up there were warnings of 2nd degree skin burns and systemic toxicity if inhaled. Yikes. Apparently I am still detoxing those very toxic chemicals. This is not the first time I have smelled ammonia after my sauna but hopefully it will be the last or soon I will have it all out. The irony is that my hair is naturally very curly now and getting curlier as I mature.

According to the Medical Medium, premature gray hair is a zinc deficiency. My mom went completely gray in her early 30's. She has beautiful silver hair. People may tell you that premature gray hair is hereditary, and there may be some truth to that. According to an article by Dr. Deanna Minich,[19] our body can't retain minerals if we have high levels of metals in our body. In fact, having minerals keeps your body from binding to and retaining metals. I take mineral drops in my lemon water every morning for a while now and I take zinc often. In the case of my family and premature gray hair, I know we have high levels of heavy metals passed down on my mom's side and a subsequent zinc deficiency. I believe getting the heavy metals out of my body and taking minerals daily has reversed and slowed my premature graying.

About ten years ago I was sending a high-quality green powder to my parents to take daily. My mom called a couple months later and said she was annoyed that her hair was growing in dark again because she used to get so many compliments on her beautiful silver hair. I jokingly asked her if it was growing in dark green, and we had a good laugh. Now that I reflect back on that, I believe she was getting zinc in that powder, releasing some metals from her body and her hair was growing in with color again. Not long ago I was getting my hair touch-up colored every 5 weeks. After I had been on a good quality

---

[19] http://deannaminich.com/the-relationship-between-minerals-and-metals-natural-protection-from-heavy-metals/

zinc supplement for over a year and got most if not all of the heavy metals out of my body and brain I was able to get my hair touch-up colored every 8 weeks.

With a recent discovery of mold and natural gas exposure in my home I realized my body was stressed. I remembered that the last few times when I had gotten my hair colored I'd get a herpes blister on my lower lip within a day of the hair appointment. That was certainly a message that the color weakened my body, which was already weakened by the mold and natural gas. Even with the obvious weakening of my body from the chemicals, deciding to stop dyeing my hair was a big decision for me. It felt like the recognition of leaving the maiden phase of life — the chapter of my journey where I brought life into this world and kept busy nurturing others. I was now going into the new unknown phase of life as the wise crone.

At the age of 55, I shifted into the nurturing of self with wisdom and realizing that ego and vanity are props no longer necessary for this next phase of my life. One of my best friends' daughter, Haley, said that she thinks that there is nothing more attractive than a fit and healthy older woman with gray hair. This is from a young woman who I admire, love, and respect in her strength (rock climber), intelligence (engineer) and humor (laughs at this interesting life often).

Air Inside Your Home

There can be many toxins in the air in your home — off-gassing from flooring, cabinets, counter tops, furniture, mattresses, paint, urethane, mold, smoke, natural gas, air fresheners, or aerosol products to name a few. The EPA has ranked indoor air pollutants as the top five environmental risks to public health. Unfortunately, when I clicked on the link to read their findings the article was no longer accessible due to the recent banning of this information from the EPA. The article I read before it was removed from the EPA website said the EPA found that stagnant indoor environments allow toxins and pollutants to build up, becoming unsafe for us to breathe. It's a good idea to air out your home regularly, use air purifiers, and have plants.

I remember when I first moved into my current house I had purchased new mattresses, new couches, chairs, and other toxically off gassing items for my kids and myself. I ended up really sick for weeks afterward. Fortunately my kids were still living with their dad part-time, so they didn't have the exposure that I did. When they were with me they were also in school and sports, while I was home a lot because I worked from home at that time.

I didn't realize that by increasing my toxin load, my body was going to be stressed and my immune system would be severely challenged. I had headaches, nausea, dizziness, and exhaustion. Since my immune system was weakened, the Epstein-Barr virus was able to rear its ugly head again. It took me many months to get better from that exposure. I didn't realize it at the time, but it makes sense now why I found myself spending most of my time at home outside on my back patio in the winter away from the new furniture toxins. I've told many friends that I did a huge amount of my healing on my old outdoor couch, listening to birdsong, breathing fresh air, and being so close to old oak trees and wildlife. The combination of those things was a perfect recipe for healing.

Please consider airing out new furniture and mattresses for several weeks outside before you move them into your house. The best option is to buy certified organic mattresses, which are much more common these days. Use good-quality air filters. If you paint, use a non-VOC or low-VOC paint and stay out of your house for several days with an air purifier running continuously. The most affordable air filters you can get are plants. Plants purify the air by taking in the toxins or pollutants and changing them into oxygen through photosynthesis. Check out this article that lists the best air purifying plants out there.[20] Let's face it, plants make us feel better as well.

---

[20] https://www.consciouslifestylemag.com/air-purifying-plants-clean-air/.

Mold

My water heater failed several years ago without me knowing it because it had an insulation blanket around it. Mold grew all around it, on the wall behind it, and I wasn't able to see it for a long time because of the insulation blanket around the water heater. When I finally saw water on the floor in my garage, mold had gone through the drywall and was growing on the wood inside the wall into the house. I was told that the drywall needed to be cut out and thrown away and that the wood where the mold was inside the walls needed bleach and water sprayed on it and then to be dried completely before new drywall was put up. Trusting the information I was given, I had a friend do this for me, and new drywall was put up. We thought the problem was solved.

A few months later when I wasn't feeling very healthy again I realized I had mold growing in the gasket of my front-load washing machine. This was the third washing machine I owned that was a front load, and it was the first one that had mold problems. I had to have the entire washer removed and disposed of even though it was only two years old. When you are sick from mold you have to do what it takes to get rid of the mold, even though it's expensive. I was able to purchase a top-loading washer, and I really like it.

Around three years after the water heater failure, I started having a feeling that something was "off" about that area in my house again. I thought the mold could have possibly grown back and spread even further into my breakfast nook on the other side of the formerly affected wall. The way my body signals me that it's stressed is that I get herpes blisters on my lips when I encounter any type of stress, whether physical or emotional. I was also tired more than usual and reaching for dark chocolate to get me through the day. I was so disappointed that this started happening again for me even though I led a very clean and supported life. I told a sister friend of mine that I felt like the mold had come back and had spread. She thought my intuition was right even though most people may have thought I was crazy. Trust your body and intuition!

This time I hired a mold expert. She was able to do initial testing and did find that I had concerning levels of mold in my walls again where the water heater was and it had spread to the areas that I sensed that it had. She made sure that the mold was gone completely this time and tested the areas suspected in my house with the highest measures. She also found a significant gas leak in the wall where the old water heater was connected. It had not been fixed properly before the walls were sealed after the new water heater was installed. Essentially we were breathing in toxic gas fumes for three years as well as the mold.

When they opened up the walls in my breakfast nook they found that the mold had spread there from the original water heater leak. They found even more mold close by in the nook that was from the planter just outside the nook that had a stone veneer installed incorrectly causing water to be trapped between the veneer and the stucco. Honor your intuition in these situations. If you have water damage of any type, please get it remediated immediately by experts in the field so you don't have to go through what I did. It also cost me a lot more money to get it fixed rather than if it had been done right initially.

Do not let anyone use bleach on the mold. Drywall and insulation need to be removed, the area completely dried out and then any wood that has mold needs to be sanded and treated with a good anti-mold product by people wearing appropriate protection. The area needs to be sealed so that the air borne mold does not contaminate other areas of the house. When the remediation is done the area needs to be tested again if you can and then it can be insulated and dry-walled again when it is mold free. Use a certified company. It is extremely important that they wear protective gear and masks and seal the area so you and your furniture are not further contaminated when the mold is removed. I also had mold in my shower and the mold expert said we needed to use the Mold Away product we bought at Home Depot all over the whole shower because the mold is invisible to our eyes until a significant amount grows and then we can see it.

GMO's

So many of our crops have succumbed to science used for net profits. From everything I've read, Monsanto has tried to take over the entire seed inventory in the world. Monsanto thinks it's safe to insert toxic pesticides and herbicides into their seeds so the company can grow hardier fruits and vegetables, even though they are toxic to us. Roundup is not safe for us in any amount — many of its ingredients are harmful.[21] Monsanto is the largest GMO seed company having inflicted GMO crops on American food supplies and also controls the non-GMO seed market.[22] GMO-based food products are **banned** in over 60 other countries. Is this the fox guarding the hen house? Monsanto's expansion strategy has panned out over the last 20 years, and it's mostly been hidden from the public. "You will find innocent-sounding names in the seed packages but not "Monsanto"[23] the actual supplier of the seeds.

I have found in my personal experience that it is not safe to breathe Round-up, eat it, drink it, touch it, or anything. I was recently cleaning out my garage cupboards and found Roundup that I didn't want on my property. I had to touch the container to get them in my car and to the landfill poison collection booth. I did not think to wear gloves at the time but found out that was a mistake. I'm sure I was also breathing in some of the toxic fumes while I was driving to the dump. The next day I was not feeling well so I went to my chiropractor who does energy testing and she said I

---

[21] https://www.scientificamerican.com/article/weed-whacking-herbicide-p/
[22] https://www.planetnatural.com/seed-control/
[23] Ibid.

was presenting with detoxing pesticides. I remembered touching the Roundup container the day before. I felt physically bad like the flu because my body was dealing with that exposure trying to detox it out of my body.

In hindsight, I should have worn gloves before touching that poison container. Isn't it interesting that Roundup (glyphosate) is that bad for us,[24] and we are eating it in our fruits and vegetables unless we're eating organic. A recent study published by winewaterwatch. org found that 10 out of 10 (100 percent) California wines tested contained Roundup in them.[25] What a buzz kill that was! Monsanto just lost a huge lawsuit ($289 million) about glyphosate (Roundup) causing cancer in people and currently has 42,000 new lawsuits regarding Roundup. Glyphosate is banned in most European Countries at this time. Again, there is no safe amount of a chemical like that in us. Our bodies in the modern world already have many toxic exposures, and additional toxins just get added to our fat stores, or the liver gets so clogged with them that it can no longer do its job. This will eventually catch up to everyone unless you start eating clean and healthy so your body can heal itself. There is a wine distributer called Dry Farm Wines who distributes wines that are organically produced that do not add sugar or other harmful ingredients.

Emotionally and Energetically Toxic People

You want and need to be around people who embody how you want to be and how you want to feel. What this looks like is valuing who you choose to spend your precious time with, what their vibe is and how much they have done of their own personal work. When you meet people and they have a lower vibration than you, it may feel like

24 https://www.theguardian.com/commentisfree/2018/dec/06/the-weedkiller-in-our-food-is-killing-us
25 https://www.theguardian.com/commentisfree/2018/dec/06/the-weedkiller-in-our-food-is-killing-us

they are a downer, a complainer, or stressed out all the time. They may appear to have darkness around them or a gray color/vibe.

These are all valid perceptions. Being around people who do not take care of their energetic body and emotional body leave themselves open to attracting lower energies and lower energy situations or experiences. In fact, like attracts like so they will be attracting more energies and situations at their same vibration so why would you want to be around those energies and situations? Wouldn't you rather be around people who inspire you and make you feel good?

I recently had someone say to me, "Why would I spend time with someone I like spending time with less than with myself?" I thought about that and found that I had to agree with him. These people are in our environment, and they can be toxic. Be the example of light and love to them, but it's not up to you to save them. They have to want to change themselves. Be kind, surround them in love from a distance, and take care of yourself first so that you can spread your light energy.

Chapter 16
Clearing Soul Contracts and Core Beliefs

"Infuse your life with action. Don't wait for it to happen. Make it happen. Make your own future. Make your own hope. And whatever your beliefs, honor your creator, not by passively waiting for grace to come down from up on high, but by doing what you can to make grace happen… yourself, right now, right down here on Earth."
— Bradley Whitford

A DEAR CLIENT GAVE ME the book *Journey of Souls: Case Studies of Life Between Lives* by Michael Newton, Ph.D. She said the book had a profound impact on her life, and she thought I'd find it interesting. I found it to be very enlightening and have told many people about it since reading it. The case studies were fascinating. Deep within me it felt like the truth. If you are afraid of death or curious about what happens when we die, this book answers those questions and concerns.

The book talks about the death transition experiences of 29 case studies. All of the case studies were similar. Basically, they say that we float gently toward a light and then on toward a destination. We are reunited with loved ones immediately or sometimes eventually. We are part of a core group of 10 to 15 souls who we feel a very strong love for and connection to. We also are part of a larger group of souls consisting of around 800 to 1,000 souls. We incarnate with them and the souls in our smaller group. Within the small groups, we study the life we just lived, reconcile it with other lives lived, and then work on a plan for our next life. In each life we have lessons and objectives to learn and grow from, moving more toward love, grace, and compassion and becoming more like the essence of our Creator.

As we create these life plans or what I call master contracts for our life, we decide within our groups who will be our parents, siblings, friends, lovers, partners, spouses, teachers, and other significant figures in our life to help us to learn these lessons. We also decide what our challenges will be in this next life, such as health challenges, public speaking fears, being a narcissist, losing a child, cancer, the death of a loved one, loose boundaries, being handicapped, wanting to "fix" everyone in our lives, sleep challenges, abandonment, scarcity, drug addiction, alcoholism, hoarding, eating disorders, not being able to have a loving, connected, romantic partnership, attracting narcissists, being an enabler, or not being able to have children. *We can grow from all of these things if we choose.* **We can clear them and we can transform ourselves, becoming closer to our true selves.** This is what this chapter is all about. It's a guide on how to clear these things that are keeping us from becoming a much better version of our current selves.

The things in our master contract for us to experience in this lifetime are also associated with our core beliefs and things that trigger us. For instance, someone can say, "I am abundant" and feel like they are or they really want to be abundant. But they will test weak when energy tested right after saying that statement because they have a contract to be in scarcity in this lifetime. I believe with some self-reflection, intention, awareness, and an abundance of gratitude for the lessons learned from these things, they can be cleared, allowing us to be freer, more joyful, and to evolve into a better version of ourselves. I have created a system for clearing these things that is allowing my clients to transform their lives. This system has also been transformational for my family and me. We feel like a better version of ourselves. We now enjoy healthier relationships, take better care of ourselves, sleep better, are more joyful, peaceful, kind, abundant, and loving to others and ourselves.

I've talked to many people about how frustrated they are about always being attracted to and choosing to be in relationship with the same type of person, even though they know it's not healthy or good for them. They feel out of control about it and frustrated that they keep suffering through the same or worse consequences because of their choices and perceived weaknesses about themselves. This is not a weakness. It's a vibration of what we contracted to do until we have awareness, intention, and gratitude for the growth in these lessons and then clear them from our master contract for this life.

I found out about master contracts when I discovered I still had an energy cord in me from someone I had cleared a cord contract with previously. This was a new occurrence, and it prompted me to go deeper in my questioning. I was guided to explore deeper. That's when I discovered a master contract or plan for this life, which corresponds to what the book *Journey of Souls* was talking about in the 29 case studies. I found that within the master contract these cord attachments are a part of what I call the boundary portion of the master contract. If we came into this life planning to have weak or poor boundaries, then we are open to people attaching energy cords to us to use us as an energy supply. This is definitely something we want to clear because it is exhausting to keep someone energized or even alive at the expense of our own energy.

Another part of the boundary portion of the master contract that I've found is that most of my clients who are sensitive empaths also have in their master contract to take on the emotions of others, thereby weakening themselves. This chapter will guide you to clear your contract of taking on these emotions and allowing people to connect into you. Chapter 17 will guide you to remove those energy cords. Chapter 18 will then guide you through clearing out all of those excess emotions you took on from all of your organs. It's my belief that everyone needs to be responsible for their own energy and their own emotions on their journey, or we are keeping others from their lessons as well. These three chapters are the essence of transformation tools and my gift to beautiful you.

I have met many healers who have taken on so many of their clients' emotions and pain to help them to heal but the healer's body is failing under the burden of all of that energetic weight. As healing facilitators we want so badly to help people and we do not even realize we are doing this and cannot find a way to stop doing it on a soul level. This protocol will help to clear this and help us to release and heal. Some of us healing facilitators have it in our boundaries portion of our master contract to take on the emotions of our clients. You can clear that, and I will guide you through clearing that in this chapter.

During sessions where I was helping clients to clear core beliefs that were no longer serving them, I found that some beliefs were more difficult to shift. We realized that they were part of a master plan/contract that they had for this lifetime. Going forward I will just say "master contract," but please keep in mind it's synonymous with "life plan." I also discovered that along with these contracts we have energies in our field (aura) that are keeping us in the vibration of the thing we want to clear. Recently, I was told in a dream by my guides that I had things playing in my background. I woke up right away and thought "this is BIG!" I was able to go back to sleep. When I woke up, I started working with it immediately on myself. What I discovered is my guides were telling me was that we also have things that are ancestral and are vibrating in our DNA. I found that we have vibrations in our DNA (lineage) that are keeping us in the vibration of the things we clear from our contracts and that are causing us challenges in this lifetime.

Recently it came into my awareness that we also have fractal repeating sequences in our field. Fractals are a mathematical, never-ending, repeating pattern. You probably agree with me that we do not want a never-ending repeating pattern of scarcity, addiction, overeating, self-harm, being a worrier, depression, illness, etc.

In summary:

1. We have a contract for this lifetime of things/challenges we are going to experience for our growth.

2. We have energies in our field (aura) that vibrate at those experiences, thoughts, emotions, etc. that keep experiences happening to us and coming to us to learn and grow from.

3. We also have vibrations in our DNA (lineage) that have to do with the contract and growth experiences that keep the learning experiences coming to us.

4. We have fractal repeating sequences in our field that keep us in the energy of the growth experiences.

I can't speak for you, but I know that I'm not interested in keeping these opportunities for growth in my life. I have been doing major clearing for several months now as I write this. I finally got to the point of being tired of — figuratively speaking — ramming my face into the same wall over and over again, or stubbing my toe on the same old B.S. I've come up with a worksheet that can help organize the clearing of these four things that we're triggering on or that are holding us back. You will find through introspection and energy testing that you may have something in your contract that is also in your field and has a fractal repeating sequence, but it doesn't have a vibration in your DNA. Or you may only have something in your field. Not everything is in all four things, which is why the worksheet I created and energy testing are helpful tools for these life-changing clearings. Or you could just release all of them for everything you clear to cover all of your bases so to speak.

With regard to the vibrations in your DNA, you can look at your family history going way back and see repeating themes such as being a victim, being a martyr, illness, scarcity, heavy metals toxicity (Parkinson's, Alzheimer's, dementia, etc.), miscarriages, worthlessness, mental illness, etc. Yes, a lot of these things have a physiological basis as well, but there is definitely a soul, energy, and contract component to them. This clearing is the big picture and is a huge transformational component to healing. With that being said, some of these lessons may not be ready to be cleared. I almost always (I'm not perfect!) energy test first to make sure things are ready to be cleared before I clear them.

I recently cleared many things and went back over my worksheet to see if they all cleared. I had one thing that I had in all four areas (contract, field, DNA & fractal) of not being able to release things easily (irony!) had not cleared. I was perplexed, but then I asked and energy tested to see if it was ready to be cleared, and it wasn't. I believe this is part of being constipated for some people. Reluctance to let go can manifest quite literally, and it could be in our master contract. Good grief! I then energy tested to see if it will be ready to be cleared soon and I got a "yes." Hallelujah!

Try this now:

Sit quietly and reflect on the things that have challenged you in this lifetime and create a list of these things. *Hint: photocopy the worksheet I included in the addendums at the back of the book and use that.*

Energy test to see if these things are:

1. A part of your master contract or agreement for this life (refer to the leg muscle test or pendulum test addendum at the back of the book for testing your statements). Write down what you are testing and if it is in your contract for this life. Then put a check mark in that column if you get a "yes" (or strong energy test) that it's in your contract.

2. Test to see if they are ready to be cleared. If "yes" or strong then continue with the next steps. If not, make a note to retest soon.

3. Test to see if there are energies in your field having to do with what's in your contract. If there is, put a check mark in that column.

4. Test to see if you have a vibration in your DNA that has to do with what's in your contract, and if "yes", put a check mark. If "no", then put a dash, so if you refer back, you can see what your testing told you.

5. Finally test to see if there is a fractal repeating sequence in your field that has to do with what you want to clear from your master contract. If "yes," put a check mark. If "no," put a dash in the column.

To test these things, say or think a statement such as "I am worthy" and energy test it.

Does it test strong or weak, yes or no?

If the test when you say "I am worthy" or "I am abundant" is strong or "yes," then your spirit believes that you are worthy or abundant and it is NOT something that needs to be cleared from your master contract or the other things and you can test something else.

If you get a weak or "no" energy test then your spirit does not believe you are worthy or abundant, and you may want to clear that so you can feel and be worthy and abundant.

Then ask if it's in your master contract for this lifetime to feel unworthy or in scarcity.

If you get a weak, or a "no," energy test, then move on to the next thing.

If you get a "yes," or a strong energy test, that it's in your master contract for this life, then ask if it's ready to be cleared. If you get a "yes," then proceed with the energy testing of the other items in the protocol.

Then ask if there is anything else that is ready to be cleared and released.

If that is strong, or a "yes," then do more reflection and testing until you have your list of things that are ready to be cleared.

This inquiry can be interesting. Inquiry is part of the process of reflection and awareness on whether these habits, thoughts, and actions are serving us and whether they are ready to be cleared and released. You can use your energy testing skills in this inquiry or use your intuition. When I work with clients I prefer to use energy testing and statements so that my clients can experience the guidance given us before and then after the clearing. I like to use energy testing on myself as well because I love feeling and seeing the immediate results of this work.

To clear these contracts do the following:

Close your eyes and get into a meditative state. Maybe play some meditation music.

1. Ask your guides that helped you to plan this life to join you. When you sense their presence you can ask them if they need to sign off on the contracts or if they are there to bear witness. Most, if not all, of the time, they

are there to support us and bear witness to our clearing and releasing. We just need to ask them for their help, guidance, and protection. You can ask them to help you to release and clear the things on your list.

2. After your guides join you, you're ready to start clearing and releasing.

3. With a heart full of gratitude, thank them for the lessons learned, the personal growth experienced, and the compassion gained from these lessons and experiences.

4. Then look in your mind's eye for a page from the master contract for each thing that you are clearing, or you may prefer to have them all on one page of the contract.

5. Sign the contract of the thing or things you are clearing, and when you are done signing it, see it go up in the violet flame to be transmuted.

Keep repeating this process until you have cleared and released everything from your master contract that you have on your worksheet that is ready to be cleared.

Now you are ready to clear the energies in your field, the vibrations in your DNA, and the fractal repeating sequences. To clear these you can do the following:

1. In your mind, create a beautiful gold cauldron in front of you.

2. Tune into your field around your body, seeing it with your mind's eye and **ask to see any and all energies in your field, vibrations in your DNA, and any fractal repeating sequences that have to do with what you are**

triggering on or what you have cleared in your master contract.

3. When you see or visualize these energies, vibrations in your DNA, and fractal repeating sequences, then see them **float gently into the cauldron you created in front of your body.**

4. Continue asking to see energies in your field, vibrations in your DNA, and fractal repeating sequences for the different things you are clearing and have them all go into the cauldron, understanding that the cauldron can increase in size if needed.

5. When everything you wish to clear is in the cauldron, then see everything in the cauldron go up in a violet flame transmuting all of those things that are no longer serving you and are not in your highest and best good.

6. Next bring your attention to above your crown chakra and **see a sparkly golden light of vitality** shining down and around you as far out as your fingertips and through all your being, filling up the spaces where those energies, vibrations in your DNA, and fractal repeating sequences were with the golden light of vitality.

7. Next, **see a beautiful sparkly silver light of neutrality** above your head shining down and around you as far out as your fingertips and through all your being, filling up the spaces where those energies, vibrations in your DNA, and fractal repeating sequences were with beautiful sparkly silver neutrality energy.

8. You can then see the cauldron float away and turn into gold dust until you need it again. Thank your guides for coming and let them go.

If you are unable to "see" anything — and by "see" I don't mean that you actually see them, just visualize the awareness or sense of the energies in your field — then call on Archangel Michael or whomever you work with to help you release them all into the cauldron. You can energy test to see if they are all in the cauldron as well when you feel like they are.

I had a client who wanted to be in a romantic relationship. She felt like she had wanted it for a long time and was frustrated that it hadn't manifested yet. I had her say, "I am ready for romantic partnership now," and she tested weak, so her spirit was not agreeing with that statement. I also had her say, "I'm worthy of romantic partnership," and she again tested weak. Sometimes it's a safety concern. The same client didn't feel safe in a sexual relationship although she wanted it. We determined with energy testing that she had experienced sexual trauma in a previous life, and that was also a theme for her current life. We checked with energy testing if she had the following things in her master contract and whether they were ready to be cleared:

She would feel unsafe in sexual relationship.
She would feel unworthy.
She would have difficulty in being in romantic relationship in this life.

They were all ready to be cleared. After clearing those three things in her master contract, her field, DNA, and fractal repeating patterns, I had her say, "I am *ready* for romantic partnership," and she tested strong. I then had her say, "I am *worthy* of romantic partnership," and she tested strong again. Finally I had her say, "I am *safe* in a sexual relationship," and she tested strong. Her spirit was in alignment with what she wanted in her heart.

Sometimes you have a master contract with a person in your current life. A lot of the time you will have an agreement with them that they can connect an energy cord to you for energy. There can be several or many things in your contract with them that are causing you challenges and learning opportunities. When this is determined through energy testing or intuition and that it is ready to be cleared, you can do the following:

1. Invite their spirit to join you. You can thank them for joining you and let them know you have a contract with them and it's ready to be cleared.

2. Let them know what part of the contract is being cleared, such as a cord or what specifically you are clearing.

3. Look for the contract with that person with the various parts in it that are ready to be cleared. Thank them for the lessons and show them where to sign off on the contract.

4. After they sign off on it see them return the contract to you and you sign it and then see it go up in the violet flame.

You are now both released from this part of your contract and can move forward with more ease. You can then thank their spirit and let them know they are free to go, and you can continue your work there, on the master contract, or you can come back to this dimension. You may have more things to clear with them later on as they become ready to be cleared. You will know this when things get "bumpy" with them again.

I had a contract with someone that they were not going to be very nice to me in this lifetime. After I cleared that contract, they were much easier to be around and were no longer unkind to me. You are doing the other person/soul a favor by clearing these things. I believe that person did not necessarily want to be mean to me but they were compelled to do it and no doubt are much happier now that they no longer have that contract with me.

I find these clearing protocols to be wonderful tools in my relationships as well. When you have a disagreement with your partner, friend, coworker, or family member, you can stop and figure out what emotions you are feeling and why. When you figure out those two things (what you are triggering on) then you can clear those energies from your field so that you do not trigger on the same or a similar situation with them in the future. If something feels like a pattern, then you can also check to see if there is a contract with that person or if it is in your master contract. If it is, you can check to see if it is ready to be cleared and released. This makes me think of the saying "You can't change someone or something but you can change your perception of someone or something, and they will change."

I had the gift of experiencing this a few months ago. I was saying to someone close to me "You're judging them!" and their response was "Hey, don't judge the judger!" We both burst out laughing and then I thought, "I have stuff to clear!" It was not in my master contract plan to judge, but I had energies in my field of judgment of myself and judgment of others. I also had in my field that I could feel judgment by others. I cleared those all out of my field, and I didn't feel that person's continued judgment anymore. I believe that my work helped them to not judge quite as much. They did not do any clearing but that's their journey and not my business. I can only change myself, which does affect the people around me in small ways. These are all things that we are here to learn how to deal with, grow from and release. Some of these things can be just an annoyance, while others can be uncomfortable to the point of being almost a 10 on a scale of 1–10, with 10 being awful. Things happen in our lives for us to notice and then hopefully release or clear, helping us to move forward with more grace on our journey.

It's not a comfortable feeling to have something happen and feel like you've been sucker punched emotionally. Other people may think you're making a big deal out of nothing and are being too sensitive, but I believe you that it's a big deal to **you**. These protocols are a way to clear these things and bring them down several notches if not completely released and neutral. Seeing a young man near death from cancer recently triggered me, and I felt sucker punched emotionally. In my master contract it was planned that I would lose my sister Karen to cancer when she was 18, and I did. Apparently, I still had residual emotions in my field about Karen dying as a young adult that were getting triggered when I saw that young man. I cleared my master contract of losing my sister (it tested ready to be cleared even though she had already passed on), and then I cleared those energies in my field. Initially what I was feeling was an 8 on a scale of 1–10, with 10 being uncomfortably triggered. It went down to a 3–4 immediately after doing the clearings, and now a year and a half later it's a 0.

I can now look at these experiences as a positive situation because they are things in my field that could be ready to be released and cleared. They are growth opportunities for us, and I see them as a gift now that I have these tools to clear them. This is a big part of how I've become happier. When you can look at discord as an opportunity to clear, release, and grow, then life goes much better.

A recent client was having relationship troubles. She had been in a challenging relationship for several years and was recently single. She wasn't single for very long before she met someone who she wanted to be just friends with, but she was very drawn to being around this person. She cared about him a lot, and they had a great time together and felt affection for each other. She wasn't able to take their relationship to a committed level because she had the following fears and concerns:

> Fears of hurting him
> Fears of him hurting her
> Fears of the relationship not working out
> Fears of having the same challenges that she had in her previous relationship
> Fears of losing herself in him, etc.

The other person wanted a committed relationship with her, and she was afraid of losing him, so she came to me for help. We discovered that she had some core beliefs/fears that were causing her distress as she progressed in their relationship. After we came up with these core beliefs that weren't serving her in what she wanted in this situation, we tested to see if any of them were in her master contract. They weren't, so we moved on to the protocol of clearing the energies from her field.

My client was leaving on a trip for the weekend with her friend, and I was very happy to hear from her several days later that the trip went great and that she was happily in a relationship!

Some examples of core beliefs that can hold you back:

I am not worthy of a healthy romantic relationship
I am not safe in a relationship
I lose myself and who I am in relationship
I only attract jerks
I am afraid of water, public speaking, snakes, spiders, etc.
I am not worthy of abundance
I am not worthy
I am not lovable

I'm unable to figure out what I want to do with my life
I am not safe
I am not attractive
I am not safe when I sleep
I do not have a purpose in life

These are just a few examples of some of the core beliefs and challenges that can be in our master contract, stuck in our field, vibrating in our DNA or a fractal repeating sequence that hold us back or trigger us.

A good rule of thumb is to stay consistent with how you state things. For instance, you can keep all the statements positive, which I recommend. Then if you test weak you know that your body or spirit doesn't believe the positive statement. I think it's always a good practice to keep things positive so that positivity becomes more of a habit. The more positivity you have in your life, the higher your vibration. It's a good practice to write down the statements and answers (yes or no), and then clear them and retest, recording the answers or outcomes again. This is huge transformational work that can help in every area of your life from work to relationships. If you wish you were healthy, then check in to see if it's in your master contract to be unhealthy in this life. If so, energy test to see if that is ready to be cleared, clear it, and then clear all of the energies of it from your field and chakras.

In conclusion, we can clear and release limiting beliefs and soul agreements from our master contracts, clear the energies attached to them in our field, the vibrations in our DNA, and any fractal repeating sequences of them that are also in our field. These clearings are releasing us from these burdens, and we are getting lighter in the process. Again, not everything we are working on clearing needs to be cleared all four ways, which is why energy testing is beneficial for determining how each thing needs to be cleared. Keep in mind though that if energy testing is difficult for you, it is ok to clear them all and then you know you covered all of your bases.

This protocol has already changed many lives for the better. You may end up doing this a slightly different way, which is great. We all have different ways of seeing things and doing things. The most important thing is your intention. Just do it, even if you're not sure you're doing it right, because intention is everything. The first time might be awkward, but with a bit of practice, it gets easier and clearer. Evolve, and choose to move toward more love, grace, and joy. I have included the complete protocol for clearing these things in an addendum for easy reference at the back of the book. Enjoy this transformational process!

Chapter 17

Empaths, Empathy, and Energy Cords

*"You must master a new way to **think** before you can master a new way to **be**."*
— Marianne Williamson

HAVE YOU EVER BEEN TOLD you are too sensitive and that you need to get over something? How about the feeling that what someone is saying isn't what they are thinking? How do you feel after you've been around a negative person? More and more people are realizing they are sensitive and are trying to figure out how to deal with these sensitivities in a very busy and over stimulated world.

Our lives are getting more and more stressful on every level. We have more, greater, and faster technology that makes us more efficient and available, and that leaves us less time to just be and recharge. There are benefits to this as far as being more efficient and productive, but the downsides are just as potent. Inevitably, all of these gifts are not really allowing us to get away from our work, other people, and too much stimulation. The goal is to be able to balance this and manage it rather than it managing us.

It's my belief that there is more drug and alcohol addiction in the last two decades due to more stimulation for sensitive people who don't know how to manage all of this input and dirty electricity coming at them all of the time. I also believe that the higher numbers of suicides are related to this as well. Not being able to experience peace and be free of constant stimulation is depressing, overwhelming, anxiety inducing, and untenable at times.

Also, since we all have heavy metals in us unless we are intentionally detoxing them on a daily basis, those of us who have a lot of heavy metals in their brain are like an antenna, and Wi-Fi is not their friend. These metals in their brain are reacting to the energy instabilities and causing them many problems. This constant input can wear you down on every level. I look at pictures of myself from 10 years ago and I look ragged. Yes this is because I had metals toxicity, but now I see that it was also from constant input and taking on of energies that were not good for me and were bleeding out my energies as well. I was not handling my own energies in a balanced way.

I know this because I am a HSP, or a Highly Sensitive Person, an Empath. I didn't realize that I was an Empath or even what that was until my 40's. This was another piece of the puzzle of my constant tiredness and sometimes wanting to just crawl into bed and pull the covers up to my eyebrows. Sound familiar? It also explains my need or want in the past of bourbon on the rocks after being at my kids' volleyball or basketball tournaments with huge amounts of energy in closed spaces for long periods of time.

Being a Highly Sensitive Person can also be a piece of the difficulty in sleeping for some people as well. It manifested for me in a number of ways. I would actually feel the symptoms of other people that I was close to. You can imagine how much fun that was when my kids were little and sick a lot. It gave a whole new meaning to the word *hypochondriac*, which people I cared about used about me all the time. It was very hurtful and I questioned myself at times as well. There are ways to protect yourself from feeling these things if you have the tools to do it. If only I knew then what I know now. How many times have we mature folks said that? I'm here to share ways to manage your energies so you don't have to feel so much or take on other people's stuff. My Daily Energy Routine which I shared with you in chapter 13 and is also in the back of this book addresses these things and protects us from these challenges. I will not get out of bed before doing my 5 minute routine.

If you are an HSP or Empath then you *never* want to say the words "I feel for you." Those words can guarantee that you *will* feel for them. We can help people better by not going to that place of physical or emotional suffering with them. When you find yourself wanting to say those words, instead say, "I'm sorry, that must be so hard" or some other version of kindness that doesn't take you into their suffering. We take on too much from our loved ones, friends, and clients without even realizing it, and that can hurt us in our physical body. I will teach you a protocol in the next chapter that is deeply healing for all of your organs and your physical body.

If we all went to that suffering place, then Earth would be hell, because hell is about suffering, pain, and fear. You need to take care of your energies first (oxygen mask) and help other people with being light and an example of healing, compassion, love, and grace. You may have skills to help people, and you will be able to better help them with your skills if you are not drawn down into that suffering place with them. You can still have compassion for people but without feeling what they're feeling and being negatively impacted by it.

Creating new habits of not saying the words "I feel for you," "I feel you," or "I feel your pain" will take time and practice. If you happen to say those words, just follow it quickly with "cancel-cancel" and then rephrase it. Practice makes perfect. I read that we have 10 seconds to reframe or cancel and rephrase our thoughts and spoken words.

Whether we do or don't have that 10-second rule, do it anyway, because it's creating a new habit. I used to say those words a lot, and now I don't even think them. I felt like all I said for almost two years was "cancel-cancel," but after a while I would smile, snort, guffaw (I always wanted to write that word!) Then I'd cancel it, rephrase it in a positive way, and move on. I hardly ever need to say, "cancel-cancel" anymore. I said it so much that my family used to say it to me all the time to mock me. Creating positive habits is the key and a sense of humor is so helpful.

HSP's or empaths are people-watchers, but what we are really doing is reading the crowd or reading people in a very innocent and mild way. We like to read the barometer of the crowd so we can sense the vibe and how things are going to play out. This is a sensitive person's form of self-preservation, but it can be energetically exhausting. I read a book about empaths called *Empowered by Empathy* by Rose Rosetree, and she suggests that you pull your awareness back to yourself if you find that you are doing this.

The author suggests three things. Stop and look at what you are wearing and find a color you like and say, "I really like the color blue. It makes me feel cool." Follow that with something that you like the feel of and something that you like the texture of, and then the sound of something that you can hear in that moment such as birds chirping or a song you like. It brings you back to you, and we need to be in ourselves and in the moment for greater joy.

The more sensitive you are, the more you feel from other people and the world. I've found that I feel much better if I surround myself with positive and like-minded people and also by establishing "my space." I use my sacred geometry octahedron (from my daily energy routine) to keep my energies in and other people's energies out. I intentionally keep my life force energies of love flowing through me and around me all day keeping my space clear. This doesn't let things, people, or anything less than the vibration of the love flowing through me and around me inside my field and it keeps my field clear if I do pick something up.

After working with energy for the past many years and trying different methods, I've found the energy of the earth, stars and love in combination with sacred geometry of the octahedron to work the best for my clients, and me which is why I use it in my daily energy hygiene routine. Many years ago when I first started trying to manage my energies by keeping my energy in me and keeping other people's energies out of my space, I would put a protective barrier or a bubble around me trying to keep it charged at protecting me. I found over time that it was exhausting to do that constantly and it did not work. In my daily energy routine I now bring the earth and celestial energies in and around me along with love energies and create the octahedron and everything is great in my space.

I was told several years ago when I was working with a client that they were a little uncomfortable with me because they usually can "read" whoever works on them energetically and they could not read me or get into me to "read" me. I just smiled and said that I do that intentionally so I can do my job better and that if they could have read me they would have only found love in me. They felt much better. It was not malicious on their part; it was what they did for their comfort and curiosity in this world. It's a great example of what's going on that we don't know about.

As you explore your gifts of tuning into yourself and then possibly to other people, please keep in mind the etiquette of having their permission to read them. I once shook hands with a woman who was a guest at a friend's house. At least I thought they were friends. I had the uncomfortable feeling that I was the topic of conversation right before I arrived and that they intentionally planned to have their guest "read me" when I shook her hand. She held onto my hand for much longer than customary and longer than I was comfortable with, and she did it again when I left. I felt violated and I was certain that they would talk about what she found when she read me without my permission. This is unethical to say the least.

I was taught in the Eden Method training about protecting your energy by working with your Central and Governing Meridians. Central Meridian runs up the front of your body from your pubic bone to above the middle of your top lip. Governing Meridian is on the back of your body starting at your tailbone and flowing straight up your back, over the top of your head, and meeting Central Meridian above the middle of your top lip. We were taught that if you trace Central Meridian up with your hands three times from your pubic bone to above your upper lip, and then trace Governing from your sacrum up and over the top of your head and down to above your top lip to meet Central, and twist the energy closed above your lip, that it will keep your energies in for you to use instead of them leaking out and you being tired. Doing this also helps to keep other energies out of you. In the Eden Method this is called the "Zip-Up," and it's part of the Eden Method Daily Energy Routine. My sacred geometry octahedron does this as well, along with other beneficial energy balancing.

Something that can hinder your ability to have an energetically healthy Central Meridian and subsequently leave you "open" energetically is if you have a belly button piercing. The metal in the piercing will stop or impede the flow of energy from the pubic bone through the belly button and up to the chin. You may feel more vulnerable or have trouble sleeping due to your Central Meridian not being able to manage your and other people's energies. When you take on others' energies you may feel more anxiety as your field fills up with too much of other people's stuff.

The very first and most important factor in this sensitivity of being an empath is not being grounded. The book *Earthing* by Clinton Ober, Stephen T. Sinatra, M.D. and Martin Zucker explains that earthing is the practice of getting your feet and hands into and on the earth on a daily basis. This not only brings healing earth energy into your body, supporting it at the electromagnetic charge that we were created at, but it also helps to disburse the negative effects of EMFs.

Being in nature and around trees is hugely supportive and healing. I used to make fun of tree huggers, and now I am one. If you can have your bare feet in the grass or dirt with your spine along a tree, you are supercharging your grounding. I find it to be a great comfort to sit with my very old oak trees in my backyard with my bare feet on the earth listening to nature. And yes, I have been known to hug them from time to time. If you've never done this, it's an experience I love, and I highly recommend it.

Another wonderful way to get grounded and connected is to

lie on a boulder. This feels great and hopefully you will feel the balancing, grounding and peace that come from the contact.

I believe that HSP's (Highly Sensitive People) are more sensitive to EMF's (electromagnetic frequencies), and it can impact our sleep and overall well-being. Not being grounded makes us feel the negative effects as well. I have found orgonite with shungite crystals in it to be beneficial with regard to EMF's. Orgonite is a hard resin with metal shavings, crystals, or crystal powder in it that produces a beneficial energetic vibration that can be healing for the environment. Shungite is helpful with neutralizing the harmful effects of EMF's. Orgonite can be attuned to different frequencies depending on which crystals are in it and the attunement it received while being created. I have orgonite in the four corners of my house and right next to my bed. Orgonite is a created energy that is comprised of crystals, metals, minerals, and resin that vibrate at a desired frequency. If the orgonite is created specifically to disburse EMF's it will usually have shungite in it, which also protects the body from other lower frequencies as well. I put orgonite near my indoor plants and in the roots of my fruit trees. My plants both inside and outside my house love orgonite. I have more fruit on my trees and continual blooms on my orchids than ever!

I've also found that the more energetic, spiritual, emotional, and physical work I do on myself and get done by other practitioners, the more unflappable I become in this messy, bumpy, and beautiful life. The more work we do, the more joyful we become. It also helps us to not sweat the small stuff. If I'm bothered by something I take a look at it and then I clear it from my energy field like I explained last chapter (clearing energy pictures, core beliefs, etc.) so that it doesn't trigger me anymore.

Sometimes I will be having a day where I'm feeling deep grief or sadness. I stop and think, "Why am I feeling this way?" I would have no reason to be feeling like that, and I'd realize that it wasn't my stuff. I've found that there are people in our lives that we are very connected to. I have someone like that in this life that I know when they are struggling or grieving. I choose to send them angels to help them and give them love, strength, and courage, and then I remove the energy cord that has connected us. I see my celestial energy washing away their emotions in my field, releasing them down my grounding energy pole into the earth, and I pull my energy back to myself. I'm grateful to know this about them so I can send them angelic support, but you can imagine how this impacted me before I figured it out. They most likely do not even realize they are connecting to me. It's more of an energetic and karmic habit from past lives together.

Energy cords are very common. I can feel them in my client's energy field and physical body and ask if they would like them removed. Almost all clients do want them removed because they can be an energy drain. I used to cut cords, but I found that did not work well for me, as it was easy for that energy to find its way back into my field.

Here is an example of what I have experienced with energy cords. My twin sister could put cords in me pretty easily, even though I do everything I can to not allow it. How I know this is a while back she was very busy, exhausted, and somewhat stressed in a happy way with some business opportunities. As I watched her get more and more exhausted preparing for an event, I started to get exhausted and was wondering how I was going to handle my life. I wasn't thinking about a cord between us, even though she was able to keep going somehow and even seemed like she was doing better.

I was getting more and more exhausted without apparent reason. I found myself wanting to eat sugar, drink caffeine, and eat less than good food to keep me going. This is old patterning for me from when I didn't know how to manage my energy. I finally stopped on the weekend and tuned in to see what was going on with me. I realized I had a cord from her in me. I then tuned into her. She had several cords in her and a lot on her plate, so of course she tapped into me.

She called me on the phone a few minutes later, and I told her. She didn't realize and apologized (not necessary), and we figured out a plan. I went ahead and removed the cord that was in me from her. I felt much better and had more energy within minutes. She was heading over for me to help her remove her cords. She got great relief from this and had much more energy to prepare for her big event. I have taught her how I do this, and she can now manage her own cord removal when she realizes it's happening.

To clear cords from your body:

Say "I AM removing any and all energy cords and their root systems in their entirety from my body and transmuting them now." You may yawn or sigh when this happens.

Then say "I AM filling these spaces with high vibrancy, divine, loving, and healing energy restoring these areas to their original highest vibrancy."

You don't necessarily need to know where cords are located, but sometimes I will be doing a scan on a client's body with my hands, and I will feel a cord in the same place that they have pain in their physical body. I always ask my client if they want to know whom the cord is attached to. Most say yes, but some just ask me to please remove it.

In a particular situation with a client, she had been having pain on the left side of her sacrum, her left hip, and lateral left thigh for around six years since she had crashed on her bicycle. She was in the healing profession, so she had tried many different modalities that had helped her, but none had gotten rid of the pain completely. We determined she had a cord there from her sister. We removed it in its entirety, but there was more to be cleared from that area, so I went deeper. After clearing everything else in that area that was ready to be cleared (such as emotions and past-life traumas), we put healing energy back in.

Two days later I received a text from her that the pain she had been dealing with for six years was gone. She was so excited because she had just gone to her regular yoga class, and it was a whole new experience for her. She said it opened her up in poses, and that it was truly a miracle.

Some of these cords have karmic contracts associated with them. I see a lot of this, where clients have a contract with a friend or family member that allows the other person to connect into them when needed or to stay connected into them all of the time. This is exhausting to say the least. I have a belief that we all need to be responsible for our own energy. If you allow someone to stay attached and you have to provide them with energy, then you are essentially enabling them to stay stagnant and not learn how to self manage their own energies. The previous chapter was about clearing contracts, and I urge you to reread that chapter and explore contracts with people in your life that you think you may have a cord contract with. Consider clearing those contracts if they are no longer serving you. Also be sure to see if you have weak boundaries (everyone is allowed to connect into you and you take on everyone's emotions) in your plan for this life and if it is ready to be cleared then clear it.

If you are eating well to support your physical body, you've removed any and all energetic cords, and you still feel off, then I would look into your energetic body. I know that I need to do my daily balancing to keep my energy functioning how it is meant to. If my daily energy routine does not resonate with you, then I encourage you to check out Donna Eden's 5-10 minute daily energy routine on YouTube — there are many videos with slight variations. The routine consists of hand and body movements that support and balance your energy body.

What I mean when I talk about the energy body is that we are all made up of energy in the form of electrons. This energy pattern is seen around our body or in our field. This is what you feel around someone when you find you don't like their vibe or perhaps you love their vibe. Empaths feel these things too much sometimes. It is also referred to as an aura. Some people, like Donna Eden, can see your aura. They can see or feel if it is collapsed, disconnected, or tattered. There is an exercise called the Celtic Weave in Donna Eden's daily routine that will address these things by bringing your aura or field out to your fingertips and also reattaching it to your physical body. I can say I feel much better when my aura is attached and at my fingertips. The octahedron from my daily energy hygiene routine I explained in a previous chapter reattaches your aura and brings it out to your fingertips along with unscrambling you and zipping you up. There are different ways to be energetically balanced and protected. You need to find a way that fits you and your lifestyle best so that it becomes part of your daily life.

A mentor of mine in the Eden Method Energy Medicine Program said that it was a detached aura on her clients that was preventing them from either releasing weight or gaining weight even though they were doing everything correct with their diet and exercise. It gets really interesting when the aura relates to physical body symptoms. There have been many miracle healings that people have experienced with just doing a daily energy routine. A colleague of mine was able to get off of 16 years of being on antidepressants by just doing the Eden Method Daily Energy Routine.

I have some final words of advice on being an empath. We are what we are, and it's a gift to be a sensitive, compassionate, and caring soul. Others can misuse it for their lessons in life. We often allow it, consciously or unconsciously, so that we learn our lessons about healthy relationships, boundaries, and distanced compassion.

There have been books written about the high incidence of empaths being married to or in partnership with narcissists or people with other personality disorders. This is more common than we realize, and it makes sense if you break it down. These relationships lead to devastating health challenges for the empaths, as they are constantly drained of their energies. The empaths are also taking on the excess emotions of the narcissist and it is making them ill. There is an excellent book about this by Dr. Christiane Northrup, *Dodging Energy Vampires*, and it is one of the best books I've read. It explained even more to me about being an empath and the relationships I have been in, past and present. It has information for everyone, including ways to heal and protect yourself from personality-disordered people and those who are unhealthy for you to be around.

Protect your energy, keep other energies out and away from you, surround yourself with kind and compassionate people, and heal yourself. Be committed to continued healing of body, mind, and spirit. Create habits to support you so that you can be your best self, and then help people by being the brightest light you can be. You are a gift!

Chapter 18

Healing Depression and Anxiety Spiritually and Emotionally by Clearing Excess Emotions from Body and Organs

*"Letting go gives us freedom, and freedom is the only condition for happiness. If, in our heart, we still cling to anything —
anger, anxiety, or possessions — we cannot be free."*
— *Thich Nhat Hanh*

OUR SPIRIT MAY BE VERY old and have lived many different lives. You have most likely referred to someone as an "old soul" or heard someone described as such. In Chapter 6, I talked about how our souls are energy and that the energetic imprint of our souls keeps going from life to life. In each life things can happen to us that can be very traumatic. It can leave us with a cellular or energetic imprint in our soul that continues with us into the next lives until they are healed or released. Maybe you have heard the saying, "I'd sell a piece of my soul for..." or "I left a piece of my soul in..." I have found these statements to be true. It is my belief that we can leave or lose pieces of our souls from trauma (physical and emotional or just emotional but not just physical). The good news is these can be retrieved and reintegrated, leaving a person feeling whole and more stable.

We are energy. Our thoughts are energy, and consequently our emotions are energy. All of this energy continues because energy never stops and does not disappear. Our soul incorporates significant life experiences into our vibration that contribute to the essence of who we are. Some of those vibrations of emotions can get stuck and cause pain or dis-ease in our body if not released or balanced. I wrote in Chapter 9 about how I needed to release the emotions from the site of my cancer.

It makes sense that the big emotional traumas that happen to us get incorporated into our energy vibration that then comes into the physical body when incarnated. Unless these traumas and emotions are cleared or released they can appear as "triggers" for us in this life or as a "ball and chain" in the form of irrational fears and beliefs that keep us from being who we are and can be. It can also be a part of someone having the essence of being a victim throughout their life, attracting to them more opportunities to be victimized. Who would want that?

I have a client who experienced severe trauma in another state. She recently moved back to the same town and is reintegrating that piece of her soul. It's a gift to see this process, and it's nice to know that we don't always need someone to help us to retrieve that piece of our soul that was left behind. We can do it ourselves. We can have the opportunity to live and heal it in the current lifetime. I help my clients to retrieve pieces of their souls in this life and previous lives through a process similar to past life regressions. Integration can take a couple weeks, although some people really feel it right away. With others it happens over time. They just become who their essence truly is and get more grounded, joyful, and unflappable. Something that may have upset them deeply in the past may now happen, and they find they are able to easily flow through it after these sessions.

It is my belief that we bring things into this life with us. We bring in gifts that are in the form of talents, knowledge, and abilities. On the other hand, we also bring in emotional wounds from past life emotional and physical traumas. I have also found with myself and with my clients in my practice, that we bring in ancestral emotions and stress that are transferred in utero. I read about this recently in the book *The Survivors Club* by Ben Sherwood. He talks about studies done of the descendants of concentration camp survivors and

911 survivors. Their cortisol levels are high even as infants because the stress was transferred to the fetus from the mother.

Ben Sherwood also talks about how some people handle trauma better than others and some of that is based on the size of their amygdala. The amygdala is part of the limbic brain and is responsible for stress and fear responses. If you are interested in how different people react to life-threatening situations I recommend reading this book. This explains why some people handle traumatic events better than others. I have found with my clients, friends, and family that what is traumatic to one person may not necessarily be traumatic enough to another person to be incorporated into their energetic body and carried with them. I believe these wounds can sometimes show up in young children in the form of night terrors. I have gone through this with one of my kids and wish I knew then what I know now. We would have all gotten much more sleep. But our tapestries would not be quite as beautiful as they are, for sure. Life is like that.

Let's think about this. If we come into this life to learn our lessons (threads in our tapestry) and to evolve, but we start out with some threads (perhaps dark in color, rough in texture) from previous lives, that is more work for us to do. These are threads perhaps of past life traumas that we have not yet been able to balance, clear, and release. Some of the most common of these is the irrational fear of certain animals or insects, public speaking, heights, airplanes, flying, deep water, and so on. Some people would call them phobias. Have you ever thought to yourself, "If only I didn't feel like my heart was going to explode when I speak in front of people.... I know I have something to say that will help them, and I could share my knowledge with them." What about "If only I wasn't so terrified of going into the water I could have a more joyful life playing with my kids at the lake"?

I've encountered or heard of many people who are, simply put, fragile. These people are a growing part of my energy medicine practice now. I'm attracting clients to me with these and other challenges that I have had and have been successful in healing. These souls cannot handle the chaos of life and out of necessity have made their life as protected and simple as possible. Some of them are not able to even function at all in society. They have to live with family and stay at home most if not all of the time. Many of these souls feel overwhelmed, and their anxiety is off the charts, so they have to control their environment to cope. Almost all of them have some form of PTSD from earlier in their lives that they have not been able to address and some from previous lives that they are not even aware of yet. Most of them are sensitive empaths and do not know or have the skills yet to handle it.

I have seen how amazingly resilient these souls have been and continue to be. They have suffered through a great many traumas that they experienced in this life or traumas from past lives whose imprints they have brought into this life to be cleared. *Life is not easy, and these are not weak people.* We will all experience emotional and physical traumas in this current life that we are living as we are all learning our lessons.

Empaths also have a tendency to take on the emotional burdens of other people. For instance, an empath may be married to a person with a lot of anger and frustration, so they unknowingly take on that anger and frustration so that their partner can have less of it and be happier and easier to be around. The empath is affected, with their liver and gallbladder getting energetically and emotionally congested from taking on excess anger from their loved ones, friends, clients, neighbors, co-workers, and even pets. The liver is responsible for processing rage, anger, resentment, and frustration. These emotions can be cleared and released so that they no longer burden us or get carried forward in our energetic blueprint to our next life. Some of the ways I've learned to address the current-life traumas are the same for past-life traumas.

You may have met someone who is very fearful, and then you meet their parents and see that one of them is very fearful as well.

Yes, there is a learned behavior, but I bet there is also fear that the empath child took on from that parent, so that the parent would be less fearful, easier to be around, and would able to be a better parent to the child. How this can present in their physical body over time if not addressed could be in the form of kidney disease or possibly bladder infections or UTI's, because the kidneys and bladder vibrate at a similar vibration as fear.

There are many different ways to clear or decrease the effect of these spiritual and emotional traumas. The best and most effective way that I have found is to release any and all excess stored emotions from the organs and body. I like to assess how all of my client's meridians are doing first by using muscle meridian tests, like the Spleen Meridian test in chapter 11 or in the back of the book as an addendum, and other tests to see if the meridians are either over- or under-energized. Remember each meridian is connected to an organ, so this is an effective way to see if the organs are operating optimally. Acupuncturists do this as well. I can then help to clear the excess emotions with my clients and then reassess the meridians and see that they all are testing balanced. You do not need to know these energy tests to do this protocol. I am here to tell you that everyone is carrying old emotions in their organs. Some people are carrying more than others. Our bodies are beautiful and perfect, and they want to be in balance. We just need to give them a hand from time to time. You do not need to assess your meridians with the muscle meridian tests before you do these clearings. Just know that you are healing by clearing these emotions from your organs.

Clearing the emotions that are clogging organs can be a hugely beneficial way to open up detox pathways. I talked about these physical pathways in Chapter 14, which is about detoxing. In Chapter 14, I talked about how emotions will congest the liver and cause it to be unable to physically detox as efficiently as we would like.

We typically hold the five main emotions in the following organs:

Bladder/Kidneys — Fear

Liver/Gallbladder — Anger, Rage, Frustration, Judgment, Shame, and Resentment

Heart/Small Intestine — Panic and Anxiety

Stomach/Spleen — Over-Worry and Over-Concern

Chest and Lungs/Large Intestine — Grief/Reluctance to Let Go

Take some time now and follow this protocol to clear your organs of excess stored emotions:

Sit quietly and tune into these different organs listed below (or use a pendulum to ask). See if you are carrying emotions in them for the following:

Yourself

Your loved ones

Your ancestors

Pets

Friends

Ex-partners

Neighbors

The world

If you work with clients in a healing capacity as a therapist, nurse, doctor, teacher, energy worker, caregiver, massage therapist, etc., you will most likely be holding onto emotions for your clients as well.

Hint: I've found that everyone I do this with initially has excess stored emotions in all of their organs so you can just clear all of your organs of the emotions they are holding.

Sit quietly and then call in whichever angels or higher power you like to work with to help you to release and transmute these emotions.

This is what I say when I clear my Liver and Gallbladder: "Archangel Michael, please come and help me to release any and all anger, rage, resentment, shame, judgment, and frustration that I'm carrying in my liver and gallbladder at this time on behalf of myself, my loved ones, my clients, my pets, my ancestors, or the world. Thank you. Please help me to release these emotions in their entirety and please transmute these emotions in the highest and best way for everyone involved. Thank you."

List whomever you are carrying them for, or you can ask to release for everyone on the list I provided above. Really be in the space of releasing them and in gratitude for the lessons they have taught you.

Next I call in Archangel Raphael and say, "Archangel Raphael, please infuse my liver and gallbladder with the most divine, high-vibrancy, loving, and healing light energy, returning them to their original highest vibrancy. Thank you."

Remember to thank your angels or higher power for all of their help and let them feel your gratitude.

Do this with each of the pairs of organs and then with any parts of your body that are giving you challenges when you determine what you are holding and for whom you are holding it. I found that some of my clients were holding onto excess fear on behalf of their pets and in one instance they were holding onto excess emotions on behalf of their clients or the world, which was an extreme amount to be storing. How can you be vibrantly healthy and happy and be carrying these burdens?

You can also do this with places on your body that are causing you challenges or pain as well. Remember the example I shared in the previous chapter about the client who had pain in her hip and sacrum since she crashed on her bike? More than likely there is a component to the discomfort or pain that is stuck emotions of yours or a loved one. Think back to when the pain started and what was going on in your life at that time. That should give you some clues as to the emotions that are stuck in the place where the pain is. Everyone can do this. You just have to want to. Ask for help and guidance from your guides, angels, God, or whomever you are connected to and work with.

As I said earlier, as empaths we don't like to be around our loved ones suffering, and in most cases unknowingly we take on some of their burden so they do better, and then we feel better around them. There is a downside to this, in that we can only carry so much for our loved ones and ourselves before we start having problems in our physical bodies. When my twin sister was going through some really difficult times with her kids, it affected all of us. I took on some of her grief, her frustration, and her fear. These emotions get stored in our organs that vibrate at those same frequencies. For me they also get stored in my neck, shoulders, hips, shoulder sockets, and knees.

My sister's grief, along with my own grief, was stored in my lungs. Her fear was stored with mine in my kidneys and bladder. And her frustration, along with mine, was stored in my liver and gallbladder. If you take on and carry enough emotions for all of your loved ones, you will notice physical symptoms such as liver congestion, gallbladder disease, kidney infections, bladder infections, and that's just skimming the surface. We can also carry ancestral emotions in our body and are more predisposed to certain ancestral emotions than others, in part because of our genetic makeup or our primary

Chinese Medicine element or rhythm, which is attuned to a specific emotion.

I am a fire element, so I would be more predisposed to carry more panic and anxiety in myself. My sister is a wood element, so she would be more predisposed to carrying anger and frustration. These are our predispositions and are the emotions we feel the most when we are stressed. This doesn't mean that those are the only emotions we carry. I know my sister took on some of my emotional burden when I was going through the difficult times in my life. I also know that my kids did as well. I also took on some of my kid's emotional burden when they were having difficulties. This is what love looks like and is yet another reason why we cannot judge people with a lot of physical problems. Physical problems have an emotional basis, and we do not know their story. I think it is a sign of deep compassion and they deserve to be loved, respected, and helped. This is one of the many important reasons why I am writing this book.

I found that my chronic neck and shoulder pain was in part due to the abundance of emotions I was carrying for my loved ones. I am finally starting to get relief as I am doing this clearing work. I have created an addendum that is at the back of the book called **Releasing Stored Emotions from Your Body and Organs** for you to reference to help you clear these emotions from your organs and body.

This is intense work, and you may be very tired afterwards. Take the time to rest and integrate these changes to your body. When you have deep emotional trauma sessions of *any* type, honor the work that has been done by clearing your schedule, sleeping until your body wakes up, and being gentle with yourself through quiet, a healthy diet, drinking lots of good water, and sleeping at least through the rest of that day if that's what your body wants. You should also avoid alcohol, drugs, sugar, large crowds, and heavy wireless exposure. You will integrate the work and the changes more deeply and quicker.

Another form of spiritual healing is past life regression sessions, where you go to a time where something happened that is causing you challenges in this time. For instance, if in a past life you died from your car going off an icy bridge into deep water at night, you could be very afraid of heights, pure dark, confined spaces, water, and driving on high cliffs. These are fears that I have or have had. I was told by an intuitive that is how I died in one life and that it was still impacting me. It sure was still impacting me in my dreams and also in a recent experience.

I was drawn to go to a Native American sweat lodge ceremony where I ended up in the very back of the sweat lodge. I was surrounded closely by people and had no way to get out without climbing on top of people. Then they closed the flap. It was so crowded that we were all touching. There was no light at all, not much room to move, and the air was thick and hot, and it felt hard to breathe. There was no chance to leave the small, cramped lodge for 3 hours. Needless to say I had a panic attack, and I had to use all of my energy medicine tools so that I did not disrupt the whole experience for everyone by completely freaking out. I was successful, thank goodness, and after doing my emotion clearing I feel more balanced around that type of situation. I am not saying I feel great about it, but I do feel better about it, and that is a relief.

In regression sessions you are guided to a past life or an earlier time in this life where something happened that is causing you challenges in this current life. You balance the emotions in those times. I do these with my clients now after being trained extensively in the Eden Method. I have had these done for me by Advanced Eden Method Practitioners who have gone through 4 years of extensive training on the nine energy systems. In these regressed states the practitioner is working with stuck energies, traumas, and emotions, helping and supporting the client to release them and then balancing the different energy systems in that time. This is important work and can be life changing. It is also something that should be done by a trained professional who has also done their work on themselves. Advanced Eden Method Energy Medicine Practitioners have to go through an extensive application process showing that they have done their own personal work to even be considered for acceptance to Year 4 training of grid and regression training. In the program they are teacher mentored as they show competency in working with their clients through regressing them before they will be certified as Advanced Practitioners.

I do not believe that we live our different lives on our journey of evolving in a linear fashion. I once had it described to me from a physicist's perspective on time. They said that if you took a head of cabbage and sliced it in half you would have a pretty good depiction or example of time continuum or dimensions. There are no past lives and future lives — rather, there are dimensions where lives are happening all at once on different planes or in different dimensions. When we as practitioners take our clients to a time where something happened that is causing them problems in this life, they may go spiritually to a time that was previous to the current lifetime or after the current lifetime, but it is impacting the client in this lifetime. Going back to the cabbage example, if you put a skewer through the cabbage and stopped at a certain point, that could represent the life and moment that we guided our clients to and then balance them energetically, emotionally, and spiritually in that moment in that time.

The powerful impact this past life regression healing has is that it trickles out to other lifetimes, and it impacts people in other lives that we are in as well. It has been referred to as ancestral healing because of the changes it makes in other lifetimes. As we heal, the people and animals around us heal, so it makes sense that if we heal something in a past life it heals others we are with in that life, and we no longer have that energy in the current life. I have witnessed this in my life as I have healed. My kids and loved ones have healed as well.

Even our pets have healed and thrived. I have a cat that used to be frightened all of the time. She still has a small amount of that around men, but most of it is gone. When I moved into my new house and new life, I wasn't able to bring my cats with me, because I didn't feel able to care for them yet. It took me 8 months to finally be able to get them and bring them home with me. Though I'd had cats my entire life, moving with them after doing a lot of my own emotional clearing was the easiest cat transition of my life. My previously timid and frightened cat walked into my house, looked around, looked at me, and meowed, like she was saying, "I like this place, what took you so long?!" It was a very loud and long meow! She is large and "in charge" in my house now. She is so happy here and has healed alongside me. From day one I didn't need to be concerned about either of the cats running away. They never go far.

As you heal you create a space for healing, and it trickles out to anyone else in that space. My mantra then and now is **"I AM LOVE."** It's a very healing mantra. It raises your vibration to the vibration of love, a high and yummy vibration. That is where I want to be and the space that I live in. I have a saying on a sign by my front door: "In this house let love abide and bless all those who step inside." That says it all.

Another way to heal old trauma that has affected the energetic body is an Eden Method protocol called the Grid. Just as a house has a foundation, so does your body. Donna Eden has found and documented a way to heal the deepest energy system that we have in our body and spirit. Donna can see energy in people and sees these particular energies in a grid pattern ("Grid" is what she named this energy system). Donna can see where a grid line has been broken from emotional trauma, which can be from physical trauma. Grids are designed to absorb the shock of severe emotional trauma so that we don't completely fall apart, never to recover.

A lot of us have many ancestral or past-life grids that come with us into this life that are broken and some current-life grids that are broken as well. Grids that have been broken or cracked usually remain broken. Fortunately, we have other energy systems that will step in and help to maintain us energetically until we can get those grids fixed. We want our grids to break rather than having an emotional breakdown. It is their job to do this and the job of the other energy systems to step in to help us until we can get the grid fixed. Donna has only seen a grid correct itself without intervention one time, and that person went and lived out in nature for 15 years and was able to heal. That was not an option for me, so I did what I needed to get several of my grids done. I believe that when someone is told that they have cracks in their soul; that is a broken grid.

From my perspective, when I have a grid that's ready to be fixed, I energetically feel like I'm in the tidal zone being flung against the rocks or up on the shore repeatedly. I feel energetically out of sorts, vulnerable, fragile, and not able to easily stay grounded, balanced, and centered. For me it's exhausting, chasing my energies that feel unstable, continuously balancing or correcting them, only to have them need to be corrected again and again in a day. Having a grid corrected feels like you are finally floating in a calm and warm tropical ocean after being flung around in the tidal zone. You feel more grounded, stable, peaceful, joyful, and just unflappable.

Because of my construction background I describe grids as being like the footings or foundation of a house or structure. The more cracks you have in the foundation of a house the less stable it is and the more vulnerable it is to everything.

In my experience we get stronger, happier, more stable and more unflappable with each grid that is fixed. After a grid gets corrected, some things that used to be hard to navigate no longer are. Things or situations that previously triggered emotions at a high intensity, fall off and decrease to nothing or almost nothing. I've found this to be so freeing for me. This is why I'm passionate about doing this work. Grids are not all ready to be repaired at once, and they integrate over several months after they are done. They have their own timing of when they are ready to be healed and can have profound effects on your life. They let us know when they are ready to be fixed, not when the client or practitioner thinks they should be. There are several energy tests that need to be assessed in order for a grid to be corrected. I'm particular about whom I allow to work with my energies, and I suggest you do the same. If you don't feel comfortable with a practitioner then honor that and find someone else. This is deep and important work. There needs to be a connection, respect, and trust between the client and practitioner.

The more grids you have out, the more fragile you are in this life. We all know and love people who just do not have the capacity that other people have. In contrast, we all know and love people that are so energetically sturdy that they just roll with life. One person is not better or stronger than the other. You can have grids out and operate in life. I sometimes see clients who are depressed and at a complete loss as to what could be wrong with them. I have found that the systems that support the grid need strengthening to keep them going. This also helps prepare them for their grid to be fixed.

One client came to me after trying just about everything else. They were deeply depressed and at their wits' end. They had heard of Donna Eden and had been doing the daily energy routine with some relief. But something bigger was off, and their depression and frustration was getting worse. They tried everything they could find to heal themselves. They were not able to handle day-to-day life well emotionally and felt like they had no joy. It was getting unbearable.

It's so hard as an empath to see someone going through this. We as empaths end up in healing work so that we can help people to not live in misery because we can empathize with that. The first session with this client was a thorough balancing and ended pretty rough. I was convinced I was not going to continue seeing them unless they were actively working with a psychotherapist. When they came for the second session, I conveyed that to them, and they laughed and said that they didn't need to do anymore therapy, because they had felt the best they had in years after our first session and knew they were in the right place. I was relieved to say the least.

I also love this work because it's like a puzzle. You do not just start with the grid, ever. With this client I found that the systems that keep us stable when grids are out were also out, so no wonder they were in such a challenging place. They continued to get more stable as we worked on balancing their systems, and they did their daily energy balancing to support our work. Eventually they got their grid done. It was wonderful watching and helping in this major transition for this person. They have since moved away but still come back to see me periodically. I'm happy to say that I have not seen them for a while now since they had their third grid fixed and integrated. I had them also do the Medical Medium protocol to get the heavy metals out of their body and brain, which also played a part in their healing. They are happier than they have ever been, and that makes my heart so happy. Having the honor of watching someone go from deep depression to profound joy is a gift that I am grateful for.

I've had many grids fixed on myself so far, and I don't know if there will be more to be fixed or not. They will present when they are ready. I do know that I will be working on things my whole life here on Earth. We are here to work and evolve, and I will be doing that and helping others to do that as well until I pass. Doing this deep energy work is a commitment and a blessing. We are energy and essentially our soul is energy, so getting this deep work done follows us into other lives. This is one big part of how we evolve and as we release and repair these old traumas we get happier and closer to the essence of who we are. On the other side after we pass, we are the essence of love and oneness. It is the goal in our lifetimes to achieve that on Earth.

There is not one perfect way or one healer for everyone. These are just some of the methods I've come across and used in my healing journey. The protocols I am sharing in this book are the protocols that I have come up with that help with clearing and balancing the most frequent challenges I work with on myself and with my clients. There are many different ways to heal and be healed. Use your intuition and go to where you are drawn for your healing. Put your oxygen mask on first, heal yourself, and then please go share your story, so that we are all exposed to all the wonderful ways to get healing help.

Chapter 19

What I Would Do to Beat Cancer Now

"If you believe it will work out, you'll see opportunities.
If you believe it won't, you will see obstacles."
— Dr. Wayne Dyer

I'M NOT A MEDICAL DOCTOR, nutritionist, nurse, or medically trained professional. But based on my previous experience with my cancer and my extensive energy medicine training, this is what I would do if I got cancer again. I recommend reading chapter 9 about my cancer scare and victory over it if you have not already. I mentioned that cancer cells are in all of us, and that it comes up for us through the perfect storm of a combination of viruses, toxins, compromised immune system and stress. That sounds like most of us, right? That is why cancer and dis-ease are on the rise. Life balance has become impossible for most people.

Stress weakens the immune system and wreaks havoc on our bodies. The viral, bacterial, and toxin overload in our body is another stress on the immune system. The immune system is what keeps cancer in check, so when our body is compromised by toxins, viruses, and bacteria, the immune system is simply too busy and too depleted to keep the cancer at bay.

Also from an energetic perspective the immune system will get depleted after constant and extreme stress because our fight, flight, or freeze meridian (Triple Warmer) will go to the Spleen Meridian for energy until that is depleted. It is the Spleen Meridian that supports our immune system energetically. After Triple Warmer (fight, flight or freeze meridian) depletes the Spleen Meridian energy, it will start pulling energy from the other meridians. This is very detrimental over time, because each meridian energetically supports an organ or organs in our body such as kidneys, lungs, liver, and large intestine. When so many of our organs are being energetically depleted over time and they are holding the vibration of excess emotions, then dis-ease has an opportunity to manifest in our physical body. This is information I have discussed previously in this book and a summary of how I would focus my energy if I had another cancer challenge.

The virus that is one of the biggest causes of cancer in our body is EBV, Epstein-Barr virus. I first learned about this virus in Anthony William's first book, *Medical Medium*. In his third book, *Thyroid Healing,* Anthony talks about the relationship between certain cancers and EBV. For women it is a part of breast cancer, and for men it is most common in prostate cancer. It plays a part in other cancers as well. I highly recommend all of his books, but *Thyroid Healing* talks in greater detail about the relationship between viruses and cancer. It will be a wealth of information for you or a loved one with thyroid or cancer challenges.

I suggest starting with opening up your detox pathways energetically and emotionally by clearing the emotions that are clogging and congesting them. In chapter 18, I went into detail how emotions can get stuck in our body and can cause dis-ease in the way that energy is able to flow or move in our body. Thoughts and emotions are energy, and if they are stuck they are blocking the natural and healthy flow of our body's energy systems. Check out the addendum **Releasing Stored Emotions from Your Body and Organs** in the back of the book and get these stuck emotions cleared from your organs before you start the following steps.

The next important thing I would do is to clear having health challenges, cancer, or dying from cancer from my master contract for this lifetime along with anything else that is ready to be cleared. I discussed clearing contracts in chapter 16 and the protocol is in an addendum **Clearing Soul Contracts, Energies in Your Field, Vibrations in DNA, and Fractal Repeating Sequences for Transformation** at the back of the book. Whether you believe in this or not, it doesn't hurt to do this clearing and releasing. It can be very freeing. I sat next to an older gentleman on a plane who owned his own actuarial firm for years, doing statistics on medical testing for insurance companies. I asked him if he had any suggestions after everything he had learned in his 80 years of life. He said he wouldn't get any medical tests done because he felt like they do more harm than good. He also talked about a mix-up with medical test results where a stage-four cancer patient was given a clean bill of health, and a healthy person was given a few months to live. The healthy person died in a few months, and the stage-four cancer patient lived and was healthy. There is something to this releasing and clearing of our master contract for this life that is very transformational and freeing. Our mindset, intentions and beliefs are key components as well.

Next, I would eat a raw-food organic diet so that my body could cleanse and release toxins. I would not be afraid of fruit, as fruit has so many healing properties that support your body in healing. I'd look at the 30-Day Cleanse that Anthony William suggests in his first book, *Medical Medium,* and eat that, or close to what he suggests. Eating all raw would allow the liver to take a break from having to work so hard breaking down fats and oils so that it can focus its energy on detoxing and healing. If you were too overwhelmed or unable to figure out the Medical Medium 30 Day Cleanse and if you can afford it, I would suggest going to Optimum Health Institute (OHI) to do a 1 to 3 week raw food and juice cleanse. Read the Medical Medium books while there, so that you can take the healing knowledge home with you to implement into your daily life.

I have mentioned OHI previously. OHI is a non-profit with a campus in San Diego, California, and a smaller campus in Austin, Texas. I have been to both of them many times, and miracles happen there. They have a testimonial day at the end of the week where you hear how people were given 6 weeks to live and told to get their affairs in order and the person sharing the testimonial was there sharing 8 years later how they went to OHI instead of getting their affairs in order and they experienced a healing miracle through raw food and juice detoxing. There were other testimonials of how people had scans of their body or a brain full of tumors and went home after eating raw and juicing and had no more tumors in their body or brain. Eating raw and allowing your body to heal is huge. They also address the emotional component of dis-ease in the body as well. The only thing I would do differently from them is to add in more fruit and fresh fruit juice to help with my healing. They do have a 3-month internship missionary program, which is a gift to make it affordable. I believe you have to be a guest there for a specified amount of time and then you can apply for the internship.

I would also consider looking into *hope4cancer.com* if I had a later stage cancer to see if their program would be a good fit for me. I would still do all of these other things I am sharing with you but would integrate everything together the best that I could. These are all options that can be implemented.

While I was doing the Medical Medium cleanse or after returning from OHI, I would also energy test myself to see if my body wanted or needed enemas or colonics to help get the toxins out of me and to help with my nausea, body aches, and exhaustion. When your body is releasing toxins and dead virus debris, it needs to get them *all the way out* of your body before they can be reabsorbed. The best way I found to do this is to do enemas or colonics.

After the 30-day cleanse I would continue to have celery juice first thing in the morning. In fact I plan to do this for the rest of my life. This is beneficial in so many ways. Anthony William says it's one of the most powerful healing juices available to us. He recommends drinking it first thing in the morning, either on an empty stomach or having lemon water first on an empty stomach and then waiting 20 to 30 minutes after the last sip of lemon water to drink the celery juice. If you drink the celery juice first, I would wait 30 minutes before drinking your lemon water. In Anthony's book *Celery Juice* he goes into depth about all of the benefits of the juice and also explains how celery juice helps your body to produce hydrochloric acid, which is necessary for digestion and a key component to all digestion challenges. It is also a powerful antiviral, antibacterial and antifungal. Anthony has found it to help with all addictions as well.

Some people do not enjoy the taste of celery juice but it is important not to add anything to it or dilute it with water, since the super healing properties of the celery juice will be compromised. Do the best you can and start with small amounts, building up to the recommended 16 ounces per morning serving. Give yourself some grace through this process.

The next things to add into your daily diet would be the 5 things that pull heavy metals from your body and brain (mentioned in chapter 12). These are from the *Medical Medium* book, chapter 18, "Freeing Your Body and Brain of Toxins." I highly recommend reading this chapter, as it will shed light on this epidemic. We all have heavy metals in us. There is no safe amount to have in our bodies. The celery juices helps to minimize the harmful effects of the metals.

If you are seeing an N.D. or an M.D. you can ask them about using Detoxamin suppositories in addition to taking the five things that I mentioned previously to help get the heavy metals out of your body and brain quicker. Have them energy test you for it and come up with the best protocol for you. My body wanted me to use one suppository every three to four days so that was what I did for 3 months until all of the metals were out. If you do this, make sure you add Atlantic dulse to your daily diet to get the metals all the way out of your body. Again, this process will go much quicker if you are able to do the Medical Medium heavy metals protocol and if your doctor thinks Detoximin is a good option for you.

I would have a salad for dinner most nights with lots of veggies in it. My dressing consisted of homemade hummus (Medical Medium recipe www.medicalmedium.com/recipes) and the juice of one lemon or lime. I sometimes used organic guacamole instead of hummus. I liked putting the Atlantic dulse flakes on my salad instead of in a smoothie. Because the liver's job is to detox and to break down animal fats and oils, I didn't use olive oil and lemon dressing because I wanted to not add the stress to my liver of having to break down the oil when it was already working so hard to detox. Hummus and guacamole have fats in them so I used them minimally, and it worked for me. Another easy, and fat-free, salad dressing is organic gluten free (chickpea) miso blended with water and some apple cider vinegar. It lasts a long time in the fridge. I love pomegranate seeds in my salad, and they have great healing properties. You can also add berries, grapes, or other fruit that sounds good to you.

If you are losing too much weight too rapidly or if you go too fast into detox and are starting to feel terrible or getting a rash, then you can slow things down by incorporating organic steamed sweet potatoes and organic steamed regular potatoes into your diet. Remember no dairy, so no butter for now, but I use salt and pepper and the juice of either lemon or lime. Also eat plenty of bananas to help heal your digestion and your brain and to get you through this time. Fruit has so many healing properties that it is essential in total healing. I ate more fruit than vegetables during my deep healing. We need the natural glucose from fruit, especially to heal our brains. And boy did my brain need it! Bananas were key to my brain and nervous system healing. Bananas and mangos also help you to sleep better at night.

Keep in mind the miserable, sick, weak, scattered brain, and exhausted feeling during detox will not last forever. You typically feel worse before you feel better. It's not a magic pill with a quick fix and overnight solution. It took a long time to get to this current toxic state, and it takes time to unwind, release, and heal. This is an in-depth, true way to heal your body. You will also start to feel your own vibration rising, which is a wonderful feeling. This new way of eating ended up being a version of how I choose to eat for the rest of my life. Finding foods that are a high healing vibration that make you feel good plus finding a way for them to taste and look appealing is a fun challenge with great rewards.

After I felt comfortable on the heavy metal detox and avoiding the foods recommended by Medical Medium, I would start the antiviral protocol he suggests. Knowing that you have and are healing from EBV and other viruses is powerful. By acknowledging that you have them, your immune system can then go after them. When you start the supplements for killing off and healing from EBV and other viruses, you will find that some of the supplements are the same as the heavy metals protocol. I started taking the following supplements after I energy tested myself to make sure they were what my body wanted. These are some of the supplements from the *Medical Medium* book that I took:

Ester C. Vitamin C is a strong immune system booster. It fights strep (bacteria), and in super high doses of around 20,000–25,000 IV it's been found to beat cancer. It is also anti-aging and great for your skin. When I did the strep protocol, I increased my C's to around 8,000 mg per day, splitting it between morning and night.

Zinc. Immune strengthening. Premature graying of hair is often from zinc deficiency, which is usually found with heavy metals in the body. I was getting my hair colored every 5 weeks before I knew about Medical Medium. After clearing the heavy metals and starting to take zinc daily, I was able to go every 8 weeks. I also went to a "green" salon — eco-friendly and less toxic than a regular salon.

Vegan-safe B-12. Brain and nervous system support. The Medical Medium says if you can only take one supplement, this is the one, because it's so beneficial and necessary.

5-MTHF. Helps to strengthen the central nervous system and endocrine system. I have found that if you are taking B-12 it is helpful to take this as well. Anthony William says it literally pushes the B-12 into your cells.

Selenium. Strengthens and protects the central nervous system.

L-Lysine. Lowers EBV load and acts as a central nervous system anti-inflammatory.

Cat's claw. Antiviral and antibacterial.

Oil of oregano. Antiviral, antibacterial, and immune stimulating.

Curcumin. Component of turmeric that is anti-inflammatory and helps strengthen the central nervous system and endocrine system.

Silver hydrosol. Decreases EBV viral load and is antibacterial.

Lemon balm. A powerful antiviral that's part of the protocol, but my body tested weak for it at that time, so I did not take it then. My body is testing strong for it a year and a half later.

There is a list of supplements to take in the *Medical Medium* book that is more comprehensive than what I took. Some supplements are for killing off the virus, and some of them are for boosting the immune system. Some are for healing and supporting the central nervous system, and others are for cleaning up the debris from EBV and healing the damage caused by the virus.

We all have viruses in our body, especially if we were as sick as I was. My immune system had been so challenged for so long that I had a body that was a perfect host for viruses and strep. It's extremely important that you hear that your immune system does not attack itself, EVER. If you're diagnosed with an autoimmune disease in your body, please question anyone who tells you that you need to take an immunosuppressant or antibiotics. Your poor immune system is already so challenged and beaten down that you need to cleanse, boost your immune system with supplements, good organic food, clean water, positive thoughts, emotional clearing of your organs, detoxification, rest, and energetically with acupuncture and/or a daily energy routine so that it can fight for you and go after the viruses, cancer, and bacteria in your body. Your immune system was designed and created to do this.

All of this can be overwhelming, and it can be a mystery what to take, eat, and do on our healing journey. Energy testing is a great tool to have to guide you, which is why I wrote chapter 11 about the various ways to use energy testing in your life for guidance and especially for what foods to eat and supplements to take that nourish or strengthen you. I dedicated a chapter to teaching you energy testing in depth so that you can learn to guide yourself and direct your supplements protocol on your healing journey.

There are more supplements suggested in the Medical Medium antiviral protocol that I did not take initially but added in later, and some that I never tested strong to take. I would energy test myself periodically to see if my body wanted them. What I found to be interesting is that my body would want certain supplements for a few weeks and then it would want a break from them for a week, and then it wanted them a week on and then a week off. This was mostly true with nettle leaf and licorice root. I would take other supplements for a while, until my body no longer wanted them. I found this with monolaurin. I took it for about two months during the strep protocol (1 bottle), and then my body didn't need it anymore.

It helps to use a pill organizer for your daily supplements. There are 1-week organizers and 2-week organizers, which don't hold as many. This saved me time. I would energy test the supplements weekly when I refilled the organizers. It took me a while to figure out this system, because I wasn't that smart back then with the intense brain fog. I hope these tips help you.

During my cleansing and healing, I would not only address my physical body but I would support my energetic body as well with a daily energy routine from chapter 13 and deeper energy support on a regular basis. First I would clear the stuck emotions from all of my organs, as discussed in chapter 18. I would boost and support my Spleen Meridian with my daily energy routine. I also use energy medicine to get my body out of being in a sympathetic nervous system that was a stress response way of life, into more of a parasympathetic nervous system that is a more balanced, calm, and healing way of life. Doing the daily energy routine several times a day helps you achieve the same results. Supporting my adrenals and thyroid energetically would be done by stretching and holding points on my body and doing yoga. I believe my cleansing and healing experience has gone faster and smoother, allowing me to participate sooner and more fully in work and life because I did the energy, emotional, and spiritual work alongside the physical-body work.

Some of the things I would do to get myself out of a sympathetic nervous system (stress) response are: most importantly, getting and staying grounded, yoga, breath work, releasing stuck emotions from my body, being outside with my bare feet on the earth, forgiveness work of myself and others, and finding gratitude and joy in most everything. I highly recommend yoga in the process of healing. The breath-work in yoga is needed to help support the cleansing of the lungs and to get into a parasympathetic nervous system. Breath is life. The breath of fire makes your stomach contract. Pushing air out rapidly helps to stimulate digestion and is also highly beneficial in getting into a more parasympathetic state. The stretching helps to release toxins from the joints and creates space for the meridian energy to flow easier. The twisting in yoga helps to release toxins from the organs as well. Yoga is about movement, energy, and breath for balance. This is the opposite of stress, which is rigid, un-moving, and shallow breathing. I know this, because I was an expert at stress for years. It was not a happy, balanced, joyful, or peaceful way to live.

After addressing the heavy metals and killing off the viruses, I suggest looking at addressing strep bacteria in your body. I learned from the Medical Medium books that if you have had strep throat, ear infections, pink eye, sinus infections, or SIBO, then you have strep in your body, and it would be highly beneficial to get it out or at least decreased. I took the following supplements recommended by the *Medical Medium* book that target strep:

Goldenseal. Is a natural antibiotic. I took 28 drops per day for 2 weeks and then a week off. I repeated this for 2 more cycles of 2 weeks of drops and a week off and then stopped completely.

Olive leaf extract capsules. Antiviral and antibacterial. I took 1 per day.

Oregano oil capsules. Antiviral and antibacterial. I took 1 per day.

Silver Hydrosol. I took 1 teaspoon 2–3 times a day for 2 weeks. Then my body wanted 1 teaspoon per day for a week, and then none. I went back on it after a week for another week. I would test it weekly to see what my body wanted to fight the strep.

Ester C. I took aprx. 8,500 mg per day (7 capsules in the morning and 7 at night).

Grains, sugar, and dairy feed strep, so I avoided them. I would drink fresh thyme tea daily with local raw honey to fight viruses. I also drank chaga mushroom powder in hot water with cinnamon and local raw honey. Chaga mushroom powder detoxifies, boosts the immune system, and is both antiviral and antibacterial.

While implementing everything I've just outlined, I would also spend time in an infrared sauna, as they are very beneficial in sweating out toxins from your body. Any other form of lymphatic support would be helpful, such as lymphatic massage (self-massage or with a massage therapist), dry brushing, and bouncing on a rebounder daily. Gentle to moderate exercise, such as walking, and yoga also helps to move the lymphatics. Chapter 14 about detoxing goes into more detail on these things.

Make sure your living environment is non-toxic. This is critical for healing from cancer or dis-ease in your body. I recently found out I was sleeping on the most toxic mattress available. I had a bitchin memory foam mattress and pillows from Costco that I loved. I found out that memory foam off-gasses for the life of the mattress. They are full of really bad chemicals such as formaldehyde and more. After just two days off of the mattress and pillows, I noticed a significant decrease of joint pain. Also get rid of scented candles, air fresheners (these are *very* toxic), cleaning chemicals, and pesticides.

You can check out www.debralynndadd.com as a resource for a non-toxic environment. Also The Environmental Working Group (EWG.com) has information on cleaning supplies and cosmetics that are safe to use. Drink good-quality water always (no plastic water bottles unless you are in a pinch, then Fiji water is said to be the best, per Anthony William). Make sure that the chlorine and fluoride are being filtered out of your water, as they both weaken your immune system and are chemicals that are not good to be ingested in any amount. I bought organic sheets from Target, thinking I was doing good, but they still treat the sheets with chemicals. Do your research. Non-toxic bedding is available.[26]

Have many plants in your house as well as a high-quality air purifier. A Himalayan salt lamp would be beneficial as well. I understand purifiers are not always a financial option. It took me many years to finally get one but in the meantime I used plants in many rooms of my house and opened doors and windows whenever possible.

Make sure your makeup, body lotions, and personal products are non-toxic as well. If you cannot put it on your tongue, then do not put it on your body. There are always nontoxic choices for everything out there that you are currently using. Take baby steps, because it

---

[26] https://reactual.com/home-and-garden/recommended-nontoxic-bedding.html

can be overwhelming, but keep moving forward to a less toxic life, and you WILL heal.

Just in case you do not know, diet sodas are extremely toxic to your body and brain. The sweeteners in them (aspartame, Splenda, etc.) are neurotoxins, and they can cross the blood-brain barrier and literally kill brain cells. The carbonation in them weakens your bones.

Wine is not something to drink if you are battling cancer or any other dis-ease in your body. Most wines in the US have Roundup in them. It's a chemical that kills pests and weeds and has been proven to cause cancer. If your liver is congested with viruses, metals, and toxins, then it's not able to process the chemicals we are continually ingesting, making us more susceptible to cancer. I used to really like wine, but I gave it up while I was healing, because it was a *huge* stress on my liver, which had a big job to do already. Now that I know about the Roundup, it's much easier to say, "No, thank you." In *Liver Rescue,* Anthony William goes into great detail about all of the harmful things to the liver. Most of us don't realize how important our liver is in being healthy and happy and how big of a burden it has from the average American lifestyle.

I've noticed that I don't really get sick anymore. I may feel like I'm starting to fight what one of my kids has, but after one day of fighting it and continuing to work or participate in my life (increasing and adding supplements, teas, herbs, fluids, and resting), I'm usually working and back to normal. I've noticed how much more sensitive my body is now that it's cleaner and healthier. This is also a function of feeling so good that I have less tolerance for not feeling really good. I can't handle being around smoke, exhaust, toxic fumes, perfumes, colognes, air fresheners, and mean or grumpy people. All of these are toxic, and my body will not allow me to be around them anymore without a strong reaction (warning). This is part of that example of living at a higher vibrancy and frequency.

Chapter 20
Adrenal Burnout, Life Force, and Constipation

"Start by doing what's necessary, then do what's possible,
and then suddenly you are doing the impossible."
— *Saint Francis of Assisi*

ADRENAL BURNOUT IS BECOMING A well-known and rather common occurrence these days. Back when I was diagnosed with it in my early 40's, I hadn't heard about it. That was my introduction to the concept that food has vibrancy or energy that can be healing and also that chronic stress can make us very sick over time. I had been living a life of chronic stress since my late teens with periods of extreme stress. That most likely describes most of us who've had a chronic illness.

When chronic stress meets extreme stress and you have toxins and viruses in your body, nothing good comes of that. When you are stressed, your adrenal glands secrete adrenaline into your body. Unless you're being chased by a tiger and need super strong limbs to run away, adrenaline is toxic to you. Our body doesn't know the difference between life-saving stress or stress from work and relationships. It responds to stress the same way, by pumping out adrenaline and cortisol.

We usually notice hair loss approximately four months after a stressful period of time. Whenever I notice that I'm shedding hair, I can always trace it back to a stressful period around four months previous. It shows you just how toxic large amounts of adrenaline can be to our body if it makes our hair fall out. Not only that, but it feeds dormant viruses, helping them to replicate and start wreaking their own havoc in your body.

I remember saying in the past that I was on the stress diet when someone had asked how I had lost so much weight. Well, you may lose weight initially in an unhealthy way, but that comes back to bite you later when your adrenals are burnt out and your other hormone levels, such as cortisol, are all wonky. That's when you see weight gain, and it's difficult to change if you don't understand the root causes and the total healing that is needed. You can also start to have difficulty sleeping through the night. You may go to sleep fine, because you are so exhausted, but you may roll over in your sleep and wake up enough that your confused adrenals start to produce cortisol and keep you awake. Cortisol helps you respond to stress, but it also helps regulate metabolism, so you can see how chronic stress can then lead to gaining weight eventually.

Through my healing process I've learned more about my adrenals and their function. Living life in this school on Earth, our adrenals get used often. They are here to support us in a fight, flight, or freeze situation to save our lives. But where things go askew (I love that word!) is when they are used and abused constantly. When I push my timing on an almost red light and I think I see a police officer, I feel like I can literally feel my adrenals squeezing out adrenaline, and my body starts to shake. You know what I am talking about here. When we do get pulled over by a cop our adrenals are often doing overtime. Then there is the day-to-day adrenal stress of not eating because we are too busy and too stressed out. That is when our adrenals get really depleted. Besides the fact that adrenaline is toxic to our system, our body was not designed to have adrenaline as our fuel. We need food for fuel, not adrenaline. The toxic adrenaline in our body needs to be broken down and detoxed. If our liver is compromised, it's not able to do that job efficiently and get the old toxic adrenaline out.

Healing from adrenal burnout can take some time. When the adrenals are burned out, they are flat out exhausted and not operating efficiently, or even normally. I noticed that when I first started to heal my adrenals I would be so exhausted that I would fall asleep no problem, but then I'd wake up 4–5 hours later. My adrenals would be confused and think it was time to be awake because they had actually rested for a little while. I would then sometimes be so exhausted and tired that I couldn't go to sleep. I call that "wired tired". What I've learned is that the adrenals are also responsible for producing sleep hormones and if they are not functioning properly from burnout, then our sleep patterns can be impacted negatively.

One of the hardest things I had to do to heal my adrenals was to get off of all stimulants — sugar, chocolate, caffeine, etc. That was rough. That was before I knew about the Medical Medium and learned how having those things in my diet was not helping me to heal, and healing was my ultimate goal. Anthony William suggests eating foods that support adrenal healing every 1.5 to 2 hours throughout the day to support your adrenals. These foods have potassium, sodium, and natural sugar in them. An example of this from his first book, *Medical Medium,* page 110, is a snack comprised of a date (potassium), two celery sticks (sodium), and an apple (sugar). He gives a couple more examples on that page as well. He dedicates a whole chapter to this topic in his first book, and it's extremely helpful in understanding this condition and how to heal from it. On page 111 he also goes into the benefit of the different foods such as sprouts, asparagus, blackberries, raspberries, wild blueberries, broccoli, kale, bananas, garlic, red-skinned apples, and romaine lettuce, which all support and heal your adrenals.

There are supplements that help to balance the body's cortisol levels, decrease inflammation, and support the adrenals. I'm not going to go into detail about them here, but you can find a list of them in the *Medical Medium* book, page 112. After you have practiced your energy self-testing, you can come up with a protocol tailored to what your body wants to help heal your adrenals. Or take the list to your practitioner that can energy test you for them and help you to design your protocol for your best and most efficient healing.

From an energetic perspective, if our adrenals are energetically weak, they will be slower in healing. Supporting our adrenals by caring for our physical body with rest, healing foods, gentle exercise and supplements and also by giving healing energy directly to our adrenal glands can help them to recover quicker and function more optimally. The adrenal points on our body that we can support are 1 inch above and 1 inch to either side of the belly button on both the front and the back of the body. When I have clients work with their own adrenal points, I also have them work with their cortisol points. I usually find if the adrenal points are weak, the cortisol points are as well. There are a few ways to give energy to these points. Donna Eden has a way to energize your adrenals called Flossing the Adrenals.

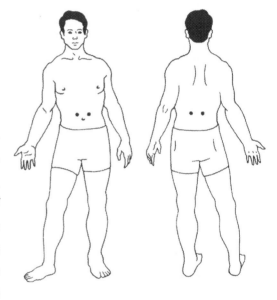

To floss or energize your adrenals you can put a thumb and a finger on the two adrenal points on the front of the body and then do the same on the back body points, which are directly behind the front adrenal points but on the back of the body. Push into the frontal points with one hand while releasing the back points with the other hand. Then push in on the back points while releasing the front points. Switching off hands, keep doing this, imagining a string between the front and the back points. I teach this to my clients so that they can support their adrenals on a daily basis. Many in the U.S. are either in adrenal fatigue or on the verge of it. Adrenals need daily support.

I also like to teach my clients to do what I call Juicing the Adrenals. I have them put their middle finger of their right hand in the top of their left arm pit and slide that finger over to the right until they are roughly in alignment with their left nipple. At the intersection of the top of the arm pit and the nipple is the heart electric point. This is a point that can give energy to other points on the body. It should be tender — that is a good indicator for finding the point. Keep your middle finger of your right hand on the heart electric point and then put your thumb and finger from your left hand on the adrenal points on the front of the body. Hold this until you feel buzzing in the adrenal points.

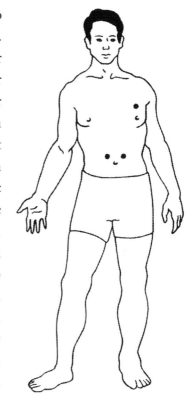

You'll find you usually yawn or sigh after about 1–3 minutes. You can then move your left hand to your back adrenal points to juice them as well. Even if you do not feel anything hold the points for 3-4 minutes with the intention that you are giving healing energy to the points.

Your cortisol points are 1 inch below and 1 inch to either side of your belly button. You can juice your cortisol points after you are done juicing your adrenal points by keeping your right middle finger in your heart electric point but then moving your left thumb and finger into the cortisol points to give them some healing energy and support. I've experienced great healing results for my clients and myself with this in conjunction with working with an under-energized Kidney Meridian, which runs right through the adrenal and cortisol points. When you have an under-energized Kidney

Melissa G Richardson

Meridian and/or adrenal burnout, you feel very tired. If you have not released excess fear from your kidneys and bladder as described in Chapter 18, then these meridians are most likely under energized, causing you to feel exhausted.

When you are experiencing physical and energetic challenges with your adrenals, cortisol points, and your Kidney Meridian, you are most likely experiencing constipation as well. The Kidney Meridian runs right through your ileocecal and Houston valves. (The ileocecal valve is on the right; Houston valve is on the left.) If the energy is not flowing through them, it's because your Kidney Meridian is under-energized, leading to energetic challenges with your bowel movements. We learned in the Eden Method to reset the valves for better energy flow and support. Here is the method Donna Eden came up with.

Try this now to reset your valves:

To energetically reset your ileocecal and Houston valves, put your hands in a karate chop on your hip bones (the ilium, the bone that sticks up when you lie down). Then let your hands fall over flat to the inside of your hip bones. While breathing in, drag your fingers up toward your belly button three times with each breath, digging in firmly but smoothly. Stop your fingers level with your belly button on the 3rd time up and replace them with your thumbs. Exhale and drag your thumbs down the inside of your hip bones closing the valves now and then release your hands.

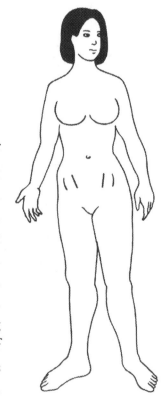

You'll be dragging about a 6-7 inch long line, pretty deep in. Moving up opens the valves, so you do the opening (upward) motion 3 times, and then you drag your thumbs in the opposite direction — down the inside of your hipbones one time — closing the valves again. See diagram below.

What you just did was to open and re-energize your ileocecal and Houston valves and then energetically close them again, which is critical. This is a reset that can be profound in conjunction with diet (plenty of plant fiber), mild to moderate exercise, plenty of water, and addressing kidney energy and adrenal support. Being grounded is a huge help also.

If you are having challenges like I discussed in this chapter, then I'd like to encourage you to take the time now to release the excess fear you are holding onto in your bladder and kidneys (if you have not already) using the **Releasing Stored Emotions from Your Body and Organs** addendum at the back of the book or the information in chapter 18. After you have done that protocol, then work with your ileocecal and Houston valves, as explained in the previous paragraph.

I had a client come see me who hadn't been able to have a bowel movement on her own for two years. They had to get colonics every week and also took magnesium citrate to help get the stool out. They had a lot of metal in their body along their spine, neck, across their sacrum, and in both hips. Energy cannot move through metal. I was able to do a deep balancing and reenergizing of their energy systems, getting the stuck energies to move that had been keeping them in constant pain. I also showed them how to do my daily energy routine and how to reset the ileocecal and Houston valves so they could do that at home. They told me later that they had a bowel movement first thing the next morning. Their pain was gone, and they were happy!

The energetic resetting of the valves is one piece of the constipation or elimination challenge in most cases. You still need to be hydrated, eat a diet high in fruit and vegetable fiber, and move your body for optimal elimination. Sometimes it's more than that. In my case it was also high level of heavy metals in my body. Everyone has heavy metals in their body at some level. It's worth looking into drinking the Medical Medium Heavy Metals Detox Smoothie as well.

Chapter 21
Sleep and "Wired Tired"

"What you seek is seeking you."
— *Rumi*

WE ALL NEED SLEEP. SOME of us need more than others. I **love** a great night's sleep. I slept great as a kid. My first recollection of disturbed sleep was immediately after I gave birth to my first child, my daughter. I remember thinking, "I'm screwed. I'll never sleep well again." The birth had triggered a core belief. I now know that we create our reality by our thoughts and words, so in a sense, I **was** screwed. I wasn't going to sleep well anymore with that core belief.

David Feinstein, Ph.D., helped me to find that I had this core belief. He is brilliant at EFT – Emotional Freedom Tapping. His book *The Promise of Energy Psychology* discusses very effective methods for EFT. David teaches EFT and energy psychology around the world. Once he picked me to come up on stage for an EFT demonstration. He talked to me briefly about my sleep challenges and started to determine what core beliefs I had that were part of these sleep challenges. He first had me say, "I am safe when I sleep." I tested strong for that, so that was a core belief that was serving me. Then he had me say, "Others are safe when I sleep," and I went really weak when he energy tested me. Because I went weak when I said that, he knew I had a core belief that others were not safe when I slept. That core belief was definitely not serving me, and it explained my anxiety around sleep. It makes sense that I started having sleep challenges when I gave birth to my daughter because I was now responsible for another soul, therefore the core belief that others are not safe while I sleep came into play.

When you find core beliefs that are not serving you, you'll want to clear them. I've been blessed to take a couple classes from Dr. Feinstein and to watch him help people clear deep fears around snakes, water, and other phobias. I've been able to take Dr. Feinstein's teachings and apply them for myself with regard to my former paralyzing fear of public speaking. I was able to use EFT to bring that fear down, and I'm now able to speak to groups. Before that, I wasn't even comfortable sitting in a circle and sharing my name. One-on-one I was fine, but the anticipation of it coming to be my turn in a circle was daunting. I've also used his teachings in my practice with clients to tap in major shifts after past-life regression sessions. Many of our core beliefs have roots in past lives.

Dr. Feinstein led me through the tapping on meridian end-points while saying things like, "Even though I have a belief that others are not safe while I sleep, it is now safe for me to sleep. I love to sleep, everyone in the world is safe while I sleep." This is a bare minimum example of what he had me do. There is a sequence to the tapping, a sequence to the words that you say, and it *works*. I highly recommend Emotional Freedom Tapping to everyone. It's a valuable tool that can be used for emotional and even physical symptoms. If you have tried EFT and it didn't resonate with you, then you could try using my protocol in the back of the book **Clearing Soul Contracts, Energies in Your Field, Vibrations in DNA, and Fractal Repeating Sequences for Transformation** and see how that works for you. I have shifted many core beliefs with both of these techniques.

Esalen Institute in Big Sur has classes for EFT taught by either David Feinstein or Dawson Church. They are both top of their field, and Esalen is a beautiful place to learn and heal. It's a retreat and learning institute on the coast of Big Sur in California. They have natural cliff-side healing mineral pools to soak in, hiking, and there's a healing vortex there. The food is wonderful, and some of it is grown organically on the farm there. They offer classes on many consciousness and health topics. Donna Eden teaches there as well.

I mentioned previously that we have many layers to heal and that sometimes we need to heal something in several different ways. This was one of those situations for me. I cleared the core belief with David Feinstein. Now when I say that others are safe when I sleep, I get a strong energy test. I was still having sleep challenges after that cleared, but the intensity had decreased. I decided to try biofeedback and hypnotherapy to come at it from a different direction.

During my hypnosis session that I was doing to help with sleep, I landed in a past life where I was a Native American woman in my late teens. I had a baby girl around 9 months old that was still nursing, and my other child was a two and a half year-old boy. We were all sick, and we were dying. I had no milk for my baby, and there was no one to even get us water for our severe dehydration. I was in a teepee with my daughter lying up against my chest and my son next to her. I had my arm and hand on both of them. It was the plague that had swept through our village, and it was hell. I knew that if I fell asleep one or both of my babies would be dead if I woke up or they would need me, or I would die in my sleep. That was unbearable. I needed to stay awake to comfort them even though I was dying and could not move. I could not go to sleep and die, leaving them alone to die. This was a pretty awful past life memory but very significant with regard to that core belief I had cleared.

Now I knew where that core belief came from and that helped. I did more work on it myself by regressing myself to that time and balancing my energy systems in that lifetime. This helped me as well, but there was still more to my sleep challenges. I was taking a class by Ellen Meredith, Ph.D., EEM-AP (Eden Method Energy Medicine Advanced Practitioner), and another piece of the healing puzzle came up. We were learning dimensional healing. I was back in my hotel room that night and decided to practice. I went to that place where people, spirits, or guides can show up to give us guidance. The people in our lives most likely lived other lives with us where we were possibly other genders, and in different close relationships — parent, friend, child, partner, or many other scenarios. Someone from my current life showed up in the dimensional healing I did back in my hotel room. I didn't want to talk to that person, so I created a door and they left that dimension. I went on and did some healing with this technique, which I found fascinating, and I called it a day.

The next night after class I decided to practice the technique again. The same person showed up, and I thought ugh! I started to make a door again but then stopped and thought that I really needed to hear what they had to say because they showed up again. I said, "Why are you here?" and they said, "You haven't forgiven me." I replied, "Yes, I've forgiven you every which way possible, and I am good." They said, "No, there was another life we lived, and it was bad. I left you and our babies when you were all sick and dying. I had to go with the hunters to get food for the tribe. I was encouraged to go, instead of stay with you, because the tribe needed my hunting skills to survive. I was also very scared that I would get the plague as well, so I listened to them, and I didn't go back and help you and our babies." WOW. I was quiet for a bit, and then I replied, in my mind, "I forgive you, and you need to forgive yourself. Thank you for this, now we are good. Go with love." Wow! Holy sha-moly! You can't make this stuff up! Anyway, that was another piece of the work that needed to be done on both my journey and theirs.

Even though it can be a challenge for me to be around this person in my current life, I was very glad that they were doing this soul-level work even though they didn't seem to realize it in their current life. That experience was also another opportunity for compassion. We are not here to judge each other, because we could be that soul, living with shame and grief. That soul in this lifetime still has a lot of shame, and that is not a fun existence. We likely have been in a similar situation ourselves or we will be. Compassion, grace, and love for self and others are the way to go, because we really are that person if we are all living out these or similar lessons on our journeys.

I recently was working on myself at bedtime checking for things to clear from my contract for this life, energies in my field to clear and also DNA vibrational clearing and I realized that I had cleared my sleep challenges from my contract for this life, the energies from my field about my sleep challenges but I had not checked to see if it was vibrating in my DNA and it was! I cleared that quick and slept exceptionally well that night.

As I mentioned previously, in April 2016 I started doing the Medical Medium protocol to get heavy metals out of my body and brain. In my studies of the Medical Medium and with being in the Medical Medium Practitioner Support Network, I learned more about the connection of heavy metals in our brain and the disruption of sleep. I got the metals out and then in September of 2016 started taking the supplements to heal my brain and the deficiencies caused by the metals. The supplements I took were melatonin, 5-HTP, Pharma Gaba, and California Poppy for a while. I started out on high doses of melatonin (40mg for around two months) to help heal my brain from the oxidized metals. Then my body tested strong for 20mg melatonin for another two months, and after that I took 3mg at night, and then 1.5 mg, and eventually only sporadically and now I do not need any. The Pharma Gaba, California poppy and 5-HTP fell off after several months and have not been needed since that initial 6–9 months of brain healing from the heavy metals.

My sleep was better, but I was still having challenges with it. I had been on and off small chips of Ambien for years, and I knew that was not good for my brain. Needing to take a drug to sleep was really weighing on me. The energy of it felt yucky, but I had to sleep. I've always been one of those people who felt like I have no reason to live if I didn't get at least six hours of sleep. I figured out in my desperation that I could take small chips of Ambien, and that was how I managed for years. I always had the concern at the back of my mind that it was really not good for my brain (true!) and that I needed to figure out my sleep and be off it for good. I had done some good work in healing my brain and decreasing my anxiety at night, but there was more to do. This was my last pharmaceutical to get out of my life, and I was ready. The more work you do on yourself clearing old emotional blocks, healing physically and energetically, the higher your vibration becomes. I simply could not handle a low-vibration substance in my body anymore. Especially a drug that was harming my brain. Many people had suggested cannabis to me to help with my sleep, and when I tuned into it I saw a lower energy to it and just could not take it. It is most likely a better solution than chips of Ambien, but neither felt optimal for me. I'm a proponent now of fixing the problem, not just dulling the body's messages.

I created a quick routine of energy exercises that would help to turn my brain off so I could go to sleep. I will go into that in detail later in this chapter. After a little over a year on the supplements and finally figuring out a few energy exercises, I was finally done with Ambien. The behavioral addiction part was very hard as well. Who doesn't want to just take a small piece of something that will stop their brain from spinning and have them drift softly, gently, and quickly off to sleep? That sounds great in theory, but it didn't outweigh the negatives. I will never hold judgment around the need for pharmaceuticals, and I understand that they may be needed for a short period of time as a bridge in our healing, but it is my soul's belief that the underlying problem or challenge needs to be addressed and healed so that we can live a vibrant and healthy, happy life. It is also my soul's belief that pharmaceuticals can often do more harm than good. I've read over the years that most pharmaceuticals have ingredients in them that are not necessary and can be harmful.

I also worked on getting off Ambien with my N.D., as well as using the Medical Medium protocol to help with sleep. This was around a three-month process. I was taking melatonin occasionally and valerian drops sometimes, and I put lavender essential oil on my wrists, temples, and below my ears at bedtime. After rubbing my wrists together with the oil on them, I inhale deeply and hold it deeply as long as I can, three times. Some of you with mild sleep challenges may only need to explore taking only one of these things. I always buy my supplements from the Medical Medium recommended supplements list, because I trust they don't have harmful fillers in them. Work with your N.D., M.D., or energy test to see if a supplement strengthens you. Or have someone energy test and guide you to help you with the best supplement program for you to heal. The energy testing protocol using the Spleen Muscle Meridian test in Chapter 11 or the addendum **Spleen Meridian Energy Test** in the back of the book will tell you if the supplement strengthens you or not.

I continually apply energy techniques for sleeping better at bedtime. I first tune in to myself, and I see my analyzer switch. It looks like a dimmer switch to me, and I dim it completely and turn it off. This visualization turns my brain down or off from analyzing everything. Sometimes during the day we may want to just dim it (during yoga), but at night we definitely want it off. I then do a couple Eden Method energy techniques. The Hook Up connects body with mind and also helps to get you out of your head. To do this, place one middle finger in your belly button and the other middle finger on your third eye slightly above and between your eyebrows. Gently pull up with both fingers. Hold this until you yawn or sigh.

I also do a gentle massage of small circles around my eye socket starting at the inside bottom and working my way up and around to the inside top of my eye socket. Then I will place my fingers just above my eyebrows in the middle, and I will rub gentle circles straight up to my hairline. I feel like this tells my eye-brain connection to turn off for the night. It relaxes my face muscles and helps me a lot. I usually yawn when I do this. I also pull my energy back to me from wherever I have sent it during the day. I call this coming back into myself. When I do this I see myself in a space that looks like a big yoga room with beautiful large windows and wood floors. I follow all of this with going into my third eye to observe what is happening there. Or I see myself going down stairs, and I count backwards from 100 as I go down each step.

During the day we can take on energies in our field from other people. Also, our chakras may be ready to release energies. If we do not clear the energies from our field and release the excess energies in our chakras, we can feel "wired tired." Before I learned how to keep my space so that I do not take on other energies or pour my energy out, I used to get wired tired from being in crowds of people. Back then, I would come home and have a little whiskey and would be able to get rid of that feeling and relax. That was just masking it, though, and I was not getting rid of all of the excess energies, which is part of why I needed those chips of Ambien. Taking a shower or a salt bath can clear our energy field (aura) around our body. Or (from my daily energy routine) you can picture in your mind's eye celestial energy coming into your crown chakra going down the middle of your body mixing with your earth energies that you are bringing up from the center of the earth and then spraying out the top of your head like a fountain into your field as far out as your arms reach. Then see that energy clearing your field and washing everything you don't need from your aura down your grounding cord into the earth.

Another energy technique I do to go to sleep is to spin out my chakras releasing anything that is ready to be released. Our chakras are in constant motion spinning information out and spinning it in. They need to be cleared or have energies released from time to time. This has helped me to go to sleep. I tune into my mind's eye and see my chakras spinning like small disks in a

counterclockwise direction. It doesn't matter what direction, just spin them out about 2 feet from your body and see them opening and releasing energies that are ready to be released. I then spin them back in and go to sleep.

The things I shared with you in chapter 15 about dirty electricity also help with sleep. My bedroom is very dark at night. My phone is on airplane mode with the sound off. It's at least six feet from my bed. I have placed orgonite pyramids at the corners of my home as well for a peaceful good energy in my home. I'm looking into turning all of the electricity off to my bedroom and getting a battery-powered alarm clock.

I have removed as many fluorescent light bulbs in my house as possible. There is a frequency to them that is not good for us and will impact us sensitive folks. Before I had gotten some deep energy work done on myself and finally was able to recognize when I was ungrounded, I had a difficult time being in Home Depot. I was able to figure out eventually that it was because of the lighting in Home Depot and my challenge of staying grounded as well. Other stores affected me that way as well. As I have gotten more energetically stable (getting Grids done and staying grounded), I am able to handle that with no problem for short periods of time, but I do not want that in my home. It is called dirty electricity, and I already went into this in more depth in Chapter 15.

Some people will have difficulty sleeping if they have their bed on a wall that has a smart meter on it. Also, having an appliance such as a refrigerator on the other side of the wall from their bed is very disruptive and overall bad for your health. My bed is not on a wall with appliances, but my office is along the wall that my solar system controller and my smart meter are on, and I cannot be in my office very long before I get completely energetically scrambled. I have since moved my desk away from that wall and I feel good in my office again. Let me tell you, that it does not feel good at all to be energetically scrambled and ungrounded. I will be working on a solution to the solar controller EMF's next to help with that.

What we eat plays a part in how we sleep as well. Now that I've been off Ambien, I can see how my sleep is impacted by what I eat as well. If I eat inflammatory foods or drink alcohol (especially wine) then I will wake up every 1 to 2 hours throughout the night. I can usually go back to sleep these days, but I don't feel rested when I eventually get up. Inflammatory foods for me are anything processed, most but not all animal protein, eggs, dairy, MSG, wine, and the rest of the Medical Medium Foods to Avoid.

Drinking caffeine or any kind of stimulant can impact your sleep. Caffeine can be in your system for up to 12 hours. Even decaf coffee has caffeine in it. What time you go to sleep can also have an impact on your sleep. I've found that I usually get the best sleep when I go to sleep by or close to 10pm. Anthony William says in his books that the most important healing sleep is from 10pm to 2am.

If I want to watch a movie or need to be on my computer up to two hours before bed, I wear my blue-light blocking glasses. Blue light will interrupt the body's production of melatonin and will make it hard to go to sleep.

I have a Tibetan eye chart taped to the wall next to my bed and when I get into bed I trace it both ways with my eyes to strengthen my eye muscles and help avoid cheater glasses. If it's been a while since I have done this my vision starts to get annoyingly blurry and I may go 1–3 times in each direction. This is a routine that exercises the muscles of my eyes, making them tired. It signals my brain that I'm going to sleep soon, plus it's a great habit for helping with eyesight. You can search "Tibetan eye chart online," print it out, and tape it to your wall next to your bed.

I make sure my bedroom is very dark and cool, and that the air is filtered.

Here is my routine:

Trace eye chart then turn off light.

Turn off my brain analyzer in my mind's eye.

Hook-up energies (middle fingers in belly button and third eye, gently pull up).

Rub gentle circles around the eye socket and above middle of eyebrows to hairline. This is Donna Eden exercise.

I make sure my celestial energy is running and spraying into my field as wide as my fingertips all around me, washing out everything that is not mine and not serving me from my aura.

I spin out my chakras releasing what is ready to be released and then bring them back down to the chakras closing them.

I say a clearing prayer to clear my home of any energies that are not welcomed by me and a protection prayer for my home to be kept clear of any and all energies not welcomed by me.

I say, "**I AM** sleeping deeply and restoratively and **I AM** only remembering the dreams that are important messages." Followed by, "My body wants, needs, and desires to sleep now."

I lie on my side and rest my head on my hand so that my fingers are on my temple. This is a stress point that is calmed by being gently held. I put my other hand near the base of my throat with my fingers touching in the indentation. This is another stress point that is calmed by touching it gently. You will see children sleeping like this.

You can also energy test yourself or work with an N.D. or someone who does energy testing to determine which of the following supplements your body wants to support healing and sleeping better:

Melatonin
Gaba
5-HTP
California Poppy
SleepThru by Gaia

Other options: Valerian and/or lavender oil diffused or on skin.

Sweet dreams.

Conclusion

*"If you are lucky enough to find a way of life you love,
you have to find the courage to live it."*
— *John Irving*

I FIND MYSELF SAYING THESE words a lot to friends, family, clients, and acquaintances: "Life is beautiful, messy, and sometimes really painful." I live by this. Embrace the messy parts of life, clean them up the best you can, and enjoy the beauty of your cleaner, lighter soul on this journey with the other beautiful souls around you. And if it's a particularly rough day, tomorrow is a brand new day. Things eventually get better, or they move on.

I like to think that we are striving to be on the lazy river of life, gently floating in the energy of our life. Sometimes we hit some rapids and need to pull to shore, re-group, clear, release and heal and then move a little farther along the river of life past the rapids and get on that raft again for a while.

Our relationships are wonderful opportunities for healing and clearing. When I notice that things are a little bumpy with friends or family, I tune in to what I'm bumping into and feeling to cause me to be out of flow. Then I clear it. I strive to remember, we cannot change the people in our lives *but* we can change ourselves, and therefore our perception of other people. This has helped me tremendously.

If you are feeling like someone is mean to you, then essentially you are creating that pattern. If you clear that contract, those energies in your field and that core belief, you can watch that transformation in that person with awe and gratitude. Remember I shared with you about the day I grumpily told my friend that he was judging someone? And he said to me, "Hey, don't judge the judger!" We had that huge laugh about it, and then I went off on my own (away from the rapids of life) and cleared the part of my contract that I would judge and would feel judgment; and cleared any and all energies and fractal repeating sequences in my field of me judging him and him judging others. I never did feel judgment in him or from him again. These protocols work!

I continue to clear emotions from painful areas of my body and specific organs. I'm always looking for ways to get better. I am continually looking for core beliefs and contracts that are not serving me any longer so I can clear them as I continue on my transformative and healing journey. By continuing to do this clearing work, I am getting more joyful and unflappable so that when life gets bumpy I handle it with much more grace and humor. I'm happy so much these days that it's unusual and uncomfortable for me to be anything else. Not feeling happy is a good catalyst for me to tune in and see what is causing me to feel that way. Then I either address it by clearing whatever is ready to be cleared, or I just honor it and know it will pass. You have the tools now in this book to help you to do your work and to be happy. Use the addendums in the back of this book as tools to live by.

I have substantially healed my liver since starting on the Medical Medium protocols in April 2016. The heavy metals are out and the parts of my brain from where the metals oxidized are healed. My brain is healed from years of being on chips of Ambien to help me sleep, and my sleep has improved dramatically. I'm continuing to eat well so I don't feed any viruses or cancers in my body. Eating well and taking some supplements to support this continued healing is only going to be good for me. It beats the alternative of not feeling very smart, not sleeping well, taking prescriptions, going for medical procedures, medical tests, not feeling well, or having less energy.

I recently realized that I had a core belief that I needed to take something (supplements at that point) to be able to sleep well at night. This is something that I believe was not serving me so I tested this by saying, "I need to take something to sleep well at night." I tested strong energetically for that being a part of my contract/plan for this life. I went through the process of clearing the contract and the pictures, energies, thoughts, and beliefs around this in my aura and my chakras and said again, "I need to take something to sleep well at night." I tested weak to that, which is a "no," or that the statement is no longer a core belief of mine. Our core beliefs are powerful and manifest in our everyday life.

Am I striving for perfection? Definitely, not. I am always heading toward vibrant health. Healthy and happy is the goal and my wish for everyone. If it was a goal of perfect health with a perfect diet 100% of the time, that would be too stressful for me and not very happy. Finding the best balance for me is my goal, and I can get clues along the way by how I'm feeling, how my sleep is, how my body feels and how my energy levels are. This is a journey, not a short trip.

I am stronger, happier, and more energetically stable than I've ever been. I'm also older than I've ever been, and I love that contrast. Life can get better as we age if we approach it with the right set of tools. We will always have lessons and work to be done in Earth school, so there's no end to that emotional and spiritual work. The world is also getting more and more toxic. If we are not eating foods that support our body in healing and cleansing, it will affect us in our health. There will be times that we don't make the best choices in food, drink, and rest, but the key is to notice it and go back to the healthier choices quicker and quicker.

I am not resting on my laurels, and if I'm being honest, I slide back on my eating a bit over the holidays and on vacations. When this happens, we need to notice the signs such as inflammation, poor sleep, low energy, stiff or sore body and we get ourselves back on track. After almost two years of a mostly raw diet of celery juice, other fruit and veggie juices, frozen fruit smoothies, salad, and some cooked veggies; my body needed a change. That was when I met with an Ayurveda consultant. She said I am Pita-Vata and that the raw food and cold smoothies were dampening my digestive fire and causing me digestion challenges. This was in October, and since it was a new season, it was beneficial for me to eat more root vegetables and cooked foods. I also believe this was my body telling me that the major healing with the raw foods was over and I was ready for the next phase of my healing and healthful journey.

Since that Ayurveda session, I have been enjoying Medical Medium recipes for soups, curries, and more seasonal recipes. I make my smoothies with fresh fruits and veggies rather than frozen. I've learned how to alter recipes to have them be healthy and beneficial to me and how my body wants to eat now to be vibrant. I've found that my body likes to eat raw until dinner and then I really enjoy eating cooked healthy foods. It's a work in progress and a dance. I'll keep working on finding the best food support and balance at any given moment of my life. Our bodies continually change and so do our circumstances. Staying aware of what our bodies are telling us helps us make choices accordingly.

I mentioned previously that I have something in me that I am compelled to do. I am so grateful to be creating a healing and wellness retreat center here on the Central Coast of California and using 100% of the proceeds from this book to help to make that happen. When I was in some very low times during my healing journey, I wished that I had a place to go where I could heal my body, mind, and spirit and learn how to be vibrantly healthy. I wished that I could find a healing retreat center to go to where I could unplug from the demands of our sometimes crazy and frenetic life. Where I could learn how to meditate, what to eat that would heal me, learn how to cleanse and detoxify my body in a safe and efficient way, and how to use energy medicine to support and heal my mental, emotional, spiritual, and physical body. A place where I could learn how to take care of myself better at home to continue my healing and eventually become vibrantly healthy.

To my core, I want everyone to be able to be healthy and happy if they want to be. I'm creating a healing and wellness retreat center based on all of the information in this book and more. It will follow the teachings of both Donna Eden and Anthony William. I will add in what I've learned on myself and in my energy medicine practice to make these healing teachings even more streamlined and efficient. It will be a place where people can retreat from the chaos of this toxic world for a day, a week, or more to learn how to heal themselves with food, supplements, energy medicine and get started on their own personal healing journey. It will combine a lot of the alternative healing approaches that I used to heal myself.

Because of my feelings that everyone should have access to this alternative healing, I will create a scholarship fund with a portion of the net proceeds from the retreat center to help financially for the people who need that help.

It has been a wonderful experience sharing my journey and all the things I have done to heal myself and to help my clients. I am grateful every minute for this life I have been given and would not change it. My challenges made me who I am, and my tapestry is beautiful to me.

So many blessings and much love to you all,

Melissa ♥

Addendums

Adrenal & Cortisol Support

The adrenal points on our body that we can support are 1" above and 1" to either side of the belly button on both the front and the back of the body. When I have clients work with their own adrenal points I also have them work with their cortisol points. I usually find if the adrenal points are weak the cortisol points are as well. There are a few ways to give energy to these points.

You can put a thumb and a finger on the two adrenal points on the front of the body and the do the same on the back body points. Push into your body on those points with one hand while releasing those points on 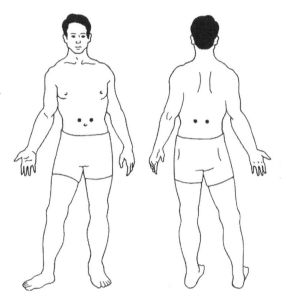 the other side of the body with the other hand and then release the points you were pushing in on while pushing in with the other hand.

Switching off hands, keep doing this imagining a string between the front and the back points.

Donna Eden calls this "Flossing the Adrenals."

I like to have my clients do something called **"Juicing the Adrenals."**

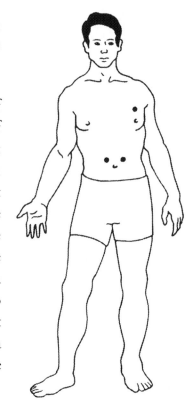

Put your middle finger of your right hand in the top of your left arm pit and slide that finger over to the right until you are roughly in alignment with your left nipple. At the intersection of the top of the arm pit and the nipple is the heart electric point. This is a point that can give energy to other points on the body. It should be tender and that is a good indicator for finding the point.

Keep your middle finger of your right hand on the heart electric and then put your thumb and finger from your left hand on the adrenal points on the front of the body. Hold this until you feel buzzing in the adrenal points and then when you yawn or sigh after about 1–4 minutes that should be good.

You can then move your left hand to your back adrenal points to juice them as well.

Your cortisol points are 1 inch below and 1 inch to either side of your belly button. You can also put your left thumb and finger in these points to give them some healing energy and support.

Clearing Chakras

Look at your body in your mind's eye and see small discs about the size of those small Frisbees spinning counter clockwise in front of your 7 chakras next to your body.

With your hands or your mind move those discs out in front/above your chakras around 2 feet. Turn them on end allowing everything in your chakras that are ready to clear to release.

Hold the intention that each disc will go back to horizontal 2 feet out from your body over the chakras when they are done clearing.

When all of the chakras have cleared and all of the discs are flat again then spin them clockwise and bring them gently (with your hands or mind) back down to your body.

This should relax you and help you to fall asleep if you are in bed.

Clearing Soul Contracts, Energies in Your Field, Vibrations in your DNA and Fractal Repeating Sequences for Transformation

1. Ask your guides that helped you to plan this life to join you. When you sense their presence you can ask them if they need to sign off on the contracts or if they are there to bear witness. Most, if not all, of the time, they are there to support us and bear witness to our clearing and releasing. We just need to ask them for their help, guidance, and protection. You can ask them to help you to release and clear the things on your list.

2. After your guides join you, you're ready to start clearing and releasing.

3. With a heart full of gratitude, thank them for the lessons learned, the personal growth experienced, and the compassion gained from these lessons and experiences.

4. Then look in your mind's eye for a page from the master contract for each thing that you are clearing, or you may prefer to have them all on one page of the contract.

5. Sign the contract of the thing or things you are clearing, and when you are done signing it, see it go up in the violet flame to be transmuted.

Keep repeating this process until you have cleared and released everything from your master contract that you have on your worksheet that is ready to be cleared.

Now you are ready to clear the energies in your field, the vibrations in your DNA, and the fractal repeating sequences. To clear these you can do the following:

1. In your mind, create a beautiful gold cauldron in front of you.

2. Tune into your field around your body, seeing it with your mind's eye and **ask to see any and all energies in your field, vibrations in your DNA, and any fractal repeating sequences that have to do with what you are triggering on or what you have cleared in your master contract.**

3. When you see, sense or visualize these energies, vibrations in your DNA, and fractal repeating sequences, then see or sense them **floating gently into the cauldron you created in front of your body**.

4. Continue asking to see energies, vibrations in your DNA, and fractal repeating sequences for the different things you are clearing and have them all go into the cauldron, understanding that the cauldron can increase in size if needed.

5. When everything you wish to clear is in the cauldron, then see everything in the cauldron go up in a violet flame transmuting all of those things that are no longer serving you and are not in your highest and best good.

6. Next bring your attention to above your crown chakra and **see a sparkly golden light of vitality** shining down and around you as far out as your fingertips and through all your being, filling up the spaces where those energies, vibrations in your DNA, and fractal repeating sequences were with the golden light of vitality.

7. Next, **see a beautiful sparkly silver light of neutrality** above your head shining down and around you as far out as your fingertips and through all your being, filling up the spaces where those energies, vibrations in your DNA, and fractal repeating sequences were with beautiful sparkly silver neutrality energy.

8. You can then see the cauldron float away and turn into gold dust until you need it again. Thank your guides for coming and let them go.

If you are unable to "see" anything — and by "see" I don't mean that you actually see them, just visualize the awareness or sense of the energies in your field — then call on Archangel Michael or whomever you work with to help you release them all into the cauldron. You can energy test to see if they are all in the cauldron as well when you feel like they are.

Clearing Core Beliefs and Things Holding You Back	In Contract for This Lifetime	Energies in Your Field	Vibrating in DNA	Fractal Fepeating Sequence

Contracts —invite guides to join you, with gratitude sign off on contract and see it go up in violet flame.

Clear Energies, DNA Vibrations and Fractal Repeating Sequences.

Ignite them with Violet Flame then shine Golden Light of Vitality and Silver Light of Neutrality into self and aura.

Clearing Energy Cords From Your Body

Say "I AM removing any and all energy cords and their root systems in their entirety from my body and transmuting them now." You may yawn or sigh when this happens.

Then say "I AM filling these spaces with high vibrancy, divine, loving, and healing energy restoring these areas to their original highest vibrancy."

If you keep having cords in you and you have been doing this then you may have a contract to be cleared with that person.

You also may have a boundary part of your master contract for this life where you allow everyone to connect into you and that needs to be cleared so that you can have strong boundaries and not let anyone attach into you. I see this a lot!

Daily Energy Routine

In the morning all of this can be done in bed.

Take a deep breath and on your exhale gently close your eyes. See an energy pole coming from your root chakra down into the center of the earth. When you get to the center of the earth, attach your energy-grounding pole. Picture the earth energy that will nourish and support you on your physical journey coming up that energy pole and spraying out your crown chakra like a big fountain clearing all of the stuff out of your aura that is not yours and is not serving you. See that stuff washing down into the earth to be transmuted. See yourself keeping that energy and fountain cycling at all times.

Celestial energy —see that same energy pole going up through the center of your body, out your crown chakra, and up into the sky and stars. See it connecting to your soul star. Your soul star is your higher self — it provides you with guidance on your spiritual journey. See that celestial energy coming from your soul star, down the energy pole and into your crown chakra. See the celestial energy going down the energy pole through your body mixing with the earth energies that are coming up. Take these mixed energies and push them out from your body as far out as your fingertips around your entire body. Keep this energy flowing at all times and out at your fingertips. This will keep your aura clear, keep you grounded and connected and will establish your space so that you don't hang onto other people's "stuff" in your aura.

Octahedron — Bring your attention to the top of your head and see the top of an octahedron connected to your energy pole above your crown chakra and coming down to the four points mid body in front, behind, and to both sides at arm's length. Then see those points go down to the point right below your feet connected to your energy grounding pole. Picture your body inside the octahedron.

When you use the geometric shape of an octahedron around your body, you are energetically reinforcing your connection between heaven and earth. It creates a feeling of grounding and connection, and it creates and keeps a personal energetic space around you. I have found this to

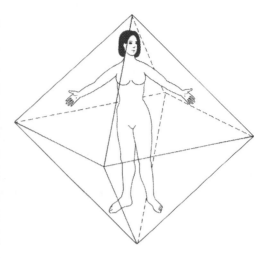

work better than all the other methods I've tried over the years to keep my energies in and other people's energies out. In combination with pushing the earth and celestial energies out to my fingertips, it unscrambles my energies and it keeps my aura out to my fingertips (with arms outstretched) unless I choose to expand my energy out further.

Energy tapping — this sequence is from Donna Eden's Daily Energy Routine with a couple minor changes from me. On the tapping parts you can use your fingertips to tap on most points, but I prefer to use my flat fist to thump my thymus. I also like to start at the top of my body and make my way down in order:

Crown Pull — put fingers from both hands at the middle of the forehead and gently slide-pull them apart toward the temples. Continue pulling apart along the midline of the head, opening the top of the head, all the way down to the neck, stretching the back of the neck open. (This improves circulation and can help with headaches and fuzzy brain.)

Tapping cheekbones — this is very grounding. Tap your fingers on your cheekbones about an inch down from the pupils of your eyes for about 10 seconds, or until you yawn or sigh.

Neck/thyroid stretch — gently put the fingers of both hands in the middle of neck together and stretch them apart, up and down, at the front of the neck, similar to the Crown Pull. Continue doing this around the front of the neck. You can do this in all directions, including the diagonals. This brings healing energy to your thyroid. I believe doing this was part of what helped me to get off my thyroid prescription and eventually thyroid supplements.

Tap K-27's — these two points are below the collarbones, about an inch down and an inch towards the armpit from the clavicle notch. Tapping these points tells the energy in all of your meridians to move forward in the right direction.

Tap thymus (*Tarzan thump–bump in middle of chest*) — this stimulates the thymus to produce T-Cells, which kill cancer.

And at the same time:

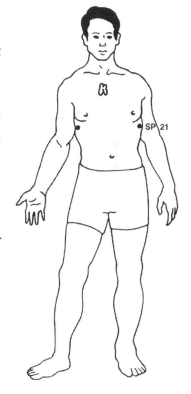

Tap spleen points — one side at a time while thumping your thymus. These points are on the "side seam" of the body — Spleen 21 (4-6 inches down from the armpit — it should be a tender spot!) on both sides of the body. Tapping these points will help to boost the immune system.

Connect head with body (*Hook Up*) — place the middle finger of one hand in the belly button, gently pulling up. The middle finger of the other hand is on the Third Eye — in-between and slightly above the eyebrows gently pulling up. Hold about 1-3 minutes or until you sigh or yawn. This energetically connects head and torso and gives you a great sense of protection and connection to your body. It also helps to get you "out of your head."

Triple Warmer Smoothie *(Chill Pill)* — do this daily when you are in a stress response mode. Lay fingers gently on temples. Take a deep breath in, and on your exhale trace your fingers around the top and back of your ears and down the side of your neck to your shoulders. At your shoulders, switch your arms (left hand on right shoulder and right hand on left shoulder) and continue tracing your fingers down your arms to your wrists and then one at a time trace them off your ring fingers. This traces your stress meridian backwards, relaxing you and helping you to get out of the stress response.

Some days I do some light lymphatic massage under my collarbones, around the sides of my breasts, and down my arm seam.

After this I'm ready to get out of bed and start my day.

Energy Testing with Your Leg for Food or as a General Energy Test

Sit down in a chair with feet on the ground.

Lift your right leg off the floor about 2 inches (unless your left leg is stronger and more reliable)

Think or say what food you want to test and then with your right hand above your knee apply a good amount of pressure to push that leg down right above the knee.

If your leg goes weak then your body doesn't want that food.

If your leg stays strong then your body wants that food, or at the least the food does not weaken your body.

This is particularly handy at restaurants. You can easily do this under the table while looking at the menu and no one would know.

Do the same as above for a general muscle test which can be useful when determining contract work:

Ask a question or make a statement and then apply pressure to the leg.

A strong leg that does not move toward the floor is a "yes" or True.

A weak leg that gets pushed to the floor is a no or negative.

Energy Testing and Emotion Clearing With a Pendulum

When you get a new pendulum you want to clear it with any of these suggestions; selenite will clear it, smudge it with white sage (burn white sage next to it and the smoke will clear the energies) leave it in the sun for several hours, run it under cold water for a minute — **selenite should never touch water or it will dissolve.** You can also leave your crystals out all night under a full moon to clear and recharge them.

After you have cleared the pendulum then hold it in the palm of your hand infusing it with your energy. You are ready to attune it to your intentions for guidance.

With the intention of a "yes" answer sway the pendulum up and down like a nod of your head. State "this is a yes" as you do it.

Then with the intention of a "no" answer sway it side to side and state "this is a "no".

Before asking your question or making your statement ask that the answers will come from **your higher self only.**

The reason I do this is because we can move the pendulum however we want to. Play with it and you will see.

As with any energy testing you need to hold clear intentions and practice.

To clear energies in your field or chakras:

When you are ready to clear energies hold your pendulum a couple inches above where you are clearing.

Your pendulum should start to spin counter clockwise which is the direction of clearing or releasing.

It should do this for a little while as you hold your arm and hand very still.

It should start to slow down (some people like me yawn at this point which tells me the clearing is done) and then the pendulum will come to the middle and bounce a couple times before starting to spin in a clockwise direction bringing in new and fresh healing energy to that space that was just cleared.

The pendulum will eventually stop and you will be done.

Do not be surprised if you feel emotions coming to the surface and you may cry. Honor this and just let it out.

You can do this anywhere on your body that you sense has energies that need to be cleared.

Ileocecal & Houston Valve Reset
(for Constipation)

If you have been dealing with constipation and have changed your diet to one consisting of a majority of fruits, vegetables and adequate amounts of good water and you are still constipated you could benefit from looking at it energetically. It would be beneficial to get your Kidney Meridian energy going first (see Kidney Meridian addendum) then you will want to energetically reset the two valves.

To Reset Valves:

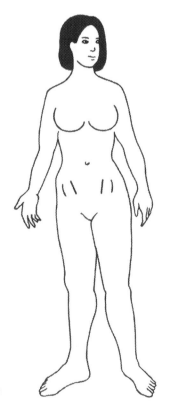

Start with your hands in a karate chop position on your two hip bones.

Keeping the sides of your hands on the bones then lay them flat to the inside of your hips.

While breathing-in drag your fingers up through the space on the inside of your hip bones around 6 – 7 inches (Ileocecal is on the right and Houston Valve is on the left.)

Exhale as you release your fingers even with your belly button.

Do this three times up slowly while breathing in **and then stop at the top of the third time (even with belly button)**

270

Place your thumbs down and while exhaling slowly drag your thumbs down the inside of your hip bones to close the now energized valves.

It is important that you close the valves energetically - do not forget that step!

I usually tap under my cheek bones (Stomach Meridian) for about 10 seconds and then tap under my collar bones (Kidney Meridian) for another 10 seconds as this sends energy through these meridians that move through or close to the valves and brings more energy movement to that area of the body where the valves are helping things to get moving.

Kidney Meridian Support

Receiving energy from the earth is our life force energy. Our Kidney Meridian begins at the bottom of our feet next to the big toe base and runs up our body through many critical points such as the ileocecal and Houston valves, adrenal and cortisol points and to right below the collar bones. Everything starts with Kidney so that is why I am including this.

If you know you have an under-energized Kidney Meridian, it would be beneficial for you to do the following:

Clear the excess Fear from your Kidneys (see Releasing Stored Emotions From Your Body and Organs Addendum)

Trace your Kidney Meridian daily until you have stability in that meridian.

Your acupuncturist can tell you if your Kidney Meridian is under energized or you can test yourself or ask someone to do this test on you:

Lie down on a bed or massage table and lift your straight leg (either one) up around two feet and twist (rotate) it out like a dancer.

Try to push your leg down and out yourself or have someone do it gently for you.

If you cannot even hold it up or it goes down easily it is an under energized Kidney Meridian and you will benefit from clearing the Fear from your Kidneys and Bladder and further energizing if necessary.

When your Kidney Meridian is under energized then it is not bringing energy up through your body adequately supporting your ileocecal and Houston valves, adrenal points, cortisol points and so many other things.

You may be experiencing constipation, adrenal burnout, exhaustion, hormonal fluctuations and more. Getting your Kidney Meridian vibrant is a big step in getting your energetic healing support for total healing.

Trace with your mind or your hands starting at the bottoms of your feet at the base of the big toe pad of your foot up the inside of your feet and circle above and around your ankle bones two times and continue up the inside of your legs to the inside and behind your knee and then up the inside of your thighs up next to your pubic bone, continuing up next to the inside of your hips (illececal & Houston valves) and up to below the collar bones on either side of your sternum just above your Thymus to the end points of the Kidney Meridian (K-27) and thump a few times when you get there.

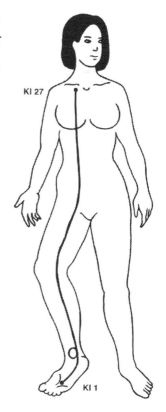

Releasing Stored Emotions from Your Body and Organs

Sit quietly and tune into or energy test the organs listed below to see if they are carrying excess emotions that they vibrate at:

Bladder/Kidneys — Fear

Liver/Gallbladder — Anger, Rage, Frustration, Judgment, Shame, and Resentment

Heart/Small Intestine — Panic and Anxiety

Stomach/Spleen — Over-Worry and Over-Concern

Breasts, Chest or Lungs — Grief

Large Intestine — Reluctance to Let Go

Then test to see who you are holding onto these emotions for so that you can release them:

Yourself

Your loved ones

Your ancestors

Pets

Friends

Neighbors

Ex partners or spouses

*Clients

Or in a lot of cases, the world

*If you work with clients in a healing capacity as a therapist, energy worker, massage therapist, etc., you will most likely be holding onto emotions for your clients as well.

You need to do this because I have discovered that all of us healing professionals take on energies in the beginning of our training and practice before we figure out our boundaries and our energy management. **This can lead us to devastating healing opportunities if we are not careful and clear these.**

You can also do this with places on your body that are causing you challenges as well. *More than likely there is a component to the discomfort or pain that is stuck emotions of yours or a loved ones.*

Sit quietly and then call in who ever you like to work with to help you to release and transmute these emotions.

This is what I say when I clear my Liver and Gallbladder:

"Archangel Michael, please come and help me to release any and all Anger, Rage, Resentment, Judgment, Shame, and Frustration that I am carrying in my Liver and Gallbladder on behalf of myself, my loved ones, my clients, my pets, my ancestors and the world. Please help me to release these emotions in their entirety and please transmute them in the highest and best way for everyone involved. Thank you."

List whoever you are carrying them for or you can ask to release for everyone on the list I provided above. Really be in the space of releasing them and in gratitude for the lessons they have taught you.

Next I call in Archangel Raphael and say "Archangel Raphael, please infuse my liver and gallbladder with the highest vibrancy, Divine, loving and healing light energy returning them to their original highest vibrancy. Thank you."

Remember to thank your angels for all of their help and let them feel your gratitude.

Do this with each of the pairs of organs and then with Lungs and Large Intestines. Also do it with any parts of your body that are giving you challenges when you determine what you are holding and for whom you are holding it.

This is intense work and you may be very tired afterward so take the time to rest and integrate these changes to your body.

Sleep Protocol

I make sure my bedroom is very dark and cool and that the air is fresh or filtered.

Trace Tibetan eye chart with your eyes then turn off light (I realize you need to keep the light on the first few times you do this until you have it set in your mind). This is not necessary for sleep but it is a habit that can signal your brain that you are getting ready to sleep. Also it really does help your eyesight!

Turn off brain analyzer in my mind's eye. This looks like a dimmer switch and an on/off switch. I can dim it during the day if I am too up in my head or I can just turn it off at bedtime.

Bring your energy back into you and then with closed eyes bring your attention to between your eyebrows inside your head where your 3rd eye is. Follow your breath.

Hook-up energies (middle fingers in belly button and 3rd eye gently pull up.)

Rub gentle circles around your eye sockets and above middle of eyebrows to hairline.

Spin out Chakras to release anything ready to be released. Spin them back in (see Chakra Clearing Addendum).

I say a clearing prayer to clear my home of any energies that are not welcomed by me and a protection prayer for my home to be kept clear of any and all energies not welcomed by me.

I say, "I AM sleeping deeply and restoratively and I AM only remembering the dreams that are important messages."

I also say, "My body wants, needs, deserves and desires to sleep now."

I trace from my temples behind my ears to my trapezius; switch/cross – hands/arms here and then trace down my arms and off my ring fingers (Triple Warmer Smoothie).

I lie on my side and rest my head on my hand so that my fingers are on my temple. This is a stress point that is calmed by being gently held.

I put my other hand near the base of my throat with my fingers touching in the indentation. This is another stress point that is calmed by touching it gently. You will see children sleeping like this.

Optional is to work with your N.D. or practitioner who does muscle testing to determine which of the following supplements your body wants to support your healing and sleeping better:

Melatonin
5 HTP
GABA
California Poppy

Other options: Valerian and/or lavender oil diffused, on skin and breathed in deeply and held.

Spleen Muscle Meridian Energy Test for Supplements

Start by assessing your Spleen muscle meridian test. Stand with your right arm hugged close to the side of your body with your hand sidewise and thumb against your body. Hold your arm in tight and strong to your body and reach over with your left hand and try to pull or push your right arm above the wrist away from your body while you try and hold it tight against your body.

This is awkward and the best way I can describe for you to do it is to slide the back of your left hand between your body and right arm just above the wrist and using your left fingers to try and move your right arm away from the right side of your body. If it is hard to push/pull away from your body then your spleen is strong. You can use either arm for this test.

*If you cannot hold your arm against your body then your Spleen Meridian is under energized and weak and you will need to go the addendum **Clearing Emotions from Your Organs and Body** to clear the over worry and over concern from your spleen and stomach and then try the test again.*

If it is still a weak test (easy to pull or push away from your body) then go back to chapter 11 on energy testing and do the recommended steps to strengthen your Spleen Meridian. Hold the intention that you will be able to do this.

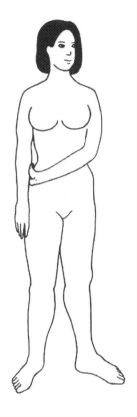

Once your Spleen Meridian is strong, we need to check and see if we can weaken your Spleen Meridian to get an accurate answer for our supplement testing. To weaken your Spleen Meridian you need to waive or flutter your right hand in front of where your spleen is in your body (this is located under your left breast.) Hold your right hand there with your palm facing your spleen and flutter your fingers together back and forth in front of your spleen weakening it and then try the muscle test again.

Right arm/thumb (perpendicular) snug against right
    side of body,
Back of left hand between right arm above wrist and
    right side of body
Push/pull to bring right arm away from the body.

This should be easy to do now and very difficult for you to hold the right arm against the body because the energy has been interrupted (weakened.) This is a weak spleen energy test or a "no." To do a quick reset/reenergize of the Spleen Meridian you can move your right hand in the air in front of your spleen in a slow figure eight pattern a few times, re-test and you should have a strong spleen energy test again.

You are now ready to test some supplements. How you do this is to have your supplement that you want to test near you on a table. You need to weaken your Spleen Meridian—remember you do this by waiving your right hand in the air back and forth above where your spleen is in your body. Your spleen is located just below your left breast.

After you do this (interrupting the energy to your spleen, weakening it) you then quickly put the supplement in your shirt or bra, tucked into your waistband of your pants (you get the picture!) then do the spleen energy test with the back of your left hand against your body trying to push/pull the right arm away from the right side of your body while holding it into your body.

If it is easy to pull your right arm away then the substance/supplement does not strengthen your spleen and it is not beneficial for you in your healing.

If your spleen test is strong now after you weakened your spleen but added the supplement to your body then the supplement strengthens your body and it is beneficial in your healing.

Here are the steps without the explanations:

Test Spleen Meridian to see if strong

Weaken Spleen Meridian to see if testable

Re-energize Spleen Meridian and retest it

Have supplements near you

Weaken Spleen Meridian

Put supplements on/next to your body

Quickly retest Spleen Meridian

If it is strong after you weakened it and added supplements to your field then the supplements strengthen you and are beneficial to you.

If it stays weak after you weaken it and add the supplements to your field then your body is not strengthened by the supplements and you do not need them.

References

Acupuncture: Erika Eddy L.Ac. www.erikaeddy.com

Astrology, Reconnective Healing, Tarot, Massage: Jatae Jeter, CMT, Reiki Master www.spiritsvessel.com

Ayurveda Consulting: Sera Melini www.hamsayogaandayurveda.com

Bio Feedback and Hypnosis: Gila M. Zak, Certified Hypnotherapist and Biofeedback Specialist www.QuantumWavesHypnotherapy.com

Bio Field Tuning, Vibrational Fascia Release Tuning Fork therapies: Re-TuneToHealth.com Tammy Glavor (805) 305 0551

Chiropractic: Dr. Darci Rose; TBM and Dr. Otto training activator only adjustment. Call for apt (805) 489-5661

Chiropractor: Dr. Ron Mutch Integrative Chiropractic; gentle structural adjustment, nutritional support, spiritual clearing and guidance. Call for appt. (844) 443-7766

Chiropracter Specializing in Atlas and Occipital: Dr. David Vazquez truHealth Specific Chiropractic www.truhealthstudio.com (805) 782-9203

Colonics: Internal Wellness Colonics, Gloria de Boer, Advanced I-ACT Certified Colon Hydrotherapist, www.internalwellness4u.com

Detox Teas: Wilwand Tea Co. www.wilwandteaco.com.

Eden Method Certification Program: www.innersource.net.

Eden Method Practitioner List — find someone near you www.innersource.net.

Fung Shui Consultant: Patricia Auxier Rock, Certified Feng Shui Practitioner, fengshui888@aol.com.

Hellerwork: Brings the body's natural structure into proper balance and alignment. Christine Troples, Finding Wings (805) 550-6163.

Life Color Readings: Titanya Dahling
www.energymedicinewoman.com

Marketing: Mental Marketing; Infinite Marketing Solutions. Maryann O'Brien Stansfield www.mentalmarketing.com

N.D and Energy Work: Dr. Susan Lundgren dr.slundgren@gmail.com Phone, FaceTime, and Skype sessions.

Photography: Allyson Magda www.allysonmagda.com

Space Clearing Certification Course: Denise Linn
www.deniselinn.com

Structural and Visceral Integration: Aligns your body back to normal functional condition: Leo Frost (805) 459-0697
www.rbodystudio.com, rbodymt@gmail.com

Printed in the United States
By Bookmasters